Praise for
NOW YOU SEE ME

"NOW YOU SEE ME is an amazing and enlightening story of Kathy Sanders's pathway to forgiveness. Kathy's firsthand recollections of the Oklahoma City Bombing of the Murrah Building, which took the lives of her two grandchildren, vividly paint a picture of that horrific day in U.S. history. Kathy's surprising later connection to Terry Nichols not only brought her to a level of forgiveness, but sparked a spiritual awakening in him. This story will be of enormous benefit to friends and families going through similar trauma and working to find their own paths to forgiveness."

—Jay Bradford, Arkansas insurance commissioner

"As the district attorney responsible for the state prosecution of Terry Nichols, I don't subscribe to conspiracy theories or musings on possible government cover-ups. But as a common citizen, I was profoundly impressed and even moved by the spiritual journey taken by Kathy Wilburn Sanders. Only those robbed of their loved ones can truly comprehend the pain and grief this grandmother and her family experienced at the hand of McVeigh and Nichols. The beauty of this story is that she is a walking testament that Jesus Christ does what he says he can do: bring peace and joy out of the ashes of grief and despair."

—Wes Lane

"Riveting. Forceful. Redemptive. Written like a personal journal, with shades of investigative reporting, Kathy Sanders recounts her personal journey after losing her two grandsons in the 1995 Oklahoma City federal building bombing. Moving through her tragedy, devastation, doubts, depression, then finally arriving at the first stirrings of wanting to live again, this artist reveals the pathway to healing she found. A powerful journey of faith revitalized and forgiveness rediscovered. I wasn't able to put it down until I finished."

—Dr. Kevin Clarkson, lead pastor of First Baptist
Church, Moore, Oklahoma

"Self awareness and the ability to forgive our enemies, as well as ourselves, seems impossible. This book shows how. Inspirational, thought-provoking, and insightful."

—Joe Kleine, assistant coach of UALR, fifteen-year
NBA player, member of the 1984 Olympic gold medal
basketball team and 1998 NBA champion Chicago Bulls

NOW YOU SEE ME

HOW I FORGAVE THE UNFORGIVABLE

Kathy Sanders

New York Boston Nashville

Scripture quotations are taken from the Holy Bible, King James Version (public domain).

FaithWords
Hachette Book Group
237 Park Avenue
New York, NY 10017

www.faithwords.com

Printed in the United States of America

RRD-C

First Edition: April 2014

10 9 8 7 6 5 4 3 2 1

FaithWords is a division of Hachette Book Group, Inc.
The FaithWords name and logo are trademarks of Hachette Book Group, Inc.

The Hachette Speakers Bureau provides a wide range of authors for speaking events. To find out more, go to www.hachettespeakersbureau.com or call (866) 376-6591.

The publisher is not responsible for websites (or their content) that are not owned by the publisher.

Library of Congress Cataloging-in-Publication Data

Sanders, Kathy.
    Now you see me : how I forgave the unforgivable / Kathy Sanders.
        pages cm
    Summary: "On April 19, 1995, Kathy Sanders's life was forever changed when a bomb exploded and destroyed the Alfred P. Murrah building in Oklahoma City, killing her two grandsons, Chase and Colton. For a while after her grandchildren died, Kathy struggled with coping and wondered if the God she'd worshipped all her life even existed. After struggling through bitterness and contemplating suicide, she turned to the Lord and asked what He'd have her do. She was reminded that the scriptures say that we are to forgive our enemies. Kathy then forged a relationship with Terry Nichols, a man who murdered her grandchildren. Additionally she housed, clothed, and cooked for Nichols's children, mother, sister, wife, and ex-wife. What's more, she demonstrated the same type of warmth to family members of Timothy McVeigh, the second man convicted of orchestrating the bombing. With photos, interviews, and actual letters exchanged between Kathy and Terry Nichols, NOW YOU SEE ME will tell the story of how she forgave these men and cultivated relationships with their families, and how her courageous efforts of forgiveness gave her peace and removed the bitterness from her life." — Provided by publisher.
    ISBN 978-1-4555-2619-2 (hardback) — ISBN 978-1-4789-5292-3 (audio download) — ISBN 978-1-4555-2620-8 (ebook) 1. Sanders, Kathy. 2. Oklahoma City Federal Building Bombing, Oklahoma City, Okla., 1995. 3. Terrorism victims' families—Oklahoma. 4. Forgiveness—Religious aspects—Christianity. 5. Restorative justice—Religious aspects—Christianity. I. Title.
    HV6432.6.S26 2014
    976.6'38—dc23
    [B]
                                                                                    2013038684

I dedicate this book to my loving Savior, who taught me to sing through my sadness, to laugh through my tears, and to feel His compassion.

Acknowledgments

I would like to recognize my beloved husband, Tom Sanders, who blesses my life each and every day.

My daughter, Edye, who, while coping with her own grief, provided courage and strength that sustained me through the worst of times.

Larry and Frances Jones have been with me through every step of this journey.

Lee Hough is popularly regarded as America's foremost agent representing Christian literature. Despite major health issues, up until his death, Lee was a persistent guardian of this project.

Although we had not previously exchanged e-mails or text messages, FaithWords editor Jana Burson took the time to meet me face-to-face when contemplating the publication of my story. She and I laughed and cried, and we bonded instantly with a common cause to share this book with the world.

J. Pat Carter and David Allen provided photos for this book.

—*Kathy Sanders*

Darkness cannot drive out darkness; only light can do that. Hate cannot drive out hate; only love can do that.

—*Martin Luther King Jr.*

NOW YOU SEE ME

Chapter One

Sometimes, when the hour is late and memories are unavoidable, I sit silently alone to watch videotapes of events I dread to see, the immediate aftermath of unspeakable death and destruction.

I wonder why I do that.

The bombing of Oklahoma City's Alfred P. Murrah Federal Building on April 19, 1995, was the deadliest act of terrorism ever enacted on American soil until the attack on the World Trade Center six years later.

The media called the Murrah onslaught America's worst tragedy since the assassination of President John F. Kennedy thirty-two years earlier. I don't endorse the comparison, except that the Oklahoma City Bombing served to confirm what the shock of the Kennedy assassination made us realize. That Americans were no longer safe. Even in our own country.

Within a sixteen-block radius, 324 buildings were damaged or outright destroyed. Eighty-six cars were burned or demolished. Total property damage was set at $652 million.

But all of that physical damage is woefully insignificant when compared to our precious loved ones who were taken away forever by the explosion.

The death toll reached 168, including nineteen children under the age of six. Two of those were Chase and Colton Smith, my grandchildren, ages three and two. During their short lives, they and their mother, the former Edye Smith, lived with me.

Today, my beloved grandsons live in heaven. They are remembered through videotapes, photographs, and the precious memories I'll cherish forever.

The fact is, I *do* know why I watch those tapes. After nineteen years, I look for some sign, some path, something...anything... that might prompt meaning in all of that horrific carnage. But I've never found anything remotely meaningful, and I suspect I never will.

The tapes don't show what I didn't know then and can't forget now: that a man identified as Timothy McVeigh had entered the Murrah nursery days before the explosion, pretending to be a father seeking day care for children he claimed to have but didn't.

Instead, his intentions were purely evil. McVeigh's visit was a clandestine evaluation of the nursery's infrastructure. He wanted to be sure he'd slaughter all of the unsuspecting people—especially preschoolers—who were inside the Murrah Building.

Courtroom testimony would reveal that McVeigh wanted to avenge the deaths of the children killed when ATF agents raided the Branch Davidian compound in Waco, Texas, on April 19, 1993, the exact same date as the Oklahoma City Bombing. McVeigh had actually been in Waco during the small-town siege. That date and other evidence would later confirm that the Waco tragedy was the flashpoint for the Oklahoma City Bombing.

Today, I turn off the VCR, but not my tormented thoughts. They continue to play repeatedly and at will inside my troubled mind. They start at the beginning...

Edye and I worked together in an office a block away from the Murrah Building. Two minutes after the workday began, we heard and felt a terrifying and deafening blast. Sitting at desks one floor apart, we sensed our building quiver, as the explosion literally shook the ground.

Along with other employees, Edye and I ran outside, fearing we'd face a tremor or a large blast ignited by a natural gas leak.

Once on the street, we saw smoke rising from the area of the Murrah Building, where, minutes earlier, we had dropped off Chase and Colton at its day-care center.

Occasionally in my life, I had heard about paralyzing fear...fear that immediately overwhelms you. In those first moments, inside that nightmare come to life, I *felt* it.

Fear engulfed us, and, for a second or two, I had to force my steps that otherwise wouldn't come.

Edye and I began to run down the sidewalk toward the Murrah Building, and I thought we might die as falling sheets of plate glass crashed all around us. The scene was surreal, with no cars moving and people emerging from the downtown building bewildered by the blast, fear on their faces. Someone shouted at us, urging us to move to the middle of the street to avoid the falling shards of glass.

When we realized that the great billows of smoke were rising from the very building where the day-care center was located, I screamed, "Edye, the babies!"

As we ran toward the building, it seemed that everyone else was running away from it.

Despite the flurry that would soon be a hysterical mob, I somehow felt as if Edye and I were moving in slow motion. Perhaps my brain was providing the illusion of slowing time so that I could put off the stunning blow that was about to change my world forever.

My hope for Chase and Colton somehow remained alive before Edye and I saw the extent of the damage to the Murrah Building. When we ran to the north side of the embattled structure, our optimism waned, then sank.

The entire front of the building had been torn away. It was now a nine-story abyss that looked as if it had been transplanted from war-torn Bosnia or from Berlin after World War II. The staggering sight of that much destruction reaching that high into the sky was beyond comprehension.

I was unable to breathe—and I felt certain that I was going to faint. But if I did, I would surely be trampled by the frantic mob struggling to get away from the wreckage. I managed to stay conscious and on my feet as interior and exterior walls continued to topple, like snowbanks inside an avalanche that sporadically collapse as temperatures rise.

The blast's aftermath seemed to have a sinister mind of its own. It willfully opposed the efforts of anyone who entered the zone intending to save lives or improve the situation.

My obsession to find Chase and Colton made me only partially aware of the screams of mangled and bloody people who staggered incoherently from the building. Their clothing hung in tatters. Most were covered with blood, soot, dust, and dirt. Facial features were hidden behind the gore and grime. Their screams bespoke the universal language of appalling agony, the merciless kind that comes in an instant and inflicts indelible pain for a lifetime.

My only thought was, *Where are my precious Chase and Colton in all of this?*

According to eventual media accounts, as Edye and I frantically continued to search for our babies, firemen and other rescue personnel were carrying out arms, legs, and other body parts on stretchers; someone would eventually try to match each appendage with its owner. Other rescuers hefted giant plastic bags with blood dripping from the torn bottoms, and hands or feet horrifically protruding through the sides.

A fireman reached out from a hydraulic lift to remove a man perched in an empty window. When the rescuer touched him, his torso fell apart.

I saw, but couldn't mentally process, the ghastly sights of those horrific minutes.

I fell into a rigid mental lockdown. I struggled to pray but couldn't. I found myself unable to place one word with another. I was dumbfounded.

Having been reared in a Christian home, I believed in God and had accepted Him as my personal Savior as a young girl.

How could this be happening to me? Surely this was a foretaste of hell.

I then began to ponder if this might be the second coming of Christ,

And if this is the Rapture, have I been left behind? I asked myself.

Just as quickly as it had momentarily wandered, my mind uncontrollably returned to the present.

"What about my grandbabies?" I said, my words lost to the bedlam of screaming and sirens.

Then I realized, perhaps for the first time, that they could be trapped and crying for their grandmother. Why wouldn't they? I had *always* responded to their cries of distress.

Suddenly, my love overtook logic.

Chase and Colton *had* to be alive inside that disintegrating building, and I was determined to find them.

We then encountered a man with outstretched arms ordering us to stop. He wore a yellow jacket with ATF in big blue letters across the front.

Edye, who was trudging along beside me, ducked from beneath my arm that was wound tightly around her shoulders. She broke my hold in her own futile press toward her babies; unable to get past the agent, she seemed to just run in no particular direction, with me chasing after her.

Throughout this entire ordeal, I had been oblivious to swarming newsmen whose cameras were directed at Edye and me, our faces shocking masks streaked with sweat and tears. I later learned the reporters focused on us because we were among the first civilians on the scene.

Other desperate people arrived soon enough—those who had been more than a block away when the bomb exploded. They, too, would try and fail in their rescue attempts levied against the unstable and crumbling building.

I was fervently and unashamedly praying aloud now. I begged God to let us find our babies alive.

⤝

Edye and I gazed again, this time hypnotically, inside the missing front of the Murrah Building. From that vantage point, the contents were grotesquely revealed. I could see furniture, debris, and bodies inside separate offices. The stone exterior was absent from top to bottom.

We stared upward into the second floor, past the disintegrated wall of the nursery. No children or teachers were visible.

"My babies, my babies!" screamed Edye. For the first time on our frantic quest, Edye dropped to her knees, unable to stand beneath the weight of her falling world.

Her breakdown served as my unwanted reality check. All hope that our babies were alive was gone. I put my arms around Edye, a hollow effort to comfort her.

"It will be all right," I said. "It *has* to be all right."

"Mother!" she said furiously as she again broke my embrace. "It will not be all right! Look at that building!"

Instinctively, we again moved through the debris.

Perhaps by some stroke of luck, Chase and Colton could be lying safe beneath the destruction. Maybe everything had fallen around them and now they were trapped inside a pocket of air. I had read about such miracles after coal mine explosions.

The dangers of what we were doing did not occur to Edye or to me. Neither of us possessed the mental clarity to consider the possible consequences of our efforts.

We were detained—and perhaps saved—by another ATF agent who ordered us to move back.

How dare he? I fumed to myself, intending but unable to ignore his command.

By now, Edye seemed completely out of her mind. I'd never seen my daughter cry with such intensity. Her screams came from some deep, primal place.

A man we had never seen before ran up to us. "The babies are all right!" he shouted joyfully, beside himself. "They got them out of the building!" Edye and I thought a miracle had unfolded.

He directed us across the street to a sea of children gathered on the curb. With each step, our sagging spirits lifted like a rocket.

Fighting our way through the crowd, we spotted the designated area and slowed our gait as the outlines of children's bodies began to form before us. Many of them shivered quietly; eerily, not one of them cried.

I suddenly felt as if Edye and I were running into a place from which we might soon run away.

As we got closer, our hearts sank and our pace slowed to a crawl. We gazed at the bloody, frightened children. We didn't recognize any of them and soon realized they were not from Chase and Colton's day care. These children had been enrolled at a YMCA day-care center a block away. None had attended the Murrah nursery. Neither Chase, Colton, nor any of the other Murrah children were among this group of survivors and victims. Our babies were not there!

Some of these youngsters were severely injured despite their having been a full city block from the blast.

Oh God, please let Chase and Colton be all right, I silently prayed again, as if repetition would pester God into granting my wish.

Our most promising possibility for finding our babies had

proven false. I could physically feel the spirit of optimism departing my body. It was replaced by nauseous despair.

Edye and I lapsed into an intense hysteria I had never previously experienced.

"How could this be happening?" I cried.

I was so confused. Why would God have allowed this massacre? I had hoped that my grandbabies might be spared. I desperately wanted to awaken from this nightmare.

At that moment, even with my daughter beside me, I felt totally alone. Where was God? Why wasn't He with me in my hour of total despair, the darkest of my entire life?

❧

Edye and I stood helplessly among still another group of desperate parents struggling valiantly to find their children. Their screams of desperation, anger, and angst were deafening, with each parent yelling and sobbing louder than the next.

The stress we endured was a sickening mixture of outrageous frustration and grief. My central nervous system seemed to be short-circuiting.

I realized I had not called my husband, Glenn Wilburn. I hadn't once thought about him during this entire morning of madness. How could that be?

Using a borrowed cell phone, I called Glenn repeatedly, but to no avail. All cellular transmissions were jammed.

"Glenn, the babies are gone!" I yelled when I was finally connected with his answering service.

"The babies are gone! Please help us. We are downtown at the Murrah Building!"

Seemingly from nowhere, I heard my name rising above the noise of other people and emergency vehicles. The voice belonged to Christy Rush, my neighbor. Knowing that Chase and Colton had been inside the day-care center, Christy had launched a search of her own.

"Kathy, I just saw Glenn a few minutes ago," Christy said. "He asked me to help find you!"

But as the grim morning plodded on, Glenn had become camouflaged among hundreds of newly arriving and desperate people searching for loved ones—dead or alive.

Perhaps Christy could sense how fragile I was at the moment. Perhaps that's why she failed to tell me she hadn't bumped into me by chance. She had, in fact, been sent by Glenn to search for me, as he couldn't muster the courage to encounter me face-to-face by himself.

Simply knowing that Glenn was somewhere on the scene bolstered my spirits, however minimally.

Without a word, Christy pointed to my husband, perhaps a block away. Incredibly, I saw him.

His face was pressed against a car hood, his feet planted on the ground. Even from that distance, I could see his shoulders heaving. I knew he was sobbing.

Our arms entwined, Christy, Edye, and I began to weave through the mob toward Glenn. The closer we got, the more desperation I felt. My husband, usually a pillar of composure, was broken by grief and sorrow to a degree I'd never seen.

I called out to him. He looked up and spotted us. When we reached him, the four of us melted into one another's arms. No words were needed.

From the corner of my eye, I again noticed a television newsman filming us from a distance of perhaps six feet. I never gave a thought to the fact that he'd been following Edye and me throughout the treacherous morning.

Eventually I would learn that his footage was fed from his home station in Oklahoma City to media outlets across America and the world. Before nightfall, news anchors would be calling my home.

Edye and I hadn't known that during the entire time we had been frantically searching for Chase and Colton, our faces and actions had been projected onto television screens inside millions of households by a news feed; that a New York producer for NBC's *Today* show would somehow find us before the next sunrise; that anchorwoman Katie Couric would meet Edye and me in less than twenty-four hours on the rooftop of a building standing amid the rubble in downtown Oklahoma City.

In an instant, our terror worsened. A mass of panic-stricken people started running from the north side of the bombed-out Murrah Building.

"Get back! Get back!" they screamed. "There's another bomb!"

If I thought I had seen insanity after the first explosion, it was nothing compared to the madness that erupted next. The crowd that had run helter-skelter after the first blast now responded in a unified stampede.

Glenn, Edye, Christy, and I were torn between running for our lives and remaining near the compromised structure where, by now, perhaps rescuers had miraculously found our babies.

We didn't move. After all, how could we leave without knowing what had happened to our children?

Police officers appeared from out of nowhere and forcefully steered the crowd one block over to Broadway Street in anticipation of the second blast.

As we walked along the street, headed for safety, we began to hear a rumble, as if tanks were approaching a war zone. The sounds, in fact, belonged to a convoy of bulldozers. Upon arriving at the Murrah site, they spread into formation. One by one, the machines eased into the pile of smoldering wreckage that held the dead, the dying, and the trapped.

Mysteriously, the bulldozers didn't place the rubble into waiting trucks. Then it hit me. The equipment had not been sent to permanently remove the debris. Drivers had come to search and rescue.

Not one soul was found alive.

A sickening silence descended as Edye, Glenn, Christy, and I walked to the car. None of us spoke. After all we had seen, what could be said?

"Oh God, I beg You—*please* don't let these bulldozers be the way Chase and Colton are found," I said aloud.

This time, I made no effort to conceal my prayer.

Chapter Two

From Oklahoma City, Interstate 35 shoots straight north to the Kansas State line. Some ninety minutes after the bombing, Oklahoma State Trooper Charlie Hanger was traveling north near the town of Perry. As he was about to pass an old Mercury traveling in the same direction, he noticed that it had no license plate. He pulled the car over and approached the vehicle. The driver was Timothy McVeigh, a Gulf War veteran. McVeigh had no driver's license, and when the trooper noticed a bulge in his jacket, he found that McVeigh was carrying a loaded .45-caliber Glock.

Hanger cuffed McVeigh without incident and took him to the Noble County jail in Perry. Although Trooper Hanger and the officers at the jail knew about the bombing, they gave no thought to McVeigh as a suspect. Why would they? Someone who carried out such a monstrous atrocity would not likely be fleeing the scene in an old jalopy without a tag. While being processed, McVeigh watched news accounts of the bombing, showing no reaction.

Two days later, as McVeigh was being processed for release, a deputy noticed a televised report of a worldwide manhunt for one Timothy McVeigh, the primary suspect in the Oklahoma City Bombing. McVeigh, only five minutes from freedom, was returned to his Perry cell.

A newscaster mentioned a second manhunt underway for Terry Lynn Nichols. Wanted simply for questioning, Nichols walked into the Herington, Kansas, police station, where he told officers he was wanted for the Oklahoma City Bombing. Patrolmen stared at Nichols in disbelief.

And so it was that police officers in two small-town jurisdictions inadvertently apprehended the masterminds behind the murderous Murrah bombing. The detainments transpired without firing a single shot.

Each police department contacted the FBI.

Chapter Three

❧❧

It was around noon when Glenn, Edye, and I entered Oklahoma City's Children's Hospital. As we stood among parents of missing youngsters, most of whom were presumably buried beneath the tangled ruins of the Murrah Building, each family member seemed to be praying with diminishing hope that somehow their child might be alive.

The atmosphere of the medical facility churned with desperation, fear, and misery. I don't think any of us realized the futility of our hope. We just wanted to find our children—but we were also terrified of what their condition would be when we did find them.

I tried to call my brother, Bobby, to enlist his help in our search for our precious boys. In retrospect, I realize I also simply longed for his presence. Bobby had *always* been strong and had *always* been there for me. I *needed* him.

Once again, my telephone didn't work due to overloaded circuits. But this time I would not be delayed. I dialed the operator, told her about my situation, and practically ordered her to put my call through.

Bless her heart, she did.

Soon afterward, my son, Danny, a police officer from a nearby town who happened to be off-duty that day, arrived at the hospital. He'd seen Edye and me on television and had been looking for us all day amid the chaos and the people. At last, he had found us.

Policemen, Oklahoma National Guardsmen, and members of the Department of Civil Emergency Management struggled to contain the crowd. Authorities' efforts were thwarted by people running toward the Murrah and adjacent buildings, hoping to find their loved ones. Nonetheless, officials patiently continued ordering folks to stand down and to stay behind designated perimeters.

Danny got word that an unidentified baby who survived had been located across the street inside the Veterans Administration Hospital.

Here we go again, I thought.

With our hearts in our throats, we sprinted to the facility. Danny and I approached the building through its parking garage, where unauthorized personnel were forbidden.

Unauthorized? I thought. *Who should be more* authorized *than a family searching for its children who are missing at a bomb site?*

Nevertheless, rules are rules—even in times of disaster. All Danny had to do was flash his police badge. He was admitted entrance into the VA Building—but I was not.

And so I was left alone in the half-dark, cavernous parking garage. The external cacophony of human desperation was replaced by foreboding echoes of silence. In its own way, the quiet was deafening.

Before I had time to think too much, the stillness was shattered by a tiny, distorted voice coming over a loudspeaker just above me. It announced that a bomb might be inside the VA Hospital—and it might soon detonate!

The voice ordered people in the VA Hospital to evacuate.

"Evacuate? To where?" I said aloud.

There was no one to answer. I just stood there alone beneath the weight of a multistory building that might explode any second.

Above, on ground level, I heard the rumble of footsteps and the pitch of anxious human voices as people fled the building. I wanted to run to where they were—to join the "safety" of the masses. But where I was, there was no safety. I desperately didn't want to die alone. And yet, I didn't move.

I couldn't. I was petrified! Frozen by fear.

I just stood there with fists clenched, face contorted, weeping uncontrollably. It occurred to me that my sobs might be the last sound I would ever hear before the blast would end my agony.

"Why, dear God, don't You send somebody to help me?"

After what seemed like an eternity, I heard the solitary voice of Danny.

Thank God, he's come for me! I thought.

Well, not entirely. Seeming as calm as everyone else was out of control, Danny had primarily come to say he'd seen the child.

It was a girl.

Depression hit me like two anvils, crashing heavily on my shoulders. Simultaneously, my awareness of the panicked movement of frantic people upstairs returned.

Like them, we should have dashed from the VA Building. But we didn't. Danny wouldn't leave his mother, and his mother was tired of running.

Physically depleted and emotionally despondent, I felt the reassuring strength of Danny's arm during our slow and deliberate walk back to the Children's Hospital. Who knew what awaited us there?

Maybe, just maybe, it would be the broken but live bodies of Chase and Colton. If so, I could gratefully spend the rest of my life nursing them back to health.

Once inside the hospital, we walked to where Edye and Glenn were sitting. Danny stood silently for what seemed to be a very long time. Finally, he turned me around to face him. When our eyes met, he simply said, "Mom, I will find the boys. I promise."

I knew Danny meant what he said, and I felt a sense of comfort in his good intentions.

Yet I felt no peace at all.

> ⤙

We continued our vigil inside the assigned waiting area at the Children's Hospital. I had often read that stressful situations give occasion for human bonding, and I found this to be true among the hopeful, praying families as we continued to wait.

I was well acquainted with one of the families, as their son used to play with my grandbabies. I tentatively tried to comfort them, probably to no one's benefit. Then I mingled with another family and still another.

I guess I felt a need to reach out. I wanted to touch people who needed touching, just as I did.

Meanwhile, Danny continued to search for Chase and Colton. I'd eventually learn that he'd gone straight to the Murrah Building, which had become an especially busy place with recovery teams sifting through the rubble.

Danny told us later that he'd stepped onto the America's Kids day-care center playground, once a haven of glee that resonated with laughter. He found it grievously silent with the limp bodies of dead children organized into a row and covered with blankets. Most of the tiny corpses were disfigured beyond recognition. Nevertheless, parents or family members would eventually have to identify the remains.

At approximately 3 p.m., only six hours (that seemed like three days) after the blast, Danny returned to the Children's Hospital waiting room.

I knew by the look on my son's face that something was wrong, but I would not allow myself to believe the worst.

"Mom, I think I found Colton," he said while avoiding eye contact.

"What do you mean, you *think* you found Colton?" I replied.

Danny described the color and cut of the garments worn by the child he had found. His description matched perfectly with how Colton was dressed when we'd left him at day care that morning.

Perhaps subconsciously I was thinking about the parents I had just seen whose own baby had been found alive. Maybe I was saturated with horrible news, and thought that odds were finally in my favor to hear something wonderful. For whatever reason, my spirit soared when my son indicated he'd found one of my grandchildren. My relief was short-lived.

"Mom," Danny said, still avoiding eye contact, "Colton's gone."

"No, no, not the baby!" I screamed.

Hearing my own words was like an out-of-body experience.

I heard the exclamation just like everyone else in the room, but it seemed as if someone else were screaming.

"Where's Edye? I *need* to tell her," Danny said.

Danny walked slowly around the corner to the chaplain's office. Within seconds, I heard one of the most bloodcurdling cries I had heard all day. It sounded like a dozen women having their hearts ripped from their chests.

I didn't have to move to know the grieving voice of Edye. My son had found my daughter.

⤚

I had no idea what *I* would say to Edye about our appalling loss. I had just begun rehearsing an experimental sentence when I involuntarily collapsed. Thankfully, a chair was right behind me.

Meanwhile, with his mission incomplete and feeling more determined than ever, Danny left the children's facility en route to find Chase.

Soon he telephoned to report locating an unidentified boy whose hair matched Chase's. The child was alive! But when he described him more fully, I knew the child was not my grandson.

So I hung up the phone. Our heartbreaking vigil dragged on unmercifully. Occasionally, screams of agony continued from the room near the chapel where Edye mourned and prayed and hoped.

For whatever reason, I didn't go to Edye—not immediately. Perhaps I thought the chaplain could console her better than I. I thought I was falling apart myself, and I didn't want Edye to see me suffer in a way that would underscore her own suffering.

To a degree, I think I was avoiding the chaplain. He represented a God with whom my terms were now torn. I knew I wasn't the first to think it—not in the context of this grieving crowd—but I couldn't help questioning *why* a God of love would allow this massacre of innocent babies and blameless adults.

"For God so loved the world, that he gave his only begotten Son, that whosoever believeth in him should not perish, but have everlasting life" (John 3:16).

I had heard that Scripture for all of my forty-one years. I believed in the God these words were spoken to describe. But I had begged Him to spare my babies, and yet Colton's life had been taken by the cruelest, most barbaric means. Was this how God showed His love for me?

Where is God now? I couldn't help but wonder.

I didn't have time to wait for an answer. The ringing of a telephone sounded a death knell for the second time that day.

Danny had found Chase.

My son didn't need to describe Chase's attire. The three-year-old was discovered wearing only a toe tag in a refrigerated truck being used as a makeshift morgue.

I think I fell to my knees. I'm not sure. Maybe that happened later. Or maybe it happened somewhere else. It's all a fog. There is, however, one thing I am sure of: I heard the anguished screams of a woman whose wails were hoarse and frail.

This time, I knew the sounds were coming from *me*.

Chapter Four

The exhaustive search for Chase and Colton had ended, but it would never be over, not for me. Never in my saddest dreams had I imagined life without my grandsons. Yet we began our journey home from the hospital with no little boys buckled into their car seats.

For the rest of my life, I knew I would miss the sight, sound, smell, and touch of my grandbabies as these sensations recurred in my memories—recollections fueled by photographs, videotapes, media coverage of the bombing's annual anniversary, music, and more, including my countless sightings of darling little boys everywhere. Unavoidably, I compared them to Chase and Colton.

Additional reminders came in hearing other children's laughter, bringing the pain of remembering the giggle and titter of youngsters that once rang through my household. My grandbabies hadn't been simply a decoration in my life, they'd become the fabric of my life.

The parade of memories began as I entered my house on April 19, 1995. The silence was suffocating.

Without speaking, Edye and I eased our way among telltale signs of laughing little lives that had flourished hours earlier.

Colton had left a cup of milk on the kitchen counter, and a toy car on the floor. I couldn't bring myself to pour out the milk, or to move the car. Edye and I entered the boys' room—a playground formerly enlivened by the delightful ring of giggles that ceased only when the babies slept. Now, they'd sleep forever. Happy pictures and furniture belied the bliss of innocence that was now relegated to graves three-quarters of a century too early.

I fell onto Colton's bed, and Edye onto Chase's. We said nothing to each other, to ourselves, or even to God. For the first time we allowed the agony we'd been suppressing to escape from our broken hearts and spinning minds.

Uncontrollable sobbing didn't cease for Edye or me for hours, or so it seemed.

Glenn was elsewhere in the house, where he clearly wanted to be alone. I understood, I guess. But he must have heard me wailing as he soon appeared, helped me to my feet, and gently guided me down the hall to our bedroom. I crawled into our bed where I pulled the covers over my head to create a dark, tiny, safe world of my own. There, I mourned from the depths of my soul.

But by early evening, rest was continually interrupted by the incessant ringing of the telephone and doorbell. Friends, family, and people I didn't know were now calling or dropping by my house. I tried to accept as many calls as possible. The instant I'd hang up the receiver, the phone would ring again. The second I'd close the door, the doorbell would chime still another time.

People with and without cameras milled around in my front yard. A few eased their way to the back.

Most of the telephone callers had seen Edye and me on the national news shows. Many hadn't realized that Chase and Colton were in the day care. Some didn't know the boys were gone. They would fall silent when I told them.

One family friend called to ask how we were doing. I managed to whisper, "We're fine, but the boys are dead." He screamed, loudly pleading, "Jesus, Jesus, Jesus." I can still recall his fervent cries.

Many callers promised to pray for me and my family. Some prayed fervently while I was still on the line. When they did, I would close my eyes in anger. I wondered if the God I had prayed to earlier might be listening to them now, because He sure hadn't listened to me then.

Each time I told friends or strangers that my grandbabies were dead, my spirit shattered a little more. I prayed that word of their deaths would spread rapidly—before I was irreparably broken into a million tiny shards of sorrow.

Someone suggested that the journalists would not make a definitive announcement until the boys had been officially pronounced dead by a coroner. So far, they'd been pronounced dead only by my son, Danny.

I glanced intermittently at the television throughout the evening. At one point, I saw a close-up picture of a tiny blue sandal lying among the bombing debris. Instantly, I knew it had belonged to Chase. The bomb had been so forceful that it blew his shoes off his little feet! I shrieked in terror as the full force of the day's events fell in on me like so many tons of Murrah Building wreckage.

People who were nonrelatives began to filter out of our house shortly after the 10 p.m. newscasts. Family members bedded down in the den. Glenn, Edye, and I went to our bedrooms and once again faced the hollow sound of quiet. Sheer exhaustion overcame our tears from time to time and allowed short periods of shallow sleep.

My final emotional breakdown for that day was prompted by a specific recollection of Chase.

Almost every night, like clockwork, he'd get out of bed and toddle down the hall into my bedroom. I'd open my eyes and he would be standing there with his little face only inches from mine. He always made some request for my assistance or had some kind of excuse just to be in my room.

"Nonna, I got to go pee-pee." Or, "Can I sleep with you and Pawpaw for just a little bit?"

As I lay there in the silent darkness, I realized it was about time for Chase to come in. I held my breath. Surely he would appear, suddenly as always, looking into my face. But, of course, he didn't. And he never would again.

✌

In the wee hours of the morning, I found myself stirring to music. So did Glenn. We struggled from the bed to follow the familiar sound—notes from a toy carousel that the boys had loved. It was a melody we both knew by heart. The uncanniness alarmed us. There was no one in their room to turn on the carousel.

Glenn and I watched the hypnotic circling of the tiny porcelain horses until the thing ran down.

What had prompted the music box to play? We had no earthly idea. The boys had died the previous morning. And yet, *somehow* their beloved carousel had begun playing its familiar tune. Were the boys sending us a message from heaven?

As I look back now, I think maybe they were. I choose to believe they were telling us, "It's okay, Nonna, we're with Jesus now."

I truly hope that this is true. Whatever the reason, the little carousel playing on its own brought me comfort—comfort I desperately needed more than anything else.

✌

I awoke on April 20, praying I had experienced a nightmare that had passed. Yet my worst fears were confirmed: Chase and Colton were not fast asleep in their room. On this, my first day without the boys, I could only think that they had eaten at my breakfast table the day before.

Consumed with grief the previous night, I had almost forgotten Edye's and my appointment with Katie Couric from the *Today* show, the popular morning television program. Eventually, I was sought by fifty of America's largest television shows and print media, including the *New York Times, Wall Street Journal, Los Angeles*

Times, Chicago Tribune, TIME, Newsweek, U.S. News and World Report, People, 60 Minutes, and *20/20.*

At 6 a.m., Edye and I were picked up by a limousine and driven downtown to do an interview that would air live via satellite coast-to-coast in approximately ninety minutes.

When we arrived at the broadcast site, the roof of a low-rise structure with the decimated Murrah Building in the background, we had trouble getting to our assigned spot. It seems the previous day a photojournalist had dressed up like a firefighter to covertly enter the Murrah's warped infrastructure. There, he secretly videotaped rescue workers searching for victims. As a result, security was tightened and no one—especially the media—could get near the area without a special pass that required a photo ID.

Neither Edye nor I had that.

Our admittance was nevertheless approved after the show's producer made several frantic phone calls on our behalf. I never knew to whom he spoke.

Edye and I were then situated on a pallet hoisted by a hydraulic forklift, steadily rising to our designated seats on the windy roof. Early morning temperatures hovered in the forties. Strong bursts of cold air whipped through our hair and clothes and stung our faces.

I wondered when my grandbabies' bodies might be ready for viewing, while Katie Couric was only doing her job by asking again and again how we were doing and how it felt to experience such a loss. How would we *really* know? Our loss wasn't even twenty-four hours old. I was totally numbed by shock and so was Edye.

We returned to our home where yesterday's gathering of reporters had grown markedly. Human traffic was now gathered on all four sides of my house.

Although I had been unaware of most videos taken of my family and me after the bombing, I had seen other desperate people who were aware of their media coverage. I had heard them yell profanities at cameramen while ordering them to go away.

But they didn't.

Later, I would come to understand that whenever they were
shooting on a public street, cameramen could record anything or
anyone they wanted.

The press didn't know that the previous day's carnage was not
my first dance with death.

Nine years earlier, I had called my dad two days before the beginning of a new year. I had asked him to fix my car.

Characteristically, he said he would. Working on it would create
an opportunity for him to see me, and I him. I would never outgrow being "Daddy's little girl." I loved the way his face would light
up every time he saw me.

I turned the block onto my parents' street only to see a fire truck
and ambulance parked in front of their house. During the short
drive from my house to theirs, my dad had suffered a massive heart
attack. I walked into his home where he lay dead on the living
room floor.

My mother, Edith Graham, was sixty years old when Dad died.
She'd been diagnosed with Alzheimer's disease during her fifties,
and Dad was her caregiver. After he passed, my brother, Bobby, and
I tried to take care of Mother as Dad had done.

But we couldn't fill his shoes.

Having quit my job to attend to Mom, I underwent economic
stress. After several years, I finally had to place my mother in a
nursing home so I could go back to work.

There, under professional care, Mom died an unnecessary death
straight out of a horror film. It was reported on that night's local
television news that aired in March 1990.

That was the first of two times I saw the tragic and senseless
death of a loved one played out during primetime TV. Obviously,

the next time I experienced such a public display of my family's personal tragedy came during the coverage of Chase's and Colton's deaths five years later.

In neither instance was I surprised, as reporters had interviewed me for the programs. Nevertheless, it feels very awkward to be grieving over a loved one's untimely death with hundreds of thousands or even millions of people watching—almost none of whom personally knew my beloved mother, my grandbabies, or me.

Edye had been named after my mother. Although Alzheimer's was ravaging Mom's mind, it never affected her spirit. She had a servant's heart and gently exhibited God's grace to other patients. She walked around from room to room humming and softly singing old hymns. Mom always had a song in her heart.

Mom didn't know where she was. Even so, she lovingly reached out to people she didn't know, in surroundings she didn't recognize. Many times she would hug them as she tucked them in with a blanket she'd picked up somewhere...maybe from another room. She was acting as a caretaker to these poor people even though she needed help herself.

Some residents didn't receive her warmly. I'm sure she was worrisome to some of the other patients. Most of the old people didn't want her coming into their room. They complained to management. Inside her nursing home, Mom was confined to a chair with a restraint called a Posey belt.

One day, upon entering Mom's room, I saw her frantically trying to untie the restraint, fighting it like you would if some intruder broke into your house and tied you to a chair. She was pitifully confused and afraid.

Instantly, I told a nursing home official to untie my mother.

"Don't restrain my mother to make your job of watching her easier," I said. "This is not right. My mother is horrified!"

I assumed my directive was fulfilled. I was wrong.

While I was at work, a nursing home staffer failed to tighten the Posey properly. In her struggle to untie it, Mom's position in the chair was shifting awkwardly.

A housekeeper told the nursing staff that Mom was sliding in her seat, but nothing was done.

Mom was alone as she struggled, sliding off the chair, attempting to free herself when the Posey wrapped itself around her throat. She choked to death, no doubt terrified regarding her strange whereabouts and why she couldn't breathe. The entire tragedy might have been prosecuted in court as negligent homicide. But I pressed no criminal charges, not even after launching my own investigation into Mom's demise.

Little did I know that I was acquiring some of the skills required to expose an official cover-up of an unnecessary death of a loved one. Five years later, I'd apply part of that experience to try to uncover the truth behind the unnecessary deaths of 168 people, including Chase and Colton.

Mom's death meant I had lost both parents within a few years—one to natural causes, the other to mysterious circumstances.

An investigator for the Office of the Medical Examiner of the State of Oklahoma and I were told by nursing home officials that Mom had died of a heart attack. That marked the first time I was ever misled by an official spokesperson regarding the death of a family member.

A heart attack would not have left the dark bruises on Mom's neck, bruises that indicated strangulation, the investigator surmised.

In searching the scene, the investigator found the Posey they had used to restrain Mom inside a container reserved for dirty laundry.

Why, he wondered, was the belt inside a bag with linens, many soiled from human waste? Had it been hidden there?

I found the housekeeper for my mother's room. I wanted to ask my own questions to someone who might have been among the last to see Mom alive.

Afraid to talk to me while at work, the cleaning woman gave me her home address since she had no telephone. Her craggy face and missing teeth expressed the hard life she had obviously endured. En route to her residence, a hotel room rented by the week, I bought a bottle of Scotch whiskey and a cigarette case. Inside the case, I hid a tiny tape recorder. I even smoked a cigarette to bond with my unsuspecting informant.

She told it all, how she had found my mother sitting sideways in her chair, how she tried to straighten her up (although she wasn't officially allowed to touch patients), how she reported Mom's predicament to the staff and how they ignored her.

I used that information in a civil lawsuit I filed against the facility. An out-of-court settlement was reached.

But that didn't bring my mother back. And it didn't erase the lies told by the nursing home officials. Both were hard lessons to absorb then, and to live with to this day.

And so I had become familiar with unexpected and unnecessary deaths. And now, I had to plan a funeral for two little boys.

Having departed the *Today* show interview, Edye and I met Chase and Colton's father, Tony Smith, for an appearance on *Geraldo*. My initial televised appearances were motivated by my passion to commemorate my grandbabies.

Perhaps I was selfish, as the majority of other survivors were not given the forums presented to Edye and me. And all because we had unofficially been the first parent and grandparent to attempt to rescue our babies. This fact had less to do with our love for our family and more to do with location.

I was obsessed in my search. I had noticed, but I didn't really focus on, the presence of television cameras around us.

If the bombing had happened more recently, my daughter and I would probably have become a YouTube sensation. I would have hated that. Nevertheless, our notoriety did bring some advantages. Eventually, it allowed us to pose candid questions to the Federal Bureau of Investigation; the Bureau of Alcohol, Tobacco, Firearms, and Explosives; and other law enforcement agencies.

In some instances, our questions were taken seriously enough to prompt the fabrication of facts. After all, the queries had been asked on national television.

✄

April 21, two days after the bombing, was Edye's birthday. Historically, birthdays had been celebrated in a big way at our house, especially for the boys.

On this somber occasion, however, I planned no festivity. In fact, I didn't even acknowledge the occasion to Edye, who said nothing about it either.

She and I spent her birthday looking at caskets.

The lids were open, displaying the delicately adorned satin-and-lace interiors. As I gazed around the room, I became claustrophobic among the array of coffins. I was nauseous and felt like I was going to vomit. Frantically, I fought the sensation with a gasp and a gulp.

Finally, we made a decision and selected the coffin that would cradle the bodies of our little boys. They had lived and died together, so we thought it only fitting that they be buried together.

When we decided to hold the service in our home church in nearby Del City, we were asked how many people would attend—as if we knew. And there were many other difficult questions to answer. Who would the pallbearers be? Would we want a morning or an afternoon service? What about a graveside service? Would we want our family to partake of a meal at the church before or after the funeral? The questions were endless and incredibly painful.

Our hearts were broken, our minds were shattered, and our senses were numb. We were in no shape to be making decisions.

We settled on having the funeral on Saturday, and told the funeral home director we were sure we could rely on his judgment should new questions arise. We just wanted to get out of that place.

Very little sleep, coupled with immeasurable sorrow and untold stress, has a way of robbing people of their ability to process thoughts—or to even have them.

When we returned home, we found our house filled with flowers from around the world. Television reporters whose names we didn't know were revealing our names to the globe. It all felt very uncomfortable. Yet the pressure of virtually wall-to-wall bodies was minimal when compared to our next trauma later that day.

We had just planned a funeral. We were preparing to announce the time and place to friends and family. When funeral home personnel went to pick up the bodies, the Oklahoma County coroner announced that Chase and Colton were being held for further identification as well as evidence! In fact, their bodies would not be authorized for burial until *all* bodies were recovered from the Murrah Building!

We were horrified. It would likely take days—maybe even weeks—to remove all the victims.

The coroner then took things a step further. He asked if he could dissect our babies to study the effects of a bomb blast on human anatomy. We just wanted to lay them to rest, not submit them to a scientific study!

Next, we were told the boys would have to be X-rayed for bomb fragments, the results of which would be submitted to authorities as evidence. Also, the coroner's office sent the FBI to our home to dust the children's bedroom for fingerprints.

That was it! I wasn't merely partaking of grief; grief was overtaking me.

Acting purely on reflex and my social conditioning, I fell to my knees and then on my face. From the depths of a place inside me, I prayed to God, "Please, please let me die!"

That desperate prayer was one of the most heartfelt of my entire life. Suicide was no longer a passing thought. It was my fervent intention, a self-centered fantasy picturing the only solution I could imagine of life without relentless pain.

I had endured traumas earlier in my life such as domestic battering, divorce, the loss of loved ones, and more.

But each offered the hope of a better life after the fact.

I was now convinced that I had suffered more in three days than I had during all previous agonies combined. I could imagine no pending promise of relief.

Those little boys had been my life. Now that they were gone, so was my life. How could I get my life back when the boys were never coming back? In spirit, I felt no less dead than Chase and Colton. It's just that they were physically gone.

Physical death was what I longed for myself.

Nevertheless, I knew I could never take my own life—not with Glenn's and Edye's feelings to consider. Therein lay the irony.

But I was not myself, and I was convinced I never would be again. The absence of sleep and presence of pain, mixed with unbearable grief and seemingly no way out—all of these things together had destroyed my ability to reason.

Lost within my own subjective cloud of confusion, I decided suicide would be best, and then looked for reasons to support my life-denying decision.

In my moments of sanity I wondered, *What if Glenn or Edye took their lives right now? Would I understand?* But then my craziness would creep back in. *Of course I would*, I'd answer myself. *I'd even be happy for them and for their escape.*

Such amazing self-deception! I learned it's hard to believe a liar when the liar is you.

The truth was that if Glenn or Edye had taken his or her own life, I'm sure I would have withdrawn into a vegetative, catatonic state and never come out again.

My sober recognition of this fact spoiled my fantasy of suicide. My selfish logic could not be justified. Then again, I wasn't myself. A stranger had invaded my body and taken up residence inside my hollow soul. I didn't know this person. She was a stranger who answered to my name—and sometimes she frightened me.

As if hovering above myself in an out-of-body experience, I watched my own thoughts and behavior. I wondered what I would think and do next.

I was all but hallucinating, and possessed by this strange spirit who was full of dark thoughts and feelings that were completely alien to my nature.

How will she ever start the slow climb out of her pit of unfathomable pain? I asked about myself.

I thought I had gone insane. I then realized that if I were truly insane, I wouldn't be wondering about it. That realization, at least, brought some comfort.

I would soon learn that these helter-skelter thoughts were common symptoms of intense sorrow.

It was not until I heard John Walsh, host of the TV show *America's Most Wanted*, speak to a group of survivors a few days later that I knew I could make it.

I will never forget his poignant words.

"You *will* grieve and you will grieve deeply!" he affirmed, his finger pointing from person to person.

So that's it? I thought to myself. *He's telling us we'll grieve? Why doesn't he just tell us fish are wet, or circles are round, or the sun sets in the west?*

My hopes for peace of mind were totally dashed—almost.

"BUT YOU WILL SURVIVE!" Walsh exclaimed. "BUT YOU WILL SURVIVE!!"

These four words became my road map out of darkness, my first baby step away from my purgatory of pain, my realization that I could *choose* life or death.

I chose life.

I'm certainly not saying I was instantly delivered from tribulation. I was told that my anguish would lessen in time and in stages. Walsh's words offered a ray of hope, a ladder that would help me gradually step up to a semblance of sanity.

I'm not sure the simple message would have rung with such resounding credibility had anyone other than Walsh been the one to bring it. But Walsh himself had undergone the violent loss of his son, Adam, who was abducted from a Sears department store in July 1981 and later found decapitated. The death of his son resulted from an intentional crime.

For this reason and others, I devoured Walsh's words. He was offering me hope that someday I would get better and begin to live again.

I found that miracles were still delivered by mortal couriers. God had sent me a personal messenger—his name was John Walsh.

From that point on, I reminded myself often that my babies were now with Jesus in heaven. But the reminder brought me little comfort. I wanted Chase and Colton to be here with me *now*.

Heaven seemed so far, far away.

Chapter Five

❧

Sunday, April 23, 1995, marked a National Day of Mourning for victims of the bombing. Thousands of people from around the nation and the world were expected to attend.

The eulogy would be delivered by the Reverend Billy Graham, who'd walked away from major surgery at the Mayo Clinic expressly to visit Oklahoma City.

Meanwhile, television news media were competing for shooting locations intended to draw viewers' attention to America's mourning heartland.

As the death toll mounted, some media continued to report that the Murrah bombing was the worst act of terrorism ever enacted on American soil. The description became a wrenching and shopworn slogan.

Lines of cameramen stood in shoulder-to-shoulder formations broadcasting images of talking heads. Most reporters stationed themselves in a way that showed the Murrah remains behind them.

For all the wrong reasons, the bombing had put Oklahoma City on the global map to an unprecedented degree.

By design, my family and I remained emotionally detached from participating in the coverage except when a print or broadcast reporter specifically wanted a human-interest interview. Many writers no longer pursued stories about those who died, but rather about those who struggled to live. Each day, my obsession mounted. I wanted Chase and Colton to be remembered. They hadn't lived long enough to leave legacies. They never even rode a bike or started kindergarten; they missed their first dates and high school graduation. Nonetheless, I desperately didn't want them forgotten.

The volume of telegrams and conventional mail increased dramatically, indicating that people far and wide were reaching out to Edye and me—and hoping we might reach back. I'm talking about *thousands* of pieces of correspondence.

We actually received mail simply addressed to the "Red-Headed Mother and Daughter." Feed The Children, an Oklahoma-based charity whose founder, Larry Jones, was featured daily on CNN. Often accompanied by Geraldo Rivera, Jones appealed for donations while standing in front of the demolished Murrah Building. Heartfelt viewers reportedly sent millions of dollars. A loving nation urgently blessed its broken city.

✂

Although the memorial ceremony was scheduled for 3 p.m., Edye, Glenn, and I were picked up five hours earlier by the Secret Service. Transported in a van, we were accompanied by silent men wearing earpieces and hidden pistols.

Downtown Oklahoma City was eerily quiet on this, the fourth day after the bombing. Streets that had so recently resounded with thundering feet, screaming people, and deafening sirens now lay quiet, except for the purr of machinery still extracting debris and dead bodies.

As our van cruised through Oklahoma's capital city, I felt as though I were watching an outtake from *The Twilight Zone*, an old television series that dealt with mysterious phenomena. Buildings that had once stood tall were broken down; their windows were blown out and curtains waved hauntingly in the warm spring wind. Shattered glass lined the sidewalks and streets. The thoroughfares that usually bustled with life now were placid reminders of those who would never walk here again.

We stopped briefly at the Internal Revenue Service office where Edye and I were working at 9:02 a.m. on that day when our world stood still, and had since remained stalled. My eyes were drawn to the structure I didn't want to see but couldn't avoid—the Murrah Building, or what remained of it. Steel dangled out its side like ruptured blood vessels, sending shivers down my spine.

As our van joined others in a caravan, downtown Oklahoma City was reflected in the rearview mirror. I rather wished it could remain there—that we might never have to return to the place where my reasons for living were ripped away from me.

Despite the fact that it was a high-security vehicle, our van had no tinted windows. Moving as slowly as an engine's idle, it eased through throngs of mourners milling outside the Oklahoma City Fairgrounds Arena four hours before the program would begin.

People parted ranks to allow the van access to the arena. Only a pane of glass separated me from those who were walking, their faces contorted into rigid masks of grief.

As the van snaked its way through the massive crowd, we gazed out across the sea of nameless faces. We could read their lips as they pointed toward our van and said, "Look, there's Edye." I was astounded that they knew my daughter's name.

Everybody seemed to stand at attention as we passed by. They lovingly waved and nodded to acknowledge our presence, as if we were in some kind of morbid parade.

As we exited the vehicle, people curiously watched us. Those who were close enough to speak offered words of condolence... touched us on the shoulder or hand and petitioned God's blessing.

"We're praying for you," they said, almost to a person.

As had been predicted, many tried to push through the shoulder-to-shoulder assembly to get close to Edye and me. Obviously, they felt they vicariously knew us.

Television had often taken us into the mourners' living rooms, where we'd become like a surrogate family. We weren't bonded by blood or long acquaintance, but by the misery of these times.

✄

As we slowly made our way inside the venue, each of us was given a long-stemmed rose and a teddy bear. We found ourselves surrounded by thousands of flowers—a marvelous reminder that the entire nation wept with us.

Our entourage was escorted by the Secret Service to the front row of the lower level of the arena. There, we began our long wait for the memorial service to begin.

As my eyes scanned the auditorium, I drank in the outpouring of intense love and compassion, as well as the great sense of sorrow. Strangers unashamedly held hands and tearfully embraced one another. Many still didn't know if their loved ones were dead or alive.

Onstage, the Oklahoma City Philharmonic Orchestra played soft music that underscored the gentle weeping of the bereaved. The proceedings assumed a tone of sorrow and dignity, similar to services grieving a fallen president.

Ever so faintly, I began to hear a smattering of applause. Faint echoes of cheering and whistling began to fill the voluminous venue. The increasing volume rose to a level comparable to the earsplitting boom of Wednesday's explosion—the event that had brought us all here. From my position, I could not see across the sea of heads turned toward the rear of the auditorium.

"What's going on?" I asked aloud, my question lost in the clamor.

Then I saw a man in uniform...then another and another. Police officers, firefighters, emergency medical technicians, and others who had searched, rescued, and recovered Murrah casualties and victims were streaming toward the front of the venue. It was a parade of courageous men and women who marched with eyes forward and hearts open. Theirs was a glorious presence!

A joyfully rousing standing ovation provided the sound track to their entry, and was sustained long after they were seated. These people were the true heroes and heroines of the heartland. And on this day television was sharing them with the world.

My grateful tears flowed, as did the tears of others around me. To us all, the men and women in uniform represented all things good, hopeful, and resilient. If they had formed a receiving line, everybody in that jubilant audience would have surely waited their turn to hug every one of the blessed civil servants.

A sudden sense of God's merciful grace touched the hearts of many in the arena. You could feel a holy presence.

But for me, I was devastated. I wished workers could have found our family's children alive.

The euphoria of the crowd soon expired after hearing that one hundred people who'd occupied the Murrah Building on that dark day could not be accounted for. After four days, most were assumed dead. Still, a few might be breathing somewhere deep in the bowels of the refuse.

Soon, that massive congregation sang the time-honored hymn "Amazing Grace." The lyrics seemed more poignant to me than ever. I'd heard that song all my life, but I had never been touched by anything like its lifting from fifteen thousand voices—not to mention those singing outside the arena. There was no room for them inside.

I thought again about the one hundred people who were still missing. I wished the comforting tones of that precious songfest could float a few miles to where they lay beneath immeasurable tons of concrete and steel. The anthem might have reassured the barely living that someone would soon be coming for them—whether earthly rescuers or the angels themselves.

My experiences in the previous four days had raised a raft of unanswered questions. I felt a discomforting sense that there were no answers to any of my questions, including the one I most wanted answered: How, in the world created by a merciful God, could all of this be happening?

I was struggling to believe that God would gradually restore me.

Even there, in that expansive hall accompanied by thousands of suffering souls, I confess my faith still fluctuated—high and low, like the notes of "Amazing Grace." The heavenly hymn was hurting and healing me, both at the same time.

But you do feel hope. Your hope wouldn't vacillate if you felt no hope at all, a voice inside me suggested.

This thought was like an epiphany from the Holy Spirit. There, among the ups and downs of my faith, I was weak but He was strong. I was reminded of "Jesus Loves Me," another favorite song from childhood.

As a children's choir began to sing, I wept bitterly on Glenn's shoulder. I was having a hard time believing that the good and loving God I had worshipped all my life really existed. And if He did, could I trust Him after what had happened to me? I had prayed; I begged—and still my babies died.

President Clinton, Mrs. Clinton, and the Reverend Graham no doubt spoke with stirring profoundness. I tried to listen, but my attention faded in and out. I would eventually learn that sustained stress can diminish a person's senses.

When the commemoration ended, pockets of crying and renewed hysteria shattered the silence. Rays of optimism had spread while the program was under way, but now reality had returned and people were grieving anew. My heart ached for the emotionally tattered mourners.

Few things are as sad as a hurting heart that's straining to hold in the sorrow, yet yearning to let it all out. Late that afternoon, many of the emotionally wounded did just that. Ushers discreetly took seats of their own, patiently waiting to allow the suffering to remain until they gained the inner strength to go outside.

The memorial service had brought survivors a bit closer to comforting memories of their slain loved ones. This made it hard to want to go home. Too much emptiness and too many memories awaited them there, as my own experiences with tragedy had taught me.

Secret Service agents escorted us backstage to meet the presidential entourage.

Hillary Clinton saw me before I saw her inside the guarded quarters. Gazing at us through moistened eyes, she tenderly placed her arms around Edye and then me.

"I've watched the two of you on television," she said. "Your boys were so precious. My heart goes out to you."

Meanwhile, President Clinton held my hand as if trying to absorb a part of my pain.

Clinton turned to Edye and then signed his name on the mat surrounding a large photograph of Chase and Colton that she'd clung to throughout the service.

With steely resolve, the president issued a promise. He did not raise his voice; he exhibited no aggression. In fact, his tone was calm, and that made it even more wonderfully frightening.

"The people who did this *will* be brought to justice," he said. He tenderly but unwaveringly stared into my eyes.

I knew I had become a party to a pact with the most powerful man in the world. This wasn't about politics. It was personal. I'd never previously felt such a degree of certainty that justice would be served for Chase and Colton, for me and Edye, for all who had lost loved ones—for every American.

I felt like the president had issued a vow for the entire nation.

Billy Graham looked as tired as I felt. I thought about his

forgoing scheduled surgery at the Mayo Clinic in order to preach today's mass funeral.

I was awestruck. Here before me was the preacher who embodied evangelical Christianity to my late mother and others in her generation. Under different circumstances, there were so many things I would have asked him.

He didn't want to talk about himself. His focus was on Edye and me. He exhibited the same one-on-one persona I'd felt from Clinton. And when Graham prayed to God on our behalf, it was as if he was confiding in an old friend about no one other than Edye and me.

The next morning, the *Daily Oklahoman* newspaper carried a front-page picture of Edye, Phyllis (Edye's stepmother), and me. As the day progressed, people from all over America called regarding that photograph—it had been published in newspapers nationwide.

Following the coroner's release of their bodies, Chase and Colton's funeral was held on April 25, 1995, six days after the massacre.

The entire night before, I didn't sleep at all. I seemed awake, but I was mindless like a zombie—hardly prepared to face the most dreaded event of my life.

Before leaving my house, I senselessly walked again to the boys' room, thinking that somehow, some way, they might be there. As I entered their former world, I prayed with all that was within me that the babies might be found there, miraculously alive. The Bible contained stories about people who were dead but had returned to life at God's request, such as Lazarus. Jesus Himself triumphed over death. And I had read books such as *Embraced by the Light*— an account of a woman who said she was clinically dead, went to heaven, and then awakened during her natural life.

But, of course, the boys were not there. I left the empty room that morning with my faith waning.

"If there *is* a God, where is He now?" I asked again.

The family car picked us up at 12:30 p.m. for the 2 p.m. service at First Baptist Church, my home congregation in Del City, a suburb of Oklahoma City.

Tony, Chase and Colton's father, openly sobbed all the way to the sanctuary during the otherwise silent ride.

Our having taken the family car proved to be a good thing. It was given priority among other vehicles, and we were driven to the front door of the church. The parking lot was crammed beyond capacity. I'd later learn that more than two thousand attendees had filled the building and spilled out onto the lawn.

At the end of the service, members of the congregation walked past the closed casket that held two bodies. Then, mourners on the grounds patiently walked inside the church to pass the casket before returning outside.

I hadn't expected such an outpouring of love and sympathy. Many people had come from out of state, I was later told.

Tim Langley, the music minister, introduced Steve Carroll, who sang "The Nursery Rhyme Song," a collection of traditional rhymes whose words were changed to express a spiritual message.

I was so impressed with Carroll's talent that I thought he should be a professional singer. Later I found out he was a former member of Three Dog Night, a superstar rock act from the late sixties to the mid-seventies. He had volunteered to sing on behalf of Chase and Colton—children he'd never met.

The entire congregation sang "Jesus Loves Me," a traditional children's song with lyrical poignancy I didn't realize until that day.

Our family friend Rhonda Schrum sang "Jesus Loves the Little Children" and "The Barney Song." I'd sung the former to Chase and Colton countless times at bedtime. Eventually Chase got to where he liked to change the words for the evening's final rendition:

"Jesus loves the Nanas and Papas, all the Nanas and Papas of the world,

red and yellow, black and white, they are precious in his sight, Jesus loves the Nanas and Papas of the world," he'd sing in his tiny voice.

I would have made a pact with God to willingly die at the end of that song if He'd let my grandson sing it to me one last time.

Tim sang, "Jesus, I Heard You Had a Big House," a tune that Edye had sung throughout her childhood.

Even though the agenda included adults singing mostly children's songs, the renditions were heartfelt. It had never occurred to me before that such clichéd lyrics could be delivered with such emotional power.

The vocalists weren't just singing these songs, their souls were projecting them, as if to remind everyone that the worth of every child is beyond measure, that there is wisdom in their simplicity, and that the promises of God are without compromise.

The musical climax came when those two thousand people, inside the church and outdoors, rose to sing "Amazing Grace." To me at that time, the song seemed to be more than just a time-proven hymnal anthem. Instead, it seemed to be the closest we mortals could get to talking to God Himself.

While singing those hallowed lyrics, the service took on a blessed tone. Many bereaved were transformed into grateful worshippers who raised their hands and opened their souls.

My primary emotion was hope; hope that I would one day see my grandbabies again. And for a blessed second, as those voices rose with the purity of cherubs, I wanted to believe that I truly *would* see my grandchildren again. But I was finding it hard. Where was the God whom I thought I knew so well?

My family and I departed the church sobbing. Our car joined the funeral procession on Interstate 44, the main highway through the entire state of Oklahoma that connects it with the nation. Especially in metropolitan areas, Interstate 44 is usually clogged with cars and almost as many semitrailer trucks. It was approaching

5 p.m., rush hour, when bumper-to-bumper traffic, even at slow speeds, was routine.

Not that day.

On both sides of the interstate, traffic had pulled to the shoulder of the road. Drivers and passengers stood solemnly outside parked vehicles. Some had their hands over their hearts. A few knelt and openly prayed for Edye, me, and our family. A few more held signs that cited Scripture or read "We are praying for you."

Burly motorcyclists and truck drivers stood or knelt with reverent dignity. Businessmen wearing suits, and women in tidy pantsuits, knelt and held hands with grimy, shirtless men, whom, in their everyday lives, they likely would have avoided.

That seemingly endless line of reverential well-wishers outside their parked vehicles was surely the most dramatic show of support for my suffering family, from that day to this.

How many motorists and passengers lined that asphalt shoulder between Del City and Oklahoma City? A hundred? A thousand? More?

I had no idea.

This stretch of concrete and asphalt along Interstate 44 seemed like sacred ground in my otherwise depleted world.

Following the graveside service, my family and I were approached by Tony Lippe, one of the first rescue workers to enter the Murrah Building.

He said that most of what he saw inside the partially fallen structure was an assortment of dead or dying bodies strewn amid shapeless rubble.

The roar of the rescue equipment had not yet begun. Except for the screams and moans of the injured and the chatter among rescuers, the demolished interior of Murrah was mostly silent.

The most poignant sound Lippe heard was the faint whimper of a child. It was Colton.

Lippe found my grandson with a glass shard thrust into his abdomen. It was lodged deep and immovable inside his internal organs.

Colton was bleeding profusely.

Lippe had a fleeting inclination to administer CPR, but he knew the measure would be futile. Seeing that Colton was about to die, Lippe simply held him in his arms. He wanted Colton to leave this world in someone's caring embrace.

Lippe heard, felt, and saw Colton take his last breath.

When the warning broke about a second bomb, the rescuers inside the Murrah wreckage started their frantic scramble to safety. Lippe wanted to get out, too, but he didn't want to put Colton down.

With no time to argue, two emergency workers picked Lippe up with Colton still fixed in his clutch. Once outside, Lippe carried Colton to a bench where Danny found him later that day.

Even under the threat that a second blast might take his own life, Lippe did not abandon Colton. His loving act offered a striking example of the special kind of love born of the moment among the citizens of Oklahoma City. Many good souls responded to counteract the hate that had inspired the bombing.

At the time—only minutes after Chase and Colton were placed into the ground—I couldn't think that deeply during Lippe's revelations. As had been the situation for days, I was moving on adrenaline and could barely think at all.

I couldn't start thinking and couldn't stop feeling. Far and away, the latter was my most agonizing curse.

Chapter Six

By summertime in 1995, the pressures of living with the aftermath of tragedy began to show cracks in the personalities of my three-member family.

Glenn's disdain for everyone in law enforcement and government had evolved into seething rage toward them—and toward God. My husband had heard, from an eyewitness, that the bomb squad had been in downtown Oklahoma City before the bombing occurred. Yet the official in charge of that squad insisted they weren't near the Murrah Building, or so he told Glenn.

Investigators later established that the bomb squad had actually been in the vicinity before the blast, prompting the official to withdraw his statement about their location.

Thereafter, Glenn felt as though everyone in local, state, and federal government was conspiring to conceal the truth about the bombing.

He was furious with God for allowing Chase and Colton to die when other children had survived the blast. Many mothers and fathers, while appearing on television, said they praised God for sparing their children's lives.

"Why," Glenn wanted to know, "did God spare some children but not our grandchildren?"

He never found a satisfactory answer to that emotionally charged query.

In every fiber of his being, my husband was convinced that the agencies formed decades earlier to serve and protect Americans had let us all down. Now, some of their personnel were lying about what really preceded and followed the Murrah bombing, Glenn believed.

I am not suggesting that Glenn thought the FBI and the ATF were coconspirators in the bombing. But he was convinced that some people inside those organizations had received prior warning of the pending destruction, and had done nothing to prevent the calamitous sequence of events from unfolding.

Edye, on the other hand, had become a paragon of strength. More than Glenn or me—or anyone else inside my entire family circle—Edye lived life one day at a time with eyes looking forward.

During those days, I dedicated my energies to searching for the truth about the Murrah bombing. It was my primary way to cope with the overwhelming loss of Chase and Colton.

Our home became another encampment of journalists and news reporters as our investigation spawned national attention. The more questions our family posed about the bombing, the more media from across the world flocked to us. Yet, no matter how many people surrounded me, I still felt empty and alone.

As we delved deeper toward the truth, some of the victims' families were appalled that Glenn and I were questioning what *really* happened. They didn't understand why we were willing to form an alliance with McVeigh's defense team. But we had similar interests with them. We simply wanted *everyone* involved in this crime to be prosecuted. We also wanted to know if our government really was telling us the truth.

By the time I met Joyce Wilt (mother of coconspirator Terry Nichols) in the courthouse, many of those families already considered me an outcast. Most were angry and didn't sympathize with my persistence for the truth. Occasionally I was referred to as "Tim McVeigh's newfound friend."

I quickly became tired of all that. Often, I leaned on Edye for support. She was resilient in a way I was unable to understand.

Recovery for everyone was a day-at-a-time ordeal. Unfortunately for some shattered folks, recovery had yet to begin. They felt as destroyed as they did on the morning the bomb's blast was heard around the world.

During times of prayer, I meditated on Jesus and asked His Holy Spirit to intercede for me. I found that I no longer knew how or what to pray.

I would be lying if I didn't confess that my own peace of mind and heart remained elusive. I was doing well to merely survive. I reminded myself that less than three months had passed since the tragedy. But constant pain prompts impatience. When you are hurting to the core, you want the anguish to stop immediately, not a year or a month or a week or a day from the agonizing moments when you feel it!

I didn't want to hear yet another well-meaning person recite the tired cliché that "time heals all wounds." I had already suffered a lifetime's worth of trauma in my short time on earth. To me, time seemed maddeningly fickle. While it brought healing, it also brought pain. It was as if God would grant me a new milestone in recovery, then the devil would retaliate with a battalion of demons determined to chip it away to nothing.

I continued to struggle with my faith. After all, it was all I had left. Psalm 23 played over and over in my mind. I was finding it hard to digest.

The LORD is my shepherd; I shall not want.
He maketh me to lie down in green pastures: he leadeth me beside
*   the still waters.*

He restoreth my soul: he leadeth me in the paths of righteousness for
   his name's sake.
Yea, though I walk through the valley of the shadow of death, I will
   fear no evil: for thou art with me; thy rod and thy staff they com-
   fort me.
Thou preparest a table before me in the presence of mine enemies:
   thou anointest my head with oil; my cup runneth over.
Surely goodness and mercy shall follow me all the days of my life:
   and I will dwell in the house of the LORD *forever.*

I had heard this passage read at funerals all my life and now it was taking on new meaning. I realized that I was the one walking through *"the valley of the shadow of death,"* and I was finding it hard to see my way out. In fact, I found it impossible.

The doorbell had rung countless times since the afternoon of April 19. Glenn, Edye, and I assumed the unexpected caller who rang now was another reporter. By now, most journalists were keeping their covenant with my family about scheduling an appointment before abruptly visiting our house. Who was breaking the rules of common courtesy by dropping by unannounced?

I opened the door to face a strange woman whose sorrowful countenance was indelibly etched by lines of worry and fear. Looking into her face was like looking into my own. Withered and weary, she seemed to bear the weight of the world.

Before I could ask her identity, she bolted into an explanation as to why she was standing on our stoop.

Her story began with a tearful announcement of how she had lost her two children in a runaway fire. As she struggled to continue speaking, she described how she saw Edye and me on the television and just "knew" we would understand her misery given our own loss.

I needed to hear no further words of introduction; I insisted the woman come inside. Edye and Glenn had already overheard her mournful lament through the open door. Before the visitor was fully inside our house, my family was standing with open arms to receive her.

To Edye and me, the woman was our sister in a sorority of sorrow. Even though we had yet to hear details of her heartbreaking loss, we instantly understood her anguish.

Alone, she had driven to Oklahoma City from Bangor, Maine—a distance of 1,921 miles—stopping only for gasoline and restroom breaks. As if her grief had been building with every mile, it crashed upon us like a tidal wave of merciless agony. Edye wrapped her arms around this woman, someone whom she had never met, just as she had numerous times with total strangers during those days.

This road-weary newcomer seemed to be at home with us, in a house she'd never previously entered. That was perfectly fine with my family and me.

We continued to listen in rapt attention as our visitor told us she had never traveled outside the state of Maine, where she had been facing the loss of her youngsters without emotional support from others.

Each of us shuddered at the thought. Granted, even inside crowded rooms or with each other, every member of my family sometimes felt as if he or she were alone. Nonetheless, that didn't mean we were ever truly by ourselves while enduring our agony. In fact, despite all my family had undergone, we were never without concern for one another. Nor were we ever without the heartfelt prayers of friends and television viewers in America and internationally.

Our visitor continued to speak, talking repeatedly about seeing Edye and me on television. Her recollections were specific. Thus, we had no doubt that she'd seen our tortured lives play out over the airwaves inside her own living room in New England.

She described how her desperation to be with us prompted her to rent a car and finance her tiresome journey with proceeds from a bake sale. She extended her condolences to Edye by giving her $130.00—apparently proceeds from the bake sale as well.

After a while, she expressed her utter exhaustion and the need to go to her motel for sorely needed rest.

"But first," she said, "I want to meet with the workers who rescued and aided local survivors. I will feel better letting them know that one more person is truly grateful for their sacrifices during this time of need."

"Can't you at least stay for dinner?" I asked. "You must be hungry."

She graciously declined and insisted on proceeding downtown to meet with the heroic rescue workers. There was a tearful goodbye followed by a standing invitation for our new friend to stay in touch. Then, almost as rapidly as she had appeared, she was gone.

Later that afternoon, I called the motel where she told us she was staying. The desk clerk confirmed her registration but indicated she had already checked out. I thought her incredibly brief stay in Oklahoma City was peculiar, although I didn't give much thought to why. Her behavior had been no more erratic than mine, or so I thought.

"Do you suppose we will ever see her again?" I asked. Edye and Glenn said nothing. Their silence was our answer.

A few weeks after the arrival of our unexpected guest, Edye moved into the house she had purchased before the bombing. She had yet other unforeseen visitors at her new home. Upon opening the door, Edye encountered unfamiliar men wearing business suits and neckties. Their identification cards and badges confirmed they were with the FBI.

The agents presented a picture of a woman. Without a doubt, Edye identified her as the person who'd visited my home.

The FBI informed Edye that the woman was suspected of putting a bullet through her husband's head and leaving him for dead behind a Dumpster in another state. When the woman was arrested, she claimed Edye as her alibi. The suspect insisted she had been with Edye Smith and family in Oklahoma City, Oklahoma.

Indeed, she had.

Our visitor had sat beside us, exchanged stories of loss, and been in our arms sharing condolences, *after* fleeing the scene of a murder she was now being accused of committing! And we sat inches from her in the transparent safety of our home. I didn't know what to think. The fact is, I still don't.

❦

During the middle 1990s, watching the television news became my unwanted pastime. I became weary of journalists who struggled to put new "angles" on the bombing, then reported just for reporting's sake. Many stories were nothing more than old news in new packaging.

I nonetheless felt compelled to watch, as I hoped for a legitimate update to answer my lingering questions about the bombing and its originators.

My television set played constantly, even as I multitasked other responsibilities. To a degree, the broadcasts' sights and sounds were background stimulus that visually anesthetized me.

And I wasn't the only person who felt that way, especially in the southwestern United States where the bombing had stirred so many households.

As still photographs were flashed, preoccupied viewers would sometimes confuse a picture of one person with the text about another. That was especially true if similar stories were aired consecutively, or if newspapers placed them side by side.

Such confusion developed between Edye and Susan Smith, who, like Edye, had lost two boys. The difference was that Smith had murdered her children. Television viewers were told that Smith had strapped her youngsters into car seats, then pushed the vehicle into a lake where they drowned.

Smith's victims were boys, as were Edye's children; her kids were ages three and fourteen months, not dramatically different from the ages of Edye's.

Smith was convicted of murdering her sons on July 22, 1995, a little more than three months after Edye's sons were slaughtered.

People began to stop Edye in public places. They recognized her face from saturation media coverage involving the deaths of young boys. But they didn't correctly place her name with her face.

"You're Susan Smith!" people might exclaim.

Can you imagine? Edye was struggling, heartbroken, and childless due to circumstances beyond her control. Then some people confused her with a woman who had murdered her own children!

But Edye wouldn't walk away.

"I'm Edye Smith!" she would say. "I loved my children. You have me confused with Susan Smith! I lost my children in the Murrah bombing!"

Her accusers would offer an embarrassed apology for the mistaken identity. Then they would simply walk away, leaving Edye alone with renewed sorrow.

≻⊱

I recalled in precise detail the dauntless efforts of Danny, my only son, on the blackest day of my life. He had come to help search for Chase and Colton without my having to call and tell him about the terrible thing that had happened.

Danny was beside me when I needed him amid the chaos of mass destruction. All the while, he led me through with his customarily calm demeanor. Danny was then, and is now, a "fix-it" man who keeps his focus on what needs to be done even in the most hectic situations. To me, the mere sight of him is comforting.

But, like many brave men, while remaining outwardly strong for others, Danny cries internally with invisible tears. Regrettably, instead of acknowledging his secret sorrow, I neglected it.

At a loss for how to process his strong emotions, Danny blamed himself for our pain. It was he who delivered the news of Chase's and Colton's deaths. What's more, he thought we blamed him, too.

This may seem illogical. But logic often evaporates from the minds of people who experience extreme psychological trauma. They often remain emotionally vulnerable for months.

To complicate matters, Danny was aware that Glenn and I thought that some local law enforcement agencies had been warned it was a dangerous day and their efforts to stop the Murrah bombing had been incompetent. We thought there were a few lawmen who had conspired to craft alibis to minimize how much they knew.

Danny had taken our anti-law-enforcement attitudes toward some officials personally, and for understandable reasons.

Then a police officer himself, Danny thought we judged him guilty by association. He was part of the brotherhood and all it represented. For this, he felt that we looked down on him.

I should have discerned this kind of remorse in my son. But I didn't. I was too absorbed in putting my own shattered soul back together; also Edye's. I am sure I focused on Edye because she lived at my house much of the time. Plus, she and I had gone through the bombing hand in hand. Experiences of adversity breed bonding, whether among family, friends, or even foes.

But this is no excuse. Consolation begins at home. Danny was also family, no matter where he happened to reside. I should have been more attentive to him.

Sadly, my neglect had even extended to Danny's daughter, Caitlin—my own granddaughter. I had been there when she was born. I had been there when she played with Colton, who was only three months older than she. But I was not there for her in those months after the bombing. Caitlin saw her grandmother on television far more often than she saw me face-to-face.

Caitlin had lost her baby cousins and her little tears were real. I should have been there to dry them. She missed me deep in her heart and I didn't take the time to miss her at all.

Danny repeatedly tried bringing Caitlin to visit Glenn and me in the days and weeks following the tragedy. He thought the love of an innocent child might aid in our healing. While in hindsight this seems practical, neither Glenn nor I was of a mind to see it then.

As she always had, Caitlin called me "Nonna." But I couldn't bear to hear this precious term of endearment. It only reminded me of the grandchildren I no longer had. I wanted to show my love for Caitlin, but at the time, with all my pain, I just couldn't bring myself to do it.

As one might imagine, my failure to show emotion toward Caitlin hurt Danny. Once again, I was too self-absorbed to realize the misery I was causing him. I had yet to be able to imagine life without Chase and Colton. I was stuck in a place where I seemed loveless. I failed to reach out to my other grandchild as well as my own son.

The places where I was wounded remain tender to this day, but not so tender that I remain protective of them. That is the beautiful truth about time healing all wounds.

Memories still surface to create an emotional "domino effect"— one painful memory ignites another that may spawn yet another. And the writing of this book has activated an avalanche of traumatic recollections such as I've not experienced since the days following the explosion.

Often when I least expect it, I am reminded of how far I've come. While evil still abounds in this world, my God has overcome the world. And it is well with my soul.

And certain loved ones, Danny among them, dependably walk by my side just as surely as they live in my heart. And they always will.

Chapter Seven

Oklahoma City is famous for hot summers. Temperatures sometimes rise to 110 degrees while suffocating humidity is measured above 90 percent.

I've endured many of those sweltering seasons.

The most stifling heat I can remember came during 1995. For the first time, I felt like a prisoner of the climate. I hated going outdoors, where my perspiration mixed with my tears. But I also deplored staying indoors, where investigations into the terrorism continued to be broadcast daily on both the network and the cable television channels.

The scrutiny of my family's personal lives remained in high gear as well.

For example, on August 25, 1995, four months after the bombing, I was casually scanning television stations when, to my surprise, I saw Edye on *Good Morning America*. When her segment ended, I switched to other channels and saw her again.

After Colton's birth, Edye had her tubes tied. I knew she was in Texas seeing a doctor about getting the procedure reversed. Again and again, news programs had inquired about my daughter's loss of Chase and Colton.

I didn't know that a producer for a national television talk show would find out, or that a correspondent had been sent to Austin to cover Edye's plans to make a baby. By the time reporters tipped off one another, a press corps formed.

And it got worse. As Edye left the operating room on a gurney, reporters put microphones before her face to pose questions about her highly personal surgery. By now, though, interviewers had added a new question.

"Edye, will you have more children and, if so, when?"

I felt overpowered by the smothering weather outside, and again "invaded" by the jaded mass media inside. I watched as my daughter's life unfolded on television. Despite all of the intrusions levied on us, I never imagined that "journalists" would be interested in Edye's reproductive agenda.

Edye was a wounded soul. She wanted a baby who had the same gleam in his eyes that Chase and Colton had in theirs. Tony Smith, Chase and Colton's father, seemed to be her answer.

The reunion at first seemed lovely, but the marriage soon became stormy and the ending was disastrous. The ink had barely seemed dry on the nuptials when Edye signed divorce papers.

And so my existence returned to what it had been—I was once again a member of a trio of broken family members struggling to mend one another. Glenn, Edye, and I stumbled along our lonesome valley of life, fraught with new wounds while the older ones had not yet scabbed, much less healed.

Summer's heat eased into fall's colorful radiance that signaled the leaves to drift in their downward spirals. I saw an analogy between nature's changes and those in my life.

Although the fall colors were radiant, our city still echoed with the somber repercussions of the Murrah blast.

I did feel somewhat invigorated by the frigid north winds that swept Oklahoma City in November. Winters in the Sooner State's capital city are routinely as cold as the summers are sweltering.

Yet the arrival of the Christmas season carried a sadness like no other.

I was contacted by Jannie Coverdale, a woman who had also

lost two grandchildren in the Murrah tragedy. Their names were Aaron and Elijah.

Jannie and I were quick to bond for obvious reasons. Additionally, we shared a quirk.

Neither of us wanted to hear other people brag about their "living" grandchildren. Jannie was my only friend who talked with me about our grandchildren in the past tense.

Aaron and Elijah were buried in the same cemetery near Chase and Colton. I went to the graveyard many times with Jannie, and I always found companionship and a bit of homespun therapy.

"Granny," she'd say, as though interpreting for Elijah, "what are you doing here with Chase and Colton's granny?"

For a few fleeting moments, Jannie brought our boys back to life. I loved those times together.

During that first Christmas season without our grandbabies, Jannie asked me to help other survivors decorate a tree at the bomb site in honor of the victims—especially the children. As snow swirled and winds penetrated, tears seemed to freeze on Jannie's and my cheeks as we grieved for our departed grandchildren.

How different this Christmas could have been, without the Oklahoma City Bombing. The thought of our little boys, lying cold and dead when they should have been at home, warm and decorating a tree with us, was more than we could bear. We were robbed of the holiday cheer and the laughter of our precious grandchildren. Instead, we stood outside at the site of their demise, with virtually frozen feet and hands. By this time the physical pain was almost as great as the emotional pain. We were exhausted in every way.

When we finished decorating the tree and began to trudge slowly away, I stopped and looked at Jannie. Through tears, I extended a Christmas greeting, using an adjective I *never* thought would cross my lips.

"Merry &*%$*%@ Christmas, Jannie," I said.

Jannie stared at me in disbelief. Then, with frozen tears clinging to our faces, we began to laugh and laugh until our bodies shook with hilarity in that sad place. We still don't know why that happened, but it was the only light moment in that otherwise dreadful day.

～

Long-term friendships are rooted in the things people have in common. For people who share similar sufferings, the friendships can be solid like no others.

Through the years, I've watched Jannie's spirits rise and fall much like my own. They have often vacillated in the same time frame.

Yet, when Jannie and I least expect it, we talk about our grandbabies. We're the only people who each lost two grandchildren in the blast. I'm intimately familiar with Jannie's type of hurting, and she with mine.

Jannie adamantly hated McVeigh and Nichols, and resolved to do so forever. The word "forgiveness" was not in her vocabulary—at least not for those infamous men.

I understood her rage, but I handled my grief differently. I had been so devastated by my loss that I had lost all strength to hate. I can't explain God's forgiving grace, and I myself was surprised by the work He was doing in my life.

Jannie, however, not only hated Nichols and McVeigh; she was mad at God.

For years, she was trapped inside a mental catch-22. How could she ask God to enable her to forgive the bombers when she hadn't forgiven God Himself? How could she pray to God when she wasn't even speaking to Him?

She talked about so many things that she'd once done, and I'd done as well, including lying in bed for hours, fearing to face the world.

"Some days, when I got up, it was like a crushing boulder of depression instantly fell on me," she said. "That went on year in and year out."

One day, Jannie happened to see a little Native American boy playing alone outside the apartment complex where she lived. His mother was a drug addict who often left the child unattended. Jannie approached the boy, told him she owned the *Lion King* cartoon movie, and asked if he'd like to see it. He said, "Yes."

The five-year-old ran to his mother's apartment to get his blanket and teddy bear. He never returned home. With the approval of his biological mother, Jannie legally adopted him.

For Jannie, the presence of a new child helped to mollify the pain from losing two others. Adrian, now nineteen, lives with Jannie to this day.

Wanting to be sure Adrian never worried about her, Jannie tried to schedule her daily release of grief. Sometimes, she retreated to the bathroom and stood under a forceful shower, muffling her sobs into the noisy stream. Adrian never knew.

For years after losing Chase and Colton, I, too, sought locations where I could let myself grieve, no matter how loudly. I looked for places where I felt safe to fall apart.

Jannie and I went to church together, where I sought God's solace and she continued to ask Him where He'd been during the Murrah tragedy. All the while, the preacher tried to draft Jannie into the choir.

"Can I let you in on a little secret?" she whispered to the minister. I thought she was going to tell him about her anger toward the higher power. Not so.

"I don't want to be in the choir," she whispered. "Not all black people sing."

During those days, I often thought about Jesus' command to forgive, and how He was surely asking for too much.

I would ultimately realize that while commanding me to forgive others, Christ wasn't trying to bully me. He was trying to better me and bring me peace.

For as long as we're on this earth, we who have accepted Christ will undergo His efforts to make us more like Him. And if He is about anything, He is about forgiveness. That was the overall reason for His suffering on the cross.

Sometimes, forgiveness is outright painful for some folks. But no matter the degree of discomfort, it's markedly less than the agony Christ suffered when He was crucified.

Yet, in His darkest hour, Jesus forgave His persecutors.

I would eventually embrace Joyce Wilt, Nichols's mother, even as Jannie determined not to. Jannie, like others, thought Joyce was guilty by some kind of association. She had brought a murderer into the world. As would most mothers, Joyce had stood by him during a trial for his life.

"Why do you think you wanted to hate Terry's mother?" Jannie was asked.

"I was very, very angry," she said. "I was angry with everybody. I was scaring myself because I was so angry. Years later I was still angry."

"When Terry Nichols's trial was over, I was angry because he didn't get the death penalty," she continued.

Then, shortly before another sunrise ushered the opportunity to weep again, Jannie found peace from the God she'd earlier despised.

"I was lying in bed, and a voice came to me and said there had been enough killing," she recalled. "It was God talking to me, you know? And I knew I was supposed to forgive. . . .

"Later that day, my telephone rang and it was some reporter, wanting to make an appointment for an interview. She wanted to talk to me about how I felt because Terry Nichols didn't get the death penalty. I told her there had been enough killing. Just like that, I told her."

The reporter never kept her appointment with Jannie. The writer had looked for a story about outrage, but she had encountered one about God's bestowal of compassion. Maybe such a story doesn't sell newspapers. For whatever reason, the journalist wasn't interested.

Jannie's burden of hatred dissolved totally and disappeared forever.

Forgiveness ushers a sense of peaceful relief, and the feeling is wonderfully contagious—but the forgiver must always take the first step.

Jannie had done that. And thus she was no longer condemned to merely endure life. After almost a decade, she began to *live* again.

Forgiveness carries power to the one who gives it, as well as the one who receives it. I've seen it in Jannie; I've felt it in me.

Forgiveness is surely the ultimate of all life's blessings.

Chapter Eight

My fragile happiness after the 1995 winter holidays slid into a melancholy common to many people at that time of year. The Oklahoma City sky was mostly slate gray. Sub-zero temperatures amid intermittent blizzards of blinding snow and solid ice hardened the ground.

My mood, like the climate, was gloomy.

"If you want to be happy, make others happy" is a proven rule.

"I don't trust happiness. I never will," said Robert Duvall in his Academy Award–winning role as Mac Sledge in *Tender Mercies*.

I knew how he felt.

Among all the people I had encountered in 1995, I didn't know how to feel about the two men who'd been arrested and charged with multiple murders in connection with the bombing. The defendants were the alleged organizers and principal perpetrators of the explosion.

Although neither had gone to trial, the names Timothy McVeigh and Terry Nichols held national recognition similar to Charles Manson or Ted Bundy. A third man, Michael Fortier, had reportedly been an accomplice, but he struck a plea bargain with the government and was sentenced to ten years in prison. He never had to stand trial, and his wife was granted immunity from prosecution in return for his cooperation in building a case against McVeigh and Nichols.

I, of course, knew that McVeigh and Nichols were securely

behind bars. I remembered the news report that said McVeigh was in custody in Perry, Oklahoma, and another that said Nichols had turned himself in to authorities in Herington, Kansas.

In the interim, I heard plenty of profanity from the mouths of countless people who loved to hate McVeigh and Nichols. They described torturous acts that they would like to inflict on them. Simply put, a lot of people would have happily killed McVeigh and Nichols if given the chance.

Some people also said they would eagerly go to war against terrorists, including the likes of McVeigh and Nichols. Eight months after the tragedy, vengeance remained real for many Oklahoma City residents.

Personally, I wanted to help those who were hurting and tend to the needs of the emotionally wounded, including Glenn, Edye, and me. I reached out to them—and to myself.

Please understand, I do not mean to portray myself as a saint or a super-Christian. I'm simply saying that I, as a believer, did what virtually anyone would have done, especially if they'd witnessed the bombing, and especially if they'd suffered personal loss.

Regarding Nichols and McVeigh: they weren't going anywhere, except to court and eventually to maximum-security imprisonment, or so I had always believed.

I was always curious as to why those men would do such a horrible thing. What happened in their lives that caused them to go so bad? What kind of evil filled their souls that caused them to do something so diabolical? I had no way of getting those questions answered, so I focused on loving those around me instead of despising the perpetrators.

Over time, this would change.

I remained obsessed with finding the truth hidden behind the local, state, and federal governments' misinformation surrounding the bombing. I knew I would never find peace of mind without knowing the actual chain of events that occurred before, during, and after April 19, 1995.

So I accelerated my probe into McVeigh and Nichols and their personal histories. Eventually, my search would spread to include their friends and families, as well as law enforcement agencies and other official entities.

Earlier, on August 11, 1995, a grand jury had indicted both McVeigh and Nichols on murder and conspiracy charges.

Only six weeks later, on October 20, approximately five weeks before Thanksgiving Day, United States Attorney General Janet Reno authorized prosecutors to seek the death penalty for McVeigh and Nichols. That decision was issued before a trial date had even been scheduled for either defendant.

What if one or both were to enter a guilty plea without going to court? What if the court then ordered that one or both be put to death? What if either or both entered a plea bargain with prosecutors that called for solitary confinement without visitors?

I had always heard that the wheels of justice moved exceedingly slow but sure. Regarding McVeigh and Nichols, the judicial process seemed to accelerate. How much time did I really have to determine what prompted either man's involvement in the worst act of terrorism ever enacted by Americans on American soil?

What event or circumstance in McVeigh's past could have possibly motivated his act of unspeakable evil? I determined to know as my first discovery. I began to research the man who had become the nation's most despised person.

I no longer had time to feel sorry for myself. I had to complete my pursuit of the truth before that truth became permanently unavailable. After all, McVeigh and Nichols might soon be put to death!

In my search for information, I learned that McVeigh was one of three children and the only boy. He was traumatized by his parents' 1984 divorce. I am sure that, like most children, he hoped his parents would reconcile. Divorce is hard on any child, but it doesn't cause them to become mass murderers.

I discovered that McVeigh enlisted in the United States Army in 1988 and had been assigned to the Persian Gulf War as a gunnery sergeant. He had been awarded a Bronze Star Medal for his outstanding service. What had happened to him between the time he left the military and the time he blew up the Murrah Building? Had he suffered battle fatigue?

If so, I had read nothing about it. Besides, that war was not as intense as other military actions—as determined by body counts, at least. Surely it wasn't battle fatigue that motivated McVeigh's malice. And there were no reports of his being wounded. He left the Army with an honorable discharge.

As a civilian, McVeigh wasn't the victim of work-related stress. How could he be? He was a security guard; a sleepy "rent-a-cop" at a New York building that met all of the safety codes required by city government. That's hardly hazardous duty.

After a year, McVeigh quit that job, and he began 1993 as a drifter, floating from town to town at his own pace and whims.

Except for his arrest for driving without a license tag and carrying a firearm, McVeigh had undergone no brushes with the law—except that he received a speeding ticket in 1993. But that was hardly enough to make him the new Unabomber.

But there was a catch.

McVeigh got the speeding ticket while en route to Elohim City, a compound for members of a militant right-wing movement in eastern Oklahoma. Why would he be driving to such an extremist environment?

Then, on September 12, 1994, McVeigh checked into a motel in Vian, Oklahoma, only a few miles from Elohim City, on the very date the plot to blow up the Murrah Building was most likely to have been conceived, according to grand jury testimony. Why didn't this concern government prosecutors? I believed it was more than a coincidence.

I was compiling a large list of questions that needed answers. Why was the hunt for John Doe II dropped shortly after the bombing, when twenty-two eyewitnesses reported seeing him with McVeigh downtown the day of the bombing? Not one person saw McVeigh alone. Every report said he was accompanied by an unidentified man.

Why had the information provided by Carol Howe, an ATF undercover informant working at Elohim City, been totally ignored? She had warned her handler of a potential bombing. In her handwritten report, she admitted that on three different occasions, she had rendezvoused with two individuals from Elohim City who were targeting buildings that they intended to bomb. According to the report, the targets included the IRS Building in Tulsa, Oklahoma; the IRS Building in Oklahoma City; and the Oklahoma City Federal Building.

I needed the truth and was determined to find it. If necessary, I'd dance with the devil to get it.

❧

Glenn and I read every article we could find about the Murrah bombing and the extraordinary capture within hours of Timothy McVeigh.

Patriots' Day, observed annually on April 19, was extremely important to some radical right-wing groups and to pro-American extremists such as McVeigh, our research had shown. Many key events in world history had transpired on that fearful date:

- April 19, 1775: Battles of Lexington and Concord, the first military engagements of the American Revolutionary War;
- April 19, 1943: German troops enter a Warsaw, Poland, ghetto to round up remaining Jews, beginning the Warsaw Ghetto Uprising;

- April 19, 1985: FBI seizes the compound of the Covenant, Sword, and Arm of the Lord (CSA), a radical Christian identity organization located in the small community of Elijah near the Arkansas-Missouri border;
- April 19, 1992: FBI attempts, but fails, during its initial raid at Ruby Ridge, Idaho, home of Randy Weaver, a former Green Beret considered by the U.S. government to be part of the Aryan Nations movement;
- April 19, 1993: ATF burns the Branch Davidian compound in Waco, Texas, after a fifty-one-day standoff with the Branch Davidians. The incident becomes known as the "Texas Massacre" to antigovernment militarist and white supremacist groups;
- April 19, 1995: The Alfred P. Murrah Federal Building is bombed in Oklahoma City, Oklahoma; and CSA member Richard Wayne Snell is executed in Arkansas for multiple murders. His victims include a black police officer and a businessman he erroneously believes to be a Jew.

The knowledge of Snell's execution stopped us in our tracks. With various extremist groups attaching so much significance to April 19, why would Arkansas officials execute Snell on this date? Were they unaware of the date's significance? Or did they intend for Snell's death to be a slap in the face of antigovernment factions?

As Snell was put to death, in attendance was his spiritual adviser, Robert G. Millar, a Canadian immigrant and founder of Elohim City, a far-right religious compound in Oklahoma. There, according to the deathwatch log notes, Snell requested the television in his cell to be turned on so he could view coverage of the Oklahoma City Bombing. He reportedly smiled and chuckled as he watched the horror unfold.

We later learned that McVeigh called Elohim City only minutes after he called the Ryder truck company where he procured the vehicle that hauled the fatal bomb to a drop-off zone situated under the building's day-care center.

Our questions continued to mount.

In the spring of 1996, I decided to actually visit Elohim City. Glenn couldn't go because it was tax season and he was struggling to maintain his accounting practice.

Against Glenn's wishes, I asked Edye to join me. We embarked on a three-and-a-half-hour journey to Elohim City.

We arrived at the gates of the compound where a sign proclaimed "Elohim City." A large, domed house sat imposingly at the front of the property.

As I got my camera, Edye barked, "Put the camera down, Mother. Put the camera down!"

The inflection in her voice said something was wrong. I quickly dropped the camera and looked up.

Men with guns pointed right at us rushed toward the car. Terrified, I felt my blood pressure rise with their every step.

Edye and I had planned our arrival for noon so we could attend the Elohim church service, one of several requirements to visit the Elohimites. We glanced around cautiously as armed escorts took us into the church. Its interior looked more like the set of a cheap horror flick than a house of worship.

Our hearts pounding, Edye and I were intimidated by men with sidearms strapped to their waists. I wondered if they were parishioners, ushers, or both.

We had arrived at the sanctuary a few minutes late. When we entered, Pastor Millar, an unassuming and grandfatherly figure, sat stroking his long white beard. He nodded to acknowledge us and then asked that we introduce ourselves. I told him who we were, and that we had lost children in the Oklahoma City Bombing. I ended the introduction with, "We're ATF's worst nightmare."

For that, we received thunderous applause.

The Elohimites had accepted us into their fold.

A group called the "Iron Cross Band" played as members of the congregation marched in a circle with their guns held high in the air, singing praises to God. I saw no one waving Bibles, just those brandishing pistols and rifles. Millar's sermon focused on the FBI raid of the Covenant, the Sword, and the Arm of the Lord (CSA) encampment in Arkansas on April 19, 1985, ten years to the day before the Oklahoma City Bombing.

CSA founder and leader James Ellison had been arrested in the raid. During his trial, courtroom testimony revealed that the paramilitary survivalist group had been plotting to blow up the Murrah Building with a rocket launcher in 1983. Ellison, who sat in the audience, had recently been released from prison. He now lived in Elohim City.

Millar told a colorful story about how people had hidden behind trees to avoid capture when the compound was raided. He painted "King James," his moniker for Ellison, as a hero in the CSA battle with federal law enforcement officials.

After the church service, the men quickly disappeared, leaving Edye and me alone with the ladies who had also worshipped. One of the women consented to give us a tour of the overall encampment. We were then taken to an old one-room building used as a schoolhouse where all the children, from kindergarten through twelfth grade, underwent homeschooling together.

As we continued to stroll the compound, I asked my hostess if she knew Andreas Strassmeir, head of Elohim City security and one of the men mentioned in the ATF report. She replied that she did. I asked what she thought of him. She said no one at Elohim liked him; he was always trying to get them to do bad things. But she refused to tell me what kind of bad things. She then offered to show me his house.

The ATF informant's information had proved to be true. Elohim

City was a terrorist training ground that accommodated key leaders of the Aryan Nations movement in the United States.

What was *really* going on? Who were these men that promoted bombings?

I later learned that the FBI allowed one of them to leave the country without ever interviewing him in connection with Murrah. Why? The FBI had conducted tens of thousands of interviews with potential witnesses, including McVeigh's fifth-grade schoolteacher.

Was it a coincidence that McVeigh blew up the Murrah on the day of Snell's execution?

I had to know.

I found that McVeigh, whose infamous history will be recorded in files next to Osama bin Laden's, had been a boring social misfit.

In a newspaper profile, I read that during McVeigh's military stint he'd become distrustful of the federal government. Then later, for whatever reason, he'd traveled to Waco, Texas, to witness firsthand the hostage situation involving the Branch Davidians and federal agents. The killing of civilians, especially children, outraged him, as it did millions of other Americans.

Earlier, while appearing on television news programs shackled in chains, McVeigh's demeanor seemed emotionless. His eyes were fixed in a distant, vacant stare. Wearing a bright orange jumpsuit, he looked forward but appeared to see nothing through his icy gaze. Flanked by sheriff's deputies, McVeigh even appeared oblivious to loud threats shouted at him by furious onlookers. A crowd of them assembled each time McVeigh was escorted from the jail to a waiting van that carried him to his arraignment and other pretrial procedures.

"BABY KILLER, BABY KILLER!" someone shouted.

Other tirades were open threats on McVeigh's life.

None of the harassment seemed to faze McVeigh. Restrained by those clanging chains, he toddled in baby steps toward a waiting

van. Deputies gripped his arms and never turned loose until he was
seated in the vehicle's backseat, where he sat alone, surrounded by
steel barriers.

In every television appearance he was a powerless captive. He sat
quietly and stared forward, ignoring the world around him.

That recurring image of McVeigh was branded into my mind
and prompted a gasp the first time I saw him in the flesh.

Citing McVeigh's right to an impartial jury, Judge Richard
Matsch had moved the defendant's trial from Oklahoma City to
Denver on February 20, 1996.

No longer did McVeigh exhibit the countenance of a cold and calculating mass murderer. He seemed the handsome image of "Joe
College"—a liberal arts graduate whose next step might be a job
interview.

Inside a courtroom, McVeigh received a celebrity and hero's welcome from his lawyers, all of whom rose from the defense table to
shake his hand and affectionately slap his back. Smiling, McVeigh
was delighted.

Is this guy facing trial for mass murder or running for political office?
I thought to myself. The phony, calculated behavior repulsed me.

I could feel myself building the same kind of anger I had earlier
seen observers exhibit toward McVeigh. I saw that same outraged
grimace on the faces of others in the room.

Until McVeigh's grand entrance, I'd had empathy for him. I again
wondered what happened in his young life to make him do something so horrible as to ruthlessly kill 168 people.

My feelings of compassion changed instantly.

My eyes saw only his sickening lack of remorse. Instantly, I realized why people are forbidden to carry concealed firearms into
courtrooms. It was a good thing we had all been searched with
electronic detectors before entering the proceeding or someone
would have shot McVeigh then and there, I'm certain.

I saw, and I felt, the boiling hatred inside that hall of justice. My own spirit was a part of that collective animosity.

Suddenly, I saw McVeigh look at me the way I was looking at him. I presumed he recognized me, as I knew he'd seen news footage of the bombing.

By now I was staring daggers and wishing they were real, that they could penetrate McVeigh's hate-filled heart. The more I stared, the more I wanted to continue.

The prisoner apparently felt the same, locking directly onto my stare. Like a schoolchild, I had entered the staring contest. But the competition was anything but childlike.

Neither of our heads or eyes ever moved. I could have kept that up all day.

After hour-long minutes, McVeigh lost the contest and looked away.

"What do you want?" he said in pantomime.

I answered with my stare, nothing else.

I began to feel uneasy. It was as if he'd entered my mind; he was reading me like a book. I wanted to scream at him while slapping him silly. I didn't want to kill him—but I'm not sure I would have stopped anyone who tried.

Mostly, I wanted to hear him shout that he was sorry for what he'd done. Even more, I wanted to believe him.

I fantasized about him being back in shackles. In those restraints, I imagined him being led to all of the brokenhearted parents inside that room. I envisioned him begging for their forgiveness.

The room's high ceilings had earlier echoed the wailing of people whose lives McVeigh had shattered.

Suddenly, my stare proved more powerful than I had thought. McVeigh rolled his chair back from the defense table and positioned his seat behind one of his lawyers. There, I could no longer see the coward.

The international tough guy had been bested by a silent, staring housewife.

I'd won our psychological battle through persistence. Thereafter, I could see McVeigh's sickening face whenever I closed my eyes. And for the rest of what became his brief life, I hoped he similarly saw mine.

✼

Before the trial, a reporter was scheduled to interview McVeigh in solitary confinement. I asked the writer to hand-deliver some items from me to the mass murderer.

I had printed Chase's and Colton's photographs on the back of thank-you cards intended for thousands of people who'd sent condolences to Glenn, Edye, and me. The photo, taken three days before my grandbabies' deaths, was the last one ever to capture their living images. I had written a text of gratitude and signed it "Chase and Colton."

I also had a Christmas card printed with an artist's rendering of the boys as sweet cherubs. A prayer, written in the form of a poem, adorned the card.

I wanted McVeigh to have these things; to see my grandbabies as two of the 168 human beings he'd slaughtered, and not merely as casualty statistics. The reporter delivered the package that had touched the hearts of so many people.

Not so with McVeigh.

The journalist said the hardened killer looked at the picture and the artful illustration before reading the poem:

OUR CHRISTMAS PRAYER

We question if Christmas can ever be "merry,"
Except in the heart of an innocent child
For our loss has taught us the meaning of sorrow
And sobered our spirits that once were so wild

Their green grave now covered in flowers
A headstone marking the place where they lay
And echoes of voices that no more shall greet us
Have saddened the chimes of this bright Christmas Day.
Therefore we cannot wish you a "Merry Ole Christmas,"
Since that is of shadowless childhood a part
But one that is holy and happy and peaceful,
The spirit of Christmas down deep in your heart.

"I don't know what to think of this," McVeigh told the reporter.

Based on what I had seen during that first day in court, I have no doubt he didn't.

꘎

Most people's lives tend to be scarred by ugly ironies, and mine was no exception.

In June 1996, Glenn came home looking unusually forlorn. I pressed him for an explanation. He was evasive before admitting that he was passing blood in his urine.

This announcement followed several weeks of not feeling "right." Glenn suggested that his old ulcer must be flaring up. So he began taking antacids.

Glenn and I spent a sleepless night. We were no strangers to looming hardship. It was as if we had developed a sixth sense detecting its approach.

The next morning, Glenn and I visited his primary care physician, who asked how long my husband's skin and eyes had been yellow. I, too, saw the amber tint, and I felt remorse for not having noticed it earlier. Perhaps I had no excuse, but I definitely had my unwanted reasons.

Glenn and I had cried ourselves to sleep almost every night for fourteen months. His eyes were constantly bloodshot. I noticed nothing else about them. Thinking back, the discoloration of his eyes and skin could have been symptoms of jaundice. But jaundice would not have prompted Glenn's acute stomach pain.

I kept trying to grab straws of encouragement, but Glenn wasn't interested in any of them. His attitude reminded me of the day of the bombing when I told Edye everything would be all right. She knew better, and told me so in no uncertain terms, as all of her joy and happiness in life were crushed by the collapse of the Murrah Building.

To no one's surprise, Glenn refused to see the doctor on the day his diagnosis was announced. He was simply drained of his capacity to absorb bad news. Therefore, Edye accompanied me to the medical facility where Glenn's case had earlier been remanded to an internist.

As soon as I saw the doctor's face, I knew that something was terribly wrong.

"Where's Glenn?" she asked.

"He refused to come," I said.

There was a long pause. "Why did he refuse?"

"He's afraid that the news is bad."

"I know your family has been through a lot," the doctor said, "and I wish there was some way I could offer you hope."

The doctor's nurse was crying audibly. Both women knew who we were and what we had been through. With tears running down her face and with the most tact she could muster, the doctor said Glenn was dying of "the cruelest form of cancer," incurable pancreatic cancer.

To say I was crushed would be as much of an understatement as saying I was slightly saddened by the passing of Chase and Colton. Once again, death was unexpectedly barging into my life. This time it wasn't sudden like my dad's, or criminal like Chase's and Colton's.

But the result would be just as permanent.

At that moment, the only place I refused to go was to my

husband's side. I knew that, ideally, that's where I should go. But I didn't know how to tell him. I needed time to think.

Why oh why, dear God, is this happening? I demanded to know. *How much sorrow can my family and I take?*

Glenn's doubts of God's existence had been building since the bombing. Consistently, he had disavowed his faith as I had struggled to rally mine.

Faith was all I had.

These thoughts were involuntary and runaway, just as they'd been when my father suffered a fatal heart attack; when my mother was strangled inside a nursing home; and when Chase and Colton slipped into eternity without even knowing they were dying.

Overall, my life seemed to be nothing but a series of hardships. I would undergo one tragedy, struggle to rebound, and then be slammed by another. Sometimes I felt like fate's punching bag.

How many coffins would I select before I finally died myself?

To avoid going home to Glenn, I went with Edye to her house. I needed time to think and nurse my wounds. Edye, always wanting to be strong, went outside so I couldn't see her weep. I, on the other hand, was inside Edye's house trying to call someone, anyone, who might be able to fix this. God hadn't really been listening to me. Maybe if I were able to reach someone whose prayers would be answered by God, then Glenn's life might be spared.

We took care to put on our best, if disingenuous, faces of comfort before entering my home. There, Glenn was alone and intentionally in the dark. It was as if he didn't want to see anyone, not even loved ones whom he knew to be bearing bad news.

I said nothing. The look on my face said it all. Glenn stood from the kitchen barstool on which he was sitting. He walked over to me, put his arms around me, and began to cry.

"All I needed was a little more time; all I needed was a little more time," Glenn said, as he stood holding me in his arms, crying.

He needed time to get to the bottom of his grandchildren's deaths. But his time was virtually gone.

As cold, calculating McVeigh fought for his life in a court of law, my kind and decent husband fought against his own death sentence by cancer.

Glenn battled for fitful sleep in his bed, connected to medical equipment and feeding tubes, while McVeigh slept soundly in his bunk financed by our tax dollars.

Bitter thoughts like this repeatedly leaped into my mind during those extremely stressful times.

Despite Glenn's physical condition, he would not abandon his quest for information, specifically the identities of the others seen with McVeigh the day of the bombing. Glenn's investigations had been so comprehensive, they were actually used as source material by some esteemed journalists.

Yet Glenn got little cooperation from the federal government, as he still believed the FBI and other agencies were lying to the American public. He'd often gone public with that accusation.

My dying husband harbored toxic outrage toward the local and national governments, as well as toward God. He loathed the government's lack of transparency. His thoughts became agnostic and bordered on atheistic before his untimely passing. Some people, including experts, eventually contended that Glenn's rage might have hastened his passing.

Two weeks after his fatal diagnosis, Glenn entered the hospital, where doctors removed his pancreas, gallbladder, duodenum, and one-third of his stomach.

For the rest of his short life, Glenn was unable to eat solid foods without getting violently ill. He eventually quit trying and I fed him intravenously through a triple lumen in his chest. Glenn grieved the fact that he couldn't eat. I basically had quit cooking or eating anything in front of him because I didn't want him tempted to try to eat.

"I just want to smell some food," Glenn pleaded. "Bake something, please, Kathy. I just want to smell some food."

I hated that request, as I didn't want to whet Glenn's appetite for food he couldn't consume.

So I baked dog biscuits.

While the biscuits were baking, Glenn and I sat at the dining room table, just off the kitchen. As we held hands, Glenn devoured the aroma of baking food. The dog biscuits smelled like hot bread on a fall morning. We enjoyed the aroma of the biscuits. Yet Glenn had no desire to eat the doggie treats.

Meanwhile, Glenn's investigations had prompted an inquiry by ABC's *20/20*, and journalists from that program came to our house. The network television disclosures embarrassed Oklahoma authorities, including its attorney general and underlings. Yet not one issued a renewed investigation started by a dying man.

It was as if they hoped their silence would outlast Glenn's life. His cries for justice would finally be hushed.

One day, while filming for the show, Tom Jarriel, the program's host, grabbed one of the dog biscuits from the bowl on the kitchen counter before I could warn him. I forgot to tell the *20/20* personnel to avoid the biscuits, as they did resemble vanilla wafers.

"Oh no, oh no, wait!" Glenn exclaimed.

Tom Jarriel took one bite of the biscuit and began spitting it in my sink.

"How did you like my dog biscuits?" I playfully asked.

"I feel sorry for your dog," Jarriel said.

Glenn roared with laughter.

It was the first time in months I had seen Glenn laugh. It was also his last laugh.

In a matter of days, Glenn became too weak to stand, and Edye and I tried to hold him upright. But he was much too frail to support his weight.

With an arm wrapped around Edye's shoulder and the other around mine, we dragged Glenn down the hallway to his and my bedroom. We placed him in bed, and told him good night before we silently closed the door.

We always made sure we were out of his earshot before we collapsed into tears.

Glenn went to be with Chase and Colton in heaven on July 15, 1997.

"I'd rather die young than grow old without you" is a song lyric made famous by the late country music singer George Jones. It sums up my feelings about life with Glenn. While I expected to physically exist after Glenn's passing, I thought I would never really live again.

"God help me!" I repeated often, both silently and aloud.

Today, his grave is a stone's throw from the grave of my grandbabies. I can easily walk from one headstone to another before returning to my car. There, tinted windows ensure my privacy as tears fill my eyes and I thank God for my late companion, and the two little boys who once graced my life.

Chapter Nine

I see little reason to report details in the two criminal trials of Terry Nichols. The hearings were thoroughly covered by major print and broadcast media from September 1997 through May 2004.

The 1997 proceedings in Denver, Colorado, resulted in Nichols's conviction of conspiracy to use a weapon of mass destruction and eight counts of involuntary manslaughter for killing federal law enforcement personnel. He was sentenced to life in prison without possibility of parole because the jury deadlocked regarding the death penalty.

He was later tried on state charges in Oklahoma in connection with the bombing. On May 26, 2004, a jury deadlocked again on imposing the death penalty. He was instead sentenced to 160 consecutive life terms without the possibility of parole. Today, Nichols is incarcerated at ADX Florence, a maximum-security prison in Florence, Colorado.

Despite the horrific nature of Nichols's crimes, I found myself mellowing on his behalf. He just didn't have the conspicuous streak of hate and rage so obvious in McVeigh.

To me, Nichols did not seem essentially mean. He seemed weird, lonely, withdrawn, and a social misfit. At times in his life, he'd been an utter outcast.

Additionally, Nichols was conspicuously quiet, shy, and insecure. He was like a teenager with an extreme inferiority complex, not a criminal with an obsession to kill. He became a solitary man because he had no alternative. He didn't have a lot of friends.

How much of an "island" was he? Think about this: He didn't pay income taxes, he had no Social Security number, and he had no bank account. He buried large sums of cash and then withdrew it as needed, like a rodent retrieving nuts from an underground stash whenever hungry.

During Nichols's trial I learned that his second wife, Marife, asked permission from the FBI to retrieve personal items from her Herington, Kansas, home where she and Nichols had lived. There, she pulled out $5,000 in cash that FBI agents had missed in their search of the Nichols home. The money was hidden underneath the mattress of their bed. Marife said that she'd earned the funds by babysitting, though no one could ever find the children she claimed to have babysat.

Marife was Nichols's second wife, whom he married without a facsimile of courtship. Instead, she was a sixteen-year-old mail-order bride. Nichols met and married her in the Philippines, but his new bride had to remain behind while waiting for a visa to the United States. When she arrived in the States, she was pregnant with another man's child.

Bewildered, Nichols "overlooked" her condition and accepted his new wife in her delicate state.

How many men would do that? How desperate would they have to be?

One morning, while standing in the hallway awaiting a pretrial hearing, I spotted a woman whose body language and demeanor strongly communicated her diminished spirit. Amid the clamor of incoming spectators and media personnel, she stood out by standing alone, as if she was lost and out of place.

Her attire was modest, and my first thought was her resemblance to Frances Bavier, the "Aunt Bee" character on *The Andy Griffith Show*.

That day, people stood in huddles in the courtroom whispering about the "Aunt Bee" persona in the hallway. The forgotten woman in the vestibule wore a long, heavy coat like the one sported by the pudgy and loving character who lived in television's Mayberry.

Joyce Wilt, Nichols's mother, was hopelessly out of place among the contemporary victims of the Oklahoma City Bombing.

I felt sorry for her. I realized this hapless little woman was intentionally ignored as people walked around her with no acknowledgment of her presence. She likely suffered that worst kind of loneliness, solitude inside a crowd.

People shunned her because of her son. They were convinced he was guilty of blowing up a building and killing children. In their minds, she was guilty by association. Her "crime" had been giving birth to a murderer.

But Joyce wasn't guilty of killing anyone's children. She was guilty only of loving one of her own—specifically, Terry Nichols. She was defenseless and vulnerable. My heart went out to her.

"Excuse me," I said, extending my hand. "I'm Kathy Wilburn—" I didn't get to say much more.

"I know who you are," she said, her eyes moistening. "I've seen you on television."

"I want you to know how sorry I am for what happened to your family," I said, my sympathy flowing toward this perfect stranger.

She stared at me blankly, like an orphaned child who had expected a spanking but instead received a hug. This was a moment I'd never seen coming—a pause when a wounded grandmother would encounter a wounded mother—now bonded by tragedy neither had expected.

Instantly gone was any anxiety regarding what people might think about my befriending Joyce. Over the course of time, the hated "Oklahoma City bomber" would become "my friend Joyce's son."

Only God could have arranged that.

Sometime later, during the trial in Denver, I asked Joyce and Susie McDonnell (Nichols's sister) to lunch. People who saw us in the café seemed a bit taken aback. To many I'm sure our appearance in public together seemed scandalous. I knew it, and I didn't care. Joyce and Susie were innocent victims of this crime as much as I and the other mourning families were. They didn't need anybody's forgiveness. But I would have offered mine if they had. They knew that.

After ordering our meal, Joyce, Susie, and I fell into chatty girl-talk. But before the food arrived, Susie's face conspicuously fell while unloading about her troubled life since the bombing. Clearly, she'd been waiting to talk to someone. She'd never thought it would be the grandmother of Chase and Colton Smith.

This grandmother hadn't anticipated that either.

Susie was concerned about her marriage because of the arrest of her brother. Her husband hadn't wanted her to come to Nichols's trial, but she had come anyway. She didn't know what to expect when she returned home. Her children were also suffering at school, where they were bullied for having an uncle who was the notorious Oklahoma City bomber.

Susie's in-laws were ashamed of her for admitting she was Nichols's sister. Joyce and Susie had consistently been the targets of hostile discrimination in their little town of Lapeer, Michigan.

During lunch, Susie continued to unload, admitting that she understood people's loathing for her. But Nichols was still her brother, and she wanted to be there for him during his trial.

I understood folks' hatred, but I didn't condone it. Instead, I started realizing that maybe prayers are not really for those people for whom you pray. Maybe they are ultimately for you. Whatever my prayers may have been doing for others, they were certainly changing me. I found that as I prayed for Nichols and his family, I was finding it easier to sleep at night, and I began to realize that forgiving Nichols was a lot easier than hating him. The more I prayed, the more restored I felt.

As a child I had personally seen the self-destructive power of unforgiveness in my grandmother's home. I learned firsthand that unforgiveness is like a seed planted. It grows and takes root. It robs you of joy and makes you bitter.

My mother told me that my grandfather had been unfaithful to my grandmother decades before I was born—while my mother was in kindergarten. From that day forward, Mom's childhood home was marked by the searing-hot brand of bitterness.

My grandmother would be happy and pleasant, but when my grandfather entered the room, her countenance changed. She would instantly glare daggers of disdain at him. Or she'd abruptly walk to another part of their house. Her hatred of him became her self-destructive way of life.

Divorce was an unspeakable taboo in those days. My grandmother spent more than fifty years punishing my grandfather for his transgressions. She carried the weight of unforgiveness to her grave.

Over time she had become a recluse. She was the kind of person who would either love you or hate you. There was no in between. Lucky for me, I was among her favorites.

My grandfather lived in a nursing home for two years before he died. My grandmother refused to visit him. And after he passed, she initially refused to attend his funeral. My mother and I finally persuaded her to visit the service contingent on our not opening the casket. Grandmother did not want to lay eyes on Grandfather, not even in his final rest.

I pitied my grandmother as much as I loved her. I didn't want to make the same mistake.

I never made a conscious decision to forgive Nichols. It just happened.

Suddenly, I felt that my unlikely and dramatic change of heart and mind was the right thing to do.

Nichols's body was locked in a cell. But maybe his spirit could someday be set free; free to share with other men who were also convicted of lawlessness and sentenced to terminal loneliness. Many were serving life without parole in the most solitary confinement of all—a life separated from the companionship of Christ. Yet Christ offered His acceptance to them inside their forever-darkened worlds. Perhaps human love and forgiveness could serve as the catalyst that would direct them to Him.

The presence of love is powerful. Its absence is always powerfully destructive.

I had already discovered something else about love, a virtual twin to forgiveness. The most solid and beneficial love comes to people who love and forgive themselves. Over time, I would discover that the best way to love yourself is to love and forgive others. That includes your dysfunctional family members, your annoying next-door neighbors, your cranky boss—and even ruthless mass murderers.

I'm not oversimplifying. How could I? Christ's messages about giving love and forgiveness are not complicated. He simply said to do those things.

To this day, people ask how I could even consider forgiving someone who killed my grandbabies. The answer is, I don't know. I just know that loving someone is a lot easier than hating them.

As Nichols's trial was winding down, Michael Tigar, lead attorney for Nichols's defense team, sent for me.

I didn't want bombing victims' family members to see me entering what they perceived to be the enemies' camp. Tigar had me escorted out of sight along the back stairs of the courthouse to a meeting room.

Why on earth would Tigar and his associates want to see me? I wondered.

Somehow, simply entering their quarters made me feel "guilty," as if I had agreed to consort with my adversary. Was my choice treasonous to the people whose families had been massacred? Was I betraying Chase and Colton? Was I being disloyal to Edye and Glenn?

I felt as if *I* were on trial—not for any crime, but for violating what was basically right or wrong.

After being introduced to Nichols's defenders, I was predictably asked to sit down. I didn't like that, as I was surrounded by lawyers who seemed to tower over me. I felt a bit like I was being backed into a corner, yet I knew my feelings were self-imposed.

Tigar then told me what I already knew—that the trial was in its sentencing phase. He said he was trying to save his client's life, and he thought the jury might spare it if I would ask the court to forgo a death sentence.

What did he just ask me to do? I heard my inner voice shout. *The families would hate me!*

I was already a controversial figure due to my appearance on the *20/20* television program. After my segment aired, some of the grieving families were so upset about my claim of a government cover-up that they met on the local news to defend law enforcement. Deceptive information from the government was just too horrible a possibility for the families to believe.

But the prosecution kept telling us all, "Don't worry—they will catch the rest of the conspirators. We just need to get these two guys out of the way."

That was, of course, a lie. Prosecutors never went after anybody else. Regarding that, many families that had been against me suddenly were not.

They apologized.

And now, Tigar was asking me to risk putting myself in jeopardy again. He wanted me to make a plea in open court full of family members who had lost loved ones in a tragedy that Nichols helped create. I didn't want to cause the grieving families any more pain. But I did want the truth, something I felt I was not hearing at the trial. And I am not the only one who thought we were not hearing the truth. Following the trial, the jury forewoman, Niki Deutchman, told *CNN*:

> The government dropped the ball. There was a lot of evidence that indicated others were involved in this crime. The decision was made early on to limit the investigation to Timothy McVeigh and Terry Nichols. A decision was made not to pursue the others involved.... The FBI evidence was handled sloppily. Evidence was misplaced, and some was rained on and rusted. Witnesses indicated they had been badgered by the FBI and stopped talking to them.

I was proud of Niki Deutchman that day for speaking candidly; I thought she presented a good case. The jury had weighed the facts and could not agree upon Nichols's guilt. However, Niki's statements made some families of the bombing victims very angry. They were irate with jurors for questioning the FBI's conduct and for wanting to know more about the others involved in the bombing.

What would those same families think if I asked the court to let Nichols live? Would I ever be able to show my face again? What would Glenn think if he were still living?

Why was I being asked to invoke this monumental gesture of mercy now? Was my earlier decision to forgive Nichols being tested by God? If so, was He sure I was ready for such an overpowering show of unconditional absolution? I wasn't sure I was.

Tears streamed down my face before I ever felt them swell.

"Do you know what you're asking me to do?" I said to Tigar and his associates. "I have been through so much! I have lost my grandchildren and my husband!"

They already knew that.

I waited for a compassionate reply that no one issued. Imagine— I was inside a room filled with lawyers who, for once, had nothing to say!

I attributed their quietness to humiliation. They'd lost their highprofile case and now had no basis to plead for judicial clemency. They were instead taking a chance on getting a vote of sympathy from the jury. They wanted me, of all people, to initiate that vote.

Nervous and outraged, I spoke a single question almost before I could formulate it.

"Mr. Tigar!" I said. "Can you stand there and tell me that Terry Nichols is an *innocent* man?"

Tigar replied before I sounded my last syllable. "Yes, ma'am, I can," he asserted.

I reeled in disbelief. I had heard enough testimony in the courtroom to know there were other people involved, but I was having a hard time believing Nichols was innocent.

At best, Nichols played a lesser role than the prosecution had alleged.

"If he's innocent, he should get up there and testify to that effect and explain what happened!" I said defiantly.

Tigar emphatically disagreed.

He said Nichols wouldn't present himself well because he was an odd, complicated little man. If he were to take the stand for the defense, he'd surely be devoured by the prosecuting attorney, Tigar insisted.

Quietly, I understood. I became willing to cooperate because I wanted to get to the truth. I knew Nichols was probably the only person who possessed that truth.

My mind swirled like a whirlwind. I needed to talk to Nichols. He knew what really happened. I didn't want to turn my back on an innocent man if, indeed, he was innocent. But again—how could he be? I had seen and heard evidence that strongly indicated otherwise.

And yet, in my heart, I held reasonable doubt about Nichols's alleged intention to commit mass murder. He knew the Murrah Building was going to be bombed. Of that I was certain. But did he know it would happen with people inside? That had not been established.

Should I therefore help stop the fatal sentence pending for a man who might not have intended to kill? Premeditated murder is a capital offense, but *intent* to murder simply had not been established with regard to Nichols, as it had with McVeigh.

How could I have found myself in this precarious position?

No one in the world had been more broken than Edye and I after the slaughter of our babies. I'd tried and failed to get straight answers from government officials, including the FBI and the ATF, as to what exactly happened on that fateful morning.

Ultimately, the only truth I knew was that officials had lied—to me and to other survivors, as well as to the press and the general public.

Glenn's and my relentless investigations, enacted while we were emotionally drained and Glenn was dying, had turned up nothing but a trail of deceit by officials as to why the bombing transpired, as well as to the number of perpetrators involved.

Then, and now, there were more unanswered questions about who orchestrated and executed that bombing than there are surrounding the John F. Kennedy assassination—or so it seems to me.

Yet I had persisted, hoping and praying that all of the guilty would be revealed, and that the innocent would be vindicated.

For my efforts, I was rewarded by finding myself in this

tremendously uncomfortable situation. I was being asked to spare the life of someone who'd assisted in taking 168 lives, whether he'd intended to or not. Whether his motives were malicious or his methods merely negligent, he remained a primary participant in America's most bloody act of terrorism to date.

Tears continued to course down my cheeks as I pondered the impact of Tigar's request from me.

"What would the people of Oklahoma City think?" I asked. "The families already hate me."

I had to stop and wipe the tears from my eyes and face. As I was trying to compose myself, I glanced around the room. There was not one dry eye.

While considering my options, I surprised myself when I said, "You get me a meeting with Terry Nichols. Let him tell me his version of what happened and I will do it. I will ask the judge to spare his life."

My heart was racing. I don't know where those words came from, but they were out there. I couldn't take them back.

Tigar said he would make it happen. My heart leaped, and then it sank.

I was asking to look directly into the eyes of Nichols so that he could tell me his story. And I was also going to stand before the families of those killed in the Murrah Building and ask the court to spare the life of a soft-spoken man they assumed to be a cold-blooded killer.

What would happen when survivors heard me ask the court to spare Nichols? I didn't know, but it couldn't be good. Hours later, Judge Matsch declared a hung jury. Nichols was no longer under the threat of the death penalty. Tigar didn't need me anymore.

I didn't get my meeting with Terry Nichols. Not yet.

Chapter Ten

By design, my relationship with Susie McDonnell continued for two reasons. First, I knew she could provide information, albeit minimal, that might answer a few questions regarding her brother. Second, I could help her personally by sharing Christ's love.

Don't get me wrong. I didn't preach to Susie or to anybody else. I was not into that, not then, not now. I agree with the old saying "Most folks would rather see a testimony than hear one."

Meanwhile, God's grace that spawned my forgiveness of the Murrah perpetrators was turning my life into a living testimony.

As I learned things that officials had not disclosed about people involved in the bombing, I continued to heal in mind and spirit. Knowledge is power—and often, in this case especially, knowledge is sorrow. But sorrow often precedes recovery, and my recovery was now securely pacing along in a step-by-step, day-by-day mode. All the while, I continued to reach out to people who didn't expect it.

Granted, my emotions continued to fluctuate, but not as frequently. While my life was not a figurative walk in the park, it was no longer a stumble through darkness.

My goals toward psychological recovery had been accelerated. My penetrating questions about an incident that had shaken the world were being answered by people who wanted to talk, not officials who wanted to suppress.

God had brought my layman's investigation and my wounded

heart a long way through my interactions with two people who were closest to Nichols.

Would my affiliation with Joyce and Susie lead to an otherwise impossible one-on-one chat between Nichols and me? God only knew.

The spirits of some people who shared my devastating experience were being eaten alive by their hatred.

Unforgiveness causes people to suffer. It's a decision you make that gradually robs you of your joy and a meaningful life. I found that hating your enemy is like drinking poison and then expecting your enemy to die.

How idiotic!

In retrospect, I realize my behavior aggravated the hostility of many people who had traveled from Oklahoma to Colorado just to lay eyes on Nichols, the man on whom they longed to lay killing hands.

There were mornings when I didn't ease into court inconspicuously; I made an entrance flanked by Joyce on one side, Susie on the other. We no longer assigned ourselves to the back row.

We weren't showy about our relationship, but neither were we reserved. I now realize how some people in the courtroom ferociously resented my alliance with the Nichols family. Most went out of their way to avoid me; many talked in hushed tones while looking my way but never speaking directly to me.

A reporter for the *New York Times* approached me, despite all she had to do in covering the trial for America's largest newspaper, to inquire about my unlikely bonding with Nichols's mother and sister.

"We can't hold them [family members] responsible for what happened," I was quoted as saying regarding Joyce and Susie in the December 19, 1997, *Times*. "They have been victims of this bombing just like I have."

For lack of a better word, my "crusade" had begun with my search for information about the bombing—and, hopefully, a bit of emotional closure. My quest had blossomed when God led me to show my love for others, which resulted in their love for me.

By now, I felt it was time to call in a favor from Susie. I would write a letter to Nichols himself, and ask his sister to take it to him.

And she did it...that easily. The simplicity of Susie's compliance had the ring of divine intervention, I was convinced.

Dear Terry,

I am sure you were surprised the first time I greeted you in the courtroom. I have watched you carefully these past few weeks. It saddened me when I saw tears fill your eyes at the mention of our children. You seem to be a man with a heart. I am not sure how you got mixed up in this or what really happened, but I do hope you take the stand and explain it to us.

I have enjoyed meeting your mother and sister. They seem like good people. My heart goes out to them. I told your mother that I am her friend, and as her friend, I wish the best for her boy. I meant it.

Terry, our family no longer has children to love and hold. We too have been hurt. We need to know the truth. I hope that you will help us find it.

Sincerely,
Kathy Wilburn

In retrospect, I wonder what the mass media and the public in general would have thought about that letter. I didn't want the media or the public to know about it because I didn't want the families to be hurt any further. At the time, I also wondered what Nichols himself might possibly think about me, a woman who socialized with his family, and who now dared to write him a personal letter.

But more than that, I had to question my own motives. In the beginning, I wrote Nichols because I needed answers. When someone found out I was writing him, I needed to qualify it. I did not want them to think I was weird. I explained that I would be willing to dance with the devil to get to the truth. Who would know more about the bombing than the bomber himself?

My explanation actually appeased some people while utterly outraging others.

The letter included on the previous page was the first of hundreds that I would eventually exchange with Nichols. His reply to the first came inside a thank-you card regarding the kindness I had extended to his family.

I was surprised by my emotions when his reply arrived. My mailbox was actually a mail drop—a slot on the wall through which the postman would push the mail so it just dropped into the house. I went over to the mail drop and I picked up the letter. I thought, *Oh my God. There is his handwriting. I wonder what he has to say.*

My heart raced. My face flushed. I felt butterflies fluttering in my stomach. I went to the kitchen and gingerly opened the envelope with an old kitchen knife.

I took my time before sending Nichols a second letter. When I had written the first letter, I was unsure as to whether he would reply. If I wrote him a second letter and he quickly answered that, too, would I suddenly become his newfound pen pal? Did I want that with anyone, especially the Oklahoma City bomber? I was unsure how I felt about it, but I felt compelled to answer.

So, I wrote that second letter. I went to the post office to mail it. I didn't want anyone to see the correspondence pinned on my door.

I continued to fantasize about Nichols's granting me a personal audience so he could provide answers about the bombing.

In the meantime, I was embarking on a dialogue through written words. Although that had not been my original objective, I soon came to understand how important this exchange was to both Nichols and me. I had established a personal relationship with a man I had never met, someone I had once despised and now partially began to pity.

How would I ever maintain this unlikely new bond that was totally foreign to me? I hated to write letters. And what would I say? "How's the weather where you live?"

Of course the weather was always the same for him, living deep in the bowels of the prison.

Perhaps I could ask, "Who's your favorite inmate?"

Obviously he couldn't have a "favorite." He was in solitary confinement.

Clearly, small talk offered no basis for building a relationship with Nichols.

In truth, he and I had no mutual interests except that he, willfully or not, had murdered my grandchildren.

He spent nights in a dark, solitary cell, while I spent nights in a dark, solitary house. His cell was all concrete and steel; my house at least offered all the comforts of home.

Far and away, mine was a more comfortable environment for nurturing personal pain.

And yet, both settings were confining. Nichols could leave his cell only on the wings of imagination. I could leave my home freely— but only by forcing one step ahead of the other. Each of us might reach our destination. But neither of us could ever feel we had quite arrived. Neither of our memories could escape the billowing smoke following a four-second explosion that changed our lives forever.

But wait. What was I thinking? Suddenly I realized that Nichols and I actually had a great deal in common.

Spiritually renewed, I knew how to continue our communication.

One old rule claims, "Familiarity breeds contempt." Another rule insists, "There's an exception to every rule."

In my correspondence with Nichols, the latter took precedence.

Any contempt I had held for the man had been, over time,

forgiven and forgotten. I found myself posing questions unrelated to my investigation, primarily anchored in my personal curiosity.

I was curious about mundane things, like, Who does your laundry? Where do you go and what do you do for the hour a day when they let you out of your cell? Do you exercise? Do you ever see other inmates?

In our every communication, Nichols was always upbeat, always positive. I felt he had risen above his circumstances. There I was, complaining about being stuck in a 3,300-square-foot house alone, but he never complained to me—not one time about anything.

My letters became informational icing on the cake of my earlier research of newspaper and magazine profiles about Nichols. They were a 20/20 focus of insight into the lonely heart and troubled mind of one of the twentieth century's most infamous criminals. Our correspondence was revealing a man who concerned himself mostly with unremarkable, day-to-day stuff.

For example, Nichols had a strong domestic side, as indicated by his love for farming with conventional tools, such as a hoe and hand plow. He'd once raised his own wheat, then ground it to make his own bread, like a nineteenth-century pioneer. That kind of dedication to fundamental self-sufficiency contradicted the image of a politically obsessed, sly, scheming bomber.

Nichols was a naturalist who enjoyed foods that were wholesome, not processed. He loved working with his hands and gardening. These things were simply not in keeping with what I would have expected regarding the mind and daily activities of a convicted criminal.

He was also a student of alternative medicines, and he eventually sent me lists of preventive measures I could utilize to thwart everything from common colds to potential heart attacks. These remedies were not merely prescriptions from old wives' tales, but were instead the findings of Nichols's tedious research.

During this time I had a health issue where I was vomiting a lot, and nothing I had tried was bringing any relief. Nichols checked a book out at the county jail and sent it to me. It was called *The Healing Benefits of Acupressure* by F. M. Houston. The book was stamped with a label stating that it was the "Property of" the jail where he was confined. It even had a date stamp indicating when it had to be returned.

I laughed to myself, thinking, *What would happen if I didn't return this? What would they do to Terry?*

I mailed the book back.

Terry Nichols had grown up on a farm where he learned to raise vegetables at the hands of his parents. But his work ethic was without spiritual nutrition. He had heard about God, but he had never met Him through His Son.

I wondered what Nichols would have been like if he had been taken to Sunday school or to church during his formative years. Would his life have been different? Would he be sitting in prison today? If only someone would have bothered to take him to church and if he'd had the opportunity to meet the Lord, it might have saved 168 people and their families—including mine—from suffering unbearable sorrow.

Nichols had no faith. To him, it was firmly against any notion that a higher power had ever existed. When he had questions about God, he asked the wrong people. He ultimately came to the conclusion that there was no God.

Nichols did acknowledge the wonders of creation, including the mountains and hills and sky and all else that our spectacular world comprises. But he credited it all to an unspecific notion of "Mother Nature," and none of it to the Creator we know as God.

My personal correspondence with Nichols eventually yielded a secret to me, and to a few reporters who researched Nichols's background.

On April 21, 1995, two days after the bombing, when Nichols walked into the Herington, Kansas, police station to surrender, he was placed inside a holding cell. To ensure his safety and confinement, he was transported to the El Reno Federal Prison in El Reno, Oklahoma. There, he encountered a single piece of reading material—the Bible.

This simple and confused young man, earlier terrified by his pursuit as a criminal, as reported on radio and television, desperately needed something to occupy his mind. He was seeking solace when he began to read the Bible someone had given him inside the prison. He began to wonder if he had been wrong about God. After all, who does an atheist call on in times of trouble?

At that point, I still had not met Nichols, and I had no reason to think I ever would.

But Nichols later told me that, in that time of trouble, he had read the Bible cover to cover—and that was just the first of repeated readings. Did he understand everything he read? I seriously doubt it. I have known some of the nation's tenured ministers who still don't understand everything in the Bible.

I personally understood the promise about mankind's gravitation toward Jesus: *"And I, if I be lifted up from the earth, will draw all men unto me"* (John 12:32).

The key word is "all." Christ's declaration encompassed everyone—including Terry Nichols.

Nichols did not enter confinement at Herington or at El Reno carrying a radio. Yet an unidentified person gave him a battery-operated radio in El Reno.

What are the chances that Nichols would tune in a broadcast from Bob George, a preacher in Carrollton, Texas? What is the likelihood that he would decide to let the dial rest, then listen to the teaching? What are the odds that the man of God would say things pertaining to Nichols's very questions about specific Bible verses? Inside a stone-and-steel prison surrounded by high walls extending underground, what were the chances that Nichols could even receive a radio broadcast signal from a tiny AM station?

Yet all of those components came together. There, inside iron bars that would restrain any man, Nichols found freedom in the words of the Lord.

He eventually sent me a comprehensive twenty-nine-page, single-spaced, handwritten testimonial letter. It narrated the events and circumstances preceding his penitent invitation for Christ to enter his heart and save his soul after forgiving his sins—transgressions that included mass murder and destruction.

What follows are excerpts from the totally candid above-mentioned letter from Nichols. It's published here for the first time.

"God or His word was not a part of our family life," Nichols wrote. *"Church was viewed as a place where foolish people got dressed up in their 'Sunday best' to listen to a preacher and get 'milked' of their money. With the exception of two occasions (being around age 10–12 at the invitation of two different school friends), I can recall going to church only for weddings and this was impressed on me to do as part of a ritual to show respect and thus be able to enjoy the reception afterwards of conversing with friends and relatives along with partaking in much great food."*

In that same letter, Nichols addressed his first marriage and the emptiness shared by his bride, Lana, and him. At that time, long before the bombing, his search for inner tranquillity suggested he read the Bible. He asked to read Lana's. She, like him, didn't own one at that time.

"I can see that the first 40 years of my life had no solid grounding, no foundation to fall back onto," Nichols's letter continued. *"I was basically a ship without a rudder drifting aimlessly, searching blindly for direction to a meaning in my life. There was something missing in my life, but I*

did not know what, nor did I really know where to look," he said. Nichols continued:

> *A couple of other faults of mine also added to my problems in life. I would often times try to please others whenever asked to do something, along with blindly trusting in what they would say and it would at times become detrimental to me later. It was also not uncommon for me to give in to other people's demands for a variety of reasons, but primarily out of kindness and not wanting to cause an argument. . . .*
>
> *During that first week at El Reno, I was surprised that 2 different ministries had mailed me a Bible. My first thought, of course, was—how did they get my name and address? I believe at first I did flip through them then set them aside. Later, perhaps the next day, I thought—well, I still don't have anything to read or to occupy my time—then I saw the Bibles and said to myself—well, I need all of the help I can get and if there is really a God and if there is anything to that Bible then I should see what it has to say and maybe, just maybe, some type of miracle will help me out of this mess I'm in. I read it from cover to cover. . . .*
>
> *Then, on March 31, 1996 I was transferred to the Englewood Federal Prison in Littleton, Colorado, about 30 miles South of Denver. This occurred after Judge Matsch ruled that I could not get a fair trial in Oklahoma and then my trial would be held in Denver. . . .*
>
> *This radio program was on from 5:05 p.m.–6 p.m., Monday through Friday, originating from Dallas, Texas. It was titled "People to People" and hosted by Bob George. To me Bob was a no-nonsense type of guy who clearly knew Scripture, would clearly give good sound biblical advice, and he was big on the grace of God. . . .*
>
> *I do sincerely thank Bob George, his staff, and his ministry for greatly helping me to understand the Bible in a better way as well*

as truly coming to the Lord and thus being saved—this occurring in June, 1996.

Nichols talked about his eventual move to Florence ADMAX USP. There, his radio was taken away. To my knowledge, he never heard the sermons of Bob George again.

But the teachings of Christ, divinely channeled through the teachings of George, remained intact, and seemed to grow in correlation to Nichols's growth in stature with Jesus:

> *In conclusion, being saved is an important part and time in one's life, however, what is even more important is what you do with your life after that point. Thus, truly being saved is only the very beginning of one's learning to walk in a newness of life, which is led by the Holy Spirit. And this can only be accomplished by the grace of God through faith in Him. Only when you begin to understand the love and grace that God has for you. We must realize and accept the truth that we can do no good things apart from God. . . .*
>
> *Though I do not know yet God's full purpose of allowing me to go through all these various trials and tribulations in regards to the OKC bombing, I do know and can say without a doubt that He has, and continues to work miracles in my life—the greatest of which is drawing me to Him for my salvation.*
>
> *But I do know that with those trials and tribulations we go through in our lives we have a choice to make. We can choose to accept them as a purifying process which will help us to truly become children of God and then able to share in that inheritance which He has waiting for us in heaven. Or we can choose to become embittered toward others and the world and in the end be separated from the love of God and thus spend eternity in hell. As for me I count it all joy in the testing of my faith for my citizenship is in heaven and*

thus I press toward the goal of the prize of the upward call of God in Christ Jesus. . . .

Thus my prayer and hope is that everyone will truly come to know—the width and length and depth and height of the love of Christ which passes all understanding and to be filled with the fullness of God Almighty.

Blessings,
Terry L. Nichols

Chapter Eleven

My correspondence with Nichols was mostly chatty and upbeat, and often contained little or nothing important. Many were vanilla digests of my routine days.

I concede, however, that those letters were written with a hidden agenda. I wanted to know everything Nichols knew about the planning and execution of the Alfred P. Murrah Building bombing. I was trying to peel away layers of unanswered questions, searching for the heart of truth. I knew when his state trial was over, he would tell me everything because he had told me he would.

My letters were never hardball interrogations. I simply portrayed myself as what I had truly become, a friend to a friendless person; a friend to someone whose welfare sincerely concerned me.

As I mentioned earlier, my attitude toward Nichols had slowly softened. With our ongoing interactions I gradually began to perceive him in all of his fallible humanity—as Terry, the son of my friend Joyce. By the time of his second trial, my relationship had evolved into proactive caring. I knew most people would never understand. I would not be surprised if Nichols might have been a bit bewildered himself. I know I was.

I found that the act of praying for Nichols and McVeigh was changing me. I didn't know how to pray for them, but I knew in my heart of hearts that I was supposed to.

My prayers were simple.

"Lord, I know that according to Your Word I am to pray for my enemies. I really don't know how to, but I'll give it a try. At this time I lift up Timothy McVeigh and Terry Nichols to You and ask You to touch their lives."

God helped me somehow to move beyond myself. By staying engaged with Nichols, peeling back layers of the mysteries of his humanity, I understood more. A ratification of my earlier and true forgiveness finally came to me. It did not result from my conscious decision.

Like many Christians, I had experienced what I believed to be miracles, some of them major, such as my earlier deliverance from numbing grief and thoughts of suicide. I think, however, that God's confirmation of my Christlike grace toward Nichols and McVeigh was the most monumental miracle I'd ever undergone.

My forgiveness of Nichols actually intensified. I liked the freedom I found when I reached out to the confused man who had been at the wrong place with the wrong people at the wrong time. I had become Nichols's friend.

In 1998, Nichols was charged with the involuntary manslaughter of eight law enforcement officers. When Nichols's federal trial was over, he was sent back to Oklahoma. I felt sorry for him as he awaited his state trial for the murder of 161 civilians, one count of fetal homicide, first-degree arson, and conspiracy. He was in solitary confinement, which is bad enough, but he also knew that if given a chance, any of the inmates would gladly kill him.

Unlike the federal prison, he had no television to watch, and the radio given to him in El Reno had been confiscated when he was moved to Colorado for his federal trial.

He spent his days staring at the walls in his small, dank cell, existing on jailhouse beans and bologna sandwiches.

Hoping to brighten his dismal existence, I bought him a cassette player at a garage sale and began sending him gospel music tapes and religious sermons.

Shortly after being moved to Oklahoma, Nichols discovered that phone privileges at the county jail were much more liberal than they had been while he was in federal custody.

In a letter to me, he said he would call me if I would simply send him my phone number.

After much thought, I sent him the number. Why not? I had nothing to lose and a whole lot to learn about the bombing. I needed answers that only he could give.

My phone rang a few days later. I looked at the caller ID. It was Nichols. My heart pounded as I anticipated talking to the man who had helped kill my grandchildren. I was nervous. Before picking up the phone, I cleared my throat, hoping to find a voice to speak. My mind raced as I thought about what to say. I knew I wanted to get at the truth about the bombing, but I had no idea how to do it. And I was desperately afraid that Nichols would discern my incentive. If so, he might never call me again.

On the second ring, I raised the receiver to my ear. A prerecorded message said, "You are receiving a call from inmate [his voice] Terry Nichols. Will you accept it?"

"Yes, I'll accept...

"Hi, Terry! How are you?" I asked cheerfully.

Once more, I was amazed by this strange relationship. Besides Nichols's immediate family, I had become the only person outside the jailhouse walls who had the attention of its most villainous criminal.

The people I told about my friendship with Nichols were astonished. Some expressed disdain. Because of this, it became my guarded secret. The person who understood most about my forgiveness toward Nichols was Nichols himself. His letters communicated this understanding both directly and indirectly.

I was lonely. Nichols was lonely. I looked forward to hearing from him, and I found myself comparing our lives as I underwent each day. Both of us had been destroyed by the bombing. True, we were destroyed in very different ways. But each of us was trying to reconstruct ourselves.

I was amazed by what God had done.

I came to realize something I believe to this day. When you totally surrender your will to Christ's, God will change you in ways you never expected. Almost always, Christ gives His believers more than they sought. Clearly, His blessings come with bonuses.

Simply through Nichols's handwritten letters to me, I absorbed his humanity at a personal level. My official research into his past had been invaluable. But Nichols's letters, no matter how trite, gave me insights I otherwise might never have had.

For example, I realized Nichols was no self-proclaimed soldier willing to die for a cause, like McVeigh. Instead, Nichols was a much simpler person who probably didn't realize himself just how he'd become involved in a catastrophic crime.

Additionally, I learned that Nichols lived with acute fear—the fear of being put to death by a jury of twelve.

He was even leery of his own lawyers, men and women who officially intended to "help" Nichols. With the exception of his immediate family, there was no one Nichols didn't fear, it seemed to me. His inability to trust anyone overwhelmingly lent to his loneliness.

I often got the sense that Nichols didn't really understand how he ever got involved in the bombing, at least to the degree of becoming a mass murderer. Perhaps he interacted with McVeigh, an old Army buddy, simply because he sought acceptance. Then things just got out of hand.

Nichols got in too deeply, and when he tried to back out, McVeigh wouldn't allow it, I surmised. McVeigh threatened Nichols's life and the lives of his family members. Nichols was too scared to go to the authorities that he did not trust.

All my life, I had heard that confession was good for the soul.

Maybe Nichols would eventually see how his baggage might be lightened by sharing with me the loaded circumstances preceding that massacre on a Wednesday in Oklahoma.

So I pressed forward, overtly exhibiting love, covertly seeking information. I came to realize that my dance with the devil had ended. Nichols was not a devil. He was a real human being. And I had realized that he was my friend. I knew this was unnatural. I came to understand that it was a gift from God.

To this day, Nichols harbors secrets he could take to his grave. I pray he won't, that he will realize that Christianity is all about giving—including answers that could help solve mysteries.

Growing up in a Christian home was a privilege. Here I am in 1958 with my mom, dad, and brother. I was five years old.

This is a picture of my mother, Edith Graham, and my grandmother, Ruby Lee Shelton, at the nursing home where they were residents. My mother was diagnosed with Alzheimer's in her fifties and died by strangulation after being restrained in a chair with a Posey belt. Grandma died two weeks later.

Chase was a proud big brother who enjoyed his little brother, Colton.

My husband Glenn's sons, Matt and Bart, beside their nephews, Chase and Colton.

"The Chaser," as we liked to call him, playing with his baby brother, Colton.

Here I am, a young grandmother, holding Caitlin and Colton.

Ever the hams, Chase and Colton were proud to show off their pudgy physiques by posing for the camera.

Nonna and Chase at Disney World. Little did I know this would be our first and last vacation.

Chase and Colton in their room with the dogs, Reuben and Rosie, a few days before the bombing.

Chase and Colton's last picture, taken on Easter 1995. They were buried in these clothes.

Edye, Danny, and Caitlin at my home in Oklahoma City one year before the bombing.

A group photograph of Chase's class at the America's Kids day-care shortly before the April 19 bombing. Several of these children died. Chase (standing in the doorway) holds hands with a girl.

Colton is the second child from the left in the front row. His teacher Miss Brenda (left) was also killed in the bombing.

The Alfred P. Murrah Federal Building in downtown Oklahoma City was the center of attention on Thursday, April 20, 1995, as rescue workers continue digging through the rubble after Wednesday's fatal explosion. *(J. Pat Carter)*

Mementos left by well-wishers at the bomb site in memory of those who lost their lives. *(J. Pat Carter)*

While the Murrah Building was imploding, I was exploding with frustration. I decided it was time to pose my questions to the media. *(David Allen)*

Two little boys were buried in this coffin.

My brother, Bobby, and son, Danny (at the front of the casket), served as pallbearers for Chase and Colton.

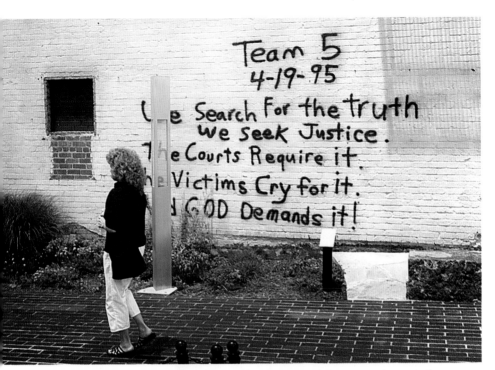

I walk past messages posted by rescue workers on Oklahoma City's Journal Record Building across the street from the Murrah.

Glenn, Edye, and me in our home shortly before Glenn lost his battle with cancer. *(David Allen)*

My good friend Jannie Coverdale and me at Christmas 2012. We've come a long way since the Oklahoma City Bombing.

I'd never flown in a helicopter. Here I am departing for Elohim City.

CHOOSE Life

27 Dec. 2001

Dear Kathy,

Just a short note to let you know that I did get three cassette tapes from Brian on Monday which you had sent to him for me. I've listened to each one already and they are truly enjoyable. You have excellent taste in music. I've even found a classical music station on my radio. Brian, I'm sure will be bringing me the latest tapes you've sent him the next time he visits me which should be next week. I should be well supplied with tapes by then and with a good variety as well because others have sent me tapes for Christmas gifts also.

Thank you as well for the $25.00 M.O., I received it on Monday. And of course I will use it to purchase a phone card so that we can stay in contact by phone.

You're in my heart, thoughts & prayers. May the Lord graciously bless you in all things. Talk with you soon my sister.

Love You,

Terry

A letter from my correspondence with Terry Nichols.

Dear Kathy,   WED., 05 SEPT. 2001

Your story about being "wired for 2:20" was easy for me to remember. In the past I did quite a bit of work around 110 & 220 wiring while on the farm & remodeling homes. In fact, years ago one day I was hooking up some 220 wiring without turning off the power (I thought I'd save a little time) and I accidentally "touched" a bare wire and it caused me to drop down on my knees. It was what one would literally call a "shocking experience". Though that experience drove me to my knees unfortunely it didn't drive me to God. Perhaps I should have held on to that wire longer to receive His message rather then just a jolt of static.

As far as my art tools they consist of red & **black** ink pens; blue, green & yellow highlighters; regular pencils; and two different thickness black roller marker pens. I would love some colored pencils or even water color paints but the jail will not allow it. But I do get some colored paper & cardstock paper from Brian at times which helps add color to my drawings.

And thank you for your thoughtfulness of sending me some colored stationary & paper. I will make good use of it. Kathy, I accept your deal (too bad Wes Lane wasn't so easy to deal with). Enclosed is "THE PRAYER OF JABEZ" on the paper as you requested. I hope it meets your expectations.

As far as my comment about me someday knocking on your door it was a combination of a jest and as a

Another correspondence letter with Terry.

Edye is now an equine dentist who travels the country "floating" horses' teeth.

Glenn and Emjay, Edye's children, make their annual Christmas pilgrimage to Chase and Colton's grave. There, I tell them stories about the brothers they never knew.

Emjay attaching a stuffed animal to one of her brothers' chairs during the 2010 memorial service. My family attends every year.

Tom Sanders and I were married in Eureka Springs, Arkansas, on September 19, 2002. He's my best friend and the finest person I've ever known. I'm so blessed to have him in my life.

Chapter Twelve

Hope can power the spirit through the saddest of circumstances. Nothing erases old hardships like new beginnings, especially a newborn baby.

Edye was expecting again.

By 1997, Edye had married Paul Stowe, a man she had met at the state fair who worked for Channel 5 news. They had moved into a house of their own, and she and I were eagerly anticipating the birth—to put it mildly. Of course, Chase and Colton would forever remain among our most precious memories. Although I could affectionately recall those memories, I couldn't put my arms around them, as I would Edye's baby. That said, I still had trouble letting go of my tributes to my departed grandchildren.

Two years after their deaths, their bedroom at my house was situated exactly as it was when they passed. No detail had been altered because, apart from my memories, these physical things were all I had left.

I felt no guilt about clinging to the past.

After all, through God's miracle, I had changed my heart and mind regarding men who killed my flesh and blood.

I was in no hurry to sacrifice my nostalgia regarding Chase and Colton, the center of my earlier world gone wrong.

In the interim, my life had been overrun with well-meaning advisers, counselors, ministers, family, and more. Most expressed opinions to me, whether solicited or not.

But my coveted memories? Only I could change those. And I refused.

Not long before Edye delivered her baby, she asked me if I would like to put up a crib in Chase and Colton's room. I really didn't want to change the room, but it seemed important to her so I agreed.

Producers from *Dateline NBC* asked to videotape Edye and me as we converted Chase and Colton's room for the new arrival, a boy named Glenn after my late husband and Edye's stepdad.

The television crew followed Edye and me as I agonized about removing sheets where my late grandchildren had slept. I cried as Edye and I physically struggled to place Chase and Colton's beds into a storage bin.

No wonder I was melancholy. That furniture represented the largest portion of memorabilia regarding my departed grand-babies. It had once held two laughing little boys, and now was destined for a dark room where it might never again be seen, just like the boys themselves.

Yet the moving of that furniture signaled another milestone in my emotional rehabilitation. Even the *Dateline* crew noticed. Moving the old pieces, and the pending arrival of an infant, somehow banished my gloom. Since the boys' deaths, walking into that room had been bittersweet and sometimes left me saddened. But the placement of new furnishings and the anticipation of the new life lifted my spirit and tapped my excitement to a degree I had never expected.

My replenished spirit also accompanied me into other settings, including the hospital where Edye delivered baby Glenn.

The birthing area and Edye's private room were filled with reporters from around the nation. I was eager for the nation to see Edye and me, both of us the happiest we'd been since before the bombing. I wanted America to see this blessed event because there had been so much heartbreak in Edye's and my lives.

The baby's doctor barely made it in time for the delivery.

Can you imagine? He was shuffling through the hospital when a nurse stepped into the hallway and yelled at him.

"If you want to see this baby born, you'd better get in here now!"

The doctor sprinted into the delivery room. Edye's guests and I went to the waiting area.

Soon after, I heard the tiny cry of a newborn baby. Glenn Brennen Stowe had announced his arrival to the world. My brother, Bobby, held me tightly as I began to weep, and then outright bawled.

Edye radiated a new mother's glow, and I continued to cry.

During that electric moment on January 12, 1998, I chose to evict the misery that had freely walked in and out of my mind for three years.

Chase and Colton would always be two precious little boys whose lives had fulfilled mine. But instead of feeling sorrowful about their absence, I felt jubilant about Glenn's presence.

For days afterward, it was as if much of the nation rejoiced over little Glenn and all he symbolized.

Edye and her baby were showered with gifts on *Oprah*. Little Glenn, Edye, and I then went to Hollywood for an appearance on *The Leeza Gibbons Show*. Mail came from fifty states and the phone rang incessantly, just as it had for weeks after the bombing.

Soon, I experienced the most wonderfully eerie happening of my life.

Edye knew how blessed I felt by little Glenn's presence, so she brought him to my house to spend the night. I thought he was too tiny and vulnerable to be moved from his home crib in the Oklahoma wintertime. But I said nothing, as Edye had thoughtfully wanted to share her new baby with me.

Edye and I visited for a while, then she went home and left the baby with me. In the dimness of nightfall, before a flickering fire, I sang lullabies to baby Glenn that I'd once sang to Chase and Colton.

Shortly afterward, I tucked baby Glenn into his crib and we retired to peaceful slumber.

I was abruptly awakened in the middle of the night by familiar music. *Where is that coming from?* I puzzled in my sleep-fogged mind. Instinctively, I tossed back the covers, stumbled to my feet, and followed the sound—to little Glenn's room.

There, bathed in moonlight, was Chase and Colton's carousel. It was one of the few possessions of theirs I had chosen to keep in the baby's room. Without provocation, it had mysteriously begun to spin and play the same tune that had played the night my grandbabies were killed.

Until baby Glenn's sleepover, it hadn't played since Chase's and Colton's deaths. Then, it stopped playing to this day.

To me, the music was a sign from Chase and Colton. It was like they were saying, "Nonna, it's okay. You can love this little boy."

I'm not a superstitious person, but there was no other explanation. I believed it was a sign from God.

The next morning, I was still relishing the warmth of beholding God's musical manifestation. I began to improvise a lullaby to tiny Glenn, wrapped snugly in a blanket and my arms.

"Falling in love again, in love again with you," were the song's first words. I don't remember the rest. I had never previously sung that song. I never sang it again. And only little Glenn and I ever heard it.

The lullaby's lyrics had flowed effortlessly from my voice by way of my heart. To me, God was helping me to channel the love I had felt for Chase and Colton to our new baby Glenn.

What a welcome and beloved task.

⤝

I remained contented by the bliss of Glenn's birth.

"A baby changes everything" has become a catchphrase during the new millennium. I can testify to its truthfulness.

But I had work to do, and it was time to do it. Rejuvenated by little Glenn, I was more determined than ever to pursue my personal search for the truth about the bombing and just who really did what during that massive slaughter. Among those people, I would find those who needed my forgiveness, for their sakes as well as my own.

I decided to dive deeply into the lives of Michael and Lori Fortier, a married couple who'd been pivotal figures in the catastrophe, according to the FBI. Courtroom testimony had indicated they were well aware of McVeigh's plans to bomb the Murrah.

On August 8, 1995, less than four months after the detonation, Michael and Lori testified before a grand jury investigating the entire Murrah ordeal. On May 27, 1998, Michael was sentenced to twelve years in prison and fined $200,000 for not warning authorities about McVeigh's plans to bomb the Murrah Building.

He remained incarcerated when I went to see his wife.

En route, I had to wonder how Michael got involved in McVeigh's diabolical plan. When asked on the witness stand about his whereabouts on the morning of the explosion, he said he had an alibi.

"I was smoking crack cocaine at a neighbor's house," he announced. The admission of one felony as defense against another doesn't ring of brilliance. Later, Michael said that Ila Hart, his mother-in-law, would provide his alibi for the day of the bombing. She did not.

Meanwhile, Lori was given immunity from prosecution in exchange for her testimony, even though she admitted to wrapping blasting caps for McVeigh in November 1994. The caps resembled Christmas presents, a sick joke regarding the "present" McVeigh would give to his forthcoming victims.

She claimed that he sat at her kitchen table, where he stacked Campbell's soup cans to illustrate how the barrels of ammonia nitrate would be stacked in the back of the Ryder truck.

Chapter Thirteen

~⚬~

Whereas my investigation for answers was rooted in my tribute to Chase, Colton, and my late husband, Glenn, it was now additionally inspired by baby Glenn's birth. Four years after the bombing, I flew to Kingman, Arizona, to call on Lori Fortier, who, among her other crimes, had also made a phony ID for McVeigh. He used the credential to rent the Ryder truck that hauled the fatal device to the Murrah Building. She listed his birth date as April 19, the very day of the bombing.

My search for Lori first led me to a modest mobile home park on the perimeter of Kingman. Lori and her husband, Michael, had lived there on McVicar Avenue before the bombing. The park had a dual personality. Everyone seemed to be either retired or selling drugs.

I asked some of the residents to search their own recollections of people coming and going from Michael and Lori's place back in the days when they lived there. Some reported activities that seemed fairly suspicious. But none could provide the kind of specifics and details I needed.

I drove to Kingman proper where I found a somewhat quaint, "village" type of settlement dotted with antique shops and out-of-the-way diners. I didn't broadcast my reason for coming to Kingman to the residents I spoke with. Neither did I conceal it. When told of my quest for the truth about Oklahoma's Murrah bombing, most residents expressed regret and remorse about the slaughter and their community's guilt by association with the Fortiers. The negative publicity had left a figurative black eye on their town. Perhaps those innocent citizens sought redemption for their town and showed it by extending courtesy to me.

I visited Kingman's TrueValue hardware store, where Michael had worked as a bookkeeper months before the bombing. Later, I would discover close ties between McVeigh, Michael, and certain members of a white supremacist group. At the hardware store, I was told that Michael had handed out literature for the militant faction.

I was also given a lead about Lori's whereabouts. Someone said she worked as a manicurist at a Kingman tanning salon. I found the business and nonchalantly strolled inside. I pretended to be interested in buying a bathing suit. Upon entering, I scanned the place as inconspicuously as possible. Somewhere in that store, I would find Lori Fortier, or so I'd been told.

There were several women giving manicures inside the salon, which made it difficult to positively identify Lori, as her appearance had surely changed in the years since I'd last seen photos of her in the media.

I could have walked into the group of nail technicians and asked which one was Lori Fortier. But doing that would have forced me to identify myself in front of her peers. I didn't want to embarrass or frighten Lori or any of her associates. So I went outside to a pay telephone. I called the salon and asked to speak to Lori. When Lori came to the phone, I identified myself as a grandmother who lost two grandchildren in the Murrah bombing and told her I was calling from a phone near the front door of the salon.

That was enough to make Lori realize I had found her. I knew exactly where she was at the very moment she and I were speaking. Our conversation, however, was friendly as I assured Lori that I harbored no anger toward her. Otherwise, she might have panicked.

Previously I had just been someone she'd seen on national television and inside a courtroom. I'm sure she never expected to see me only a few yards from the place of her livelihood.

Lori did express shock that I had found her work address. Undoubtedly, she also had to wonder if I knew where she lived.

I had come more than one thousand miles to see what she knew about an unspeakable crime. I asked Lori if she'd be willing to meet with me. She stumbled for words but did not say no, and she agreed to meet me for dinner. As I began to describe what I looked like by telling her I have red hair, she said, "Yes, ma'am, I know who you are. I know what you look like."

We made plans to meet at the Dambar & Steakhouse—the nicest restaurant in Kingman, Arizona. So far, my journey had not been in vain.

I entered the restaurant and took a seat on a bench where customers waited for a table. After a moment, I saw a young woman I believed to be Lori coming toward me. She was accompanied by an unknown woman.

The situation felt so awkward. I didn't know what to do, so I said her name. "Lori?" She answered, "Yes, ma'am," and cast her eyes to the ground. I continued, "Well, I am Kathy and it's nice to meet you."

With that, I put my arm around her and hugged her. She teared up. Then she introduced me to her friend. She was the owner of the salon where Lori worked. Then the restaurant hostess took us to our table.

I wondered if her companion was there to socialize or to protect Lori from me. The protection wouldn't be necessary.

Easing into small talk, I asked Lori her age. She was twenty-six, the same age as Edye.

I thought about the loving way Americans had reached out to Edye for years after that blast. Many of those same compassionate people would have attacked Lori for her role in the bombing. They would have been outraged had they known I intended to buy her dinner.

Fifteen minutes into our acquaintance, before I began to question Lori, I sensed her regret for assisting in the construction of the Murrah bomb. I felt inclined to believe that Lori never knew that McVeigh was going to activate the blast while people were inside the building. While wanting to avenge the deaths at Waco, Texas, Lori perhaps had intended to be a coconspirator in mass property damage, not mass murder, but I didn't know for sure.

When I thought the time was right, I eased into my questions, specifically probing about Lori's entire role in the explosion. She began to weep but abruptly cut me off, insisting her lawyers had told her not to discuss the incident. With that pronouncement, I knew that previously unpublished information would not be disclosed by Lori that day. I suppose I could have dismissed the value of my trip right then. I had come so far to learn so little.

But I did nothing of the sort. While I was ambushed by Lori's silence, I decided to tell her how the bombing had affected *my* life. I wanted to be a flesh-and-blood example of one who had lost flesh and blood.

I produced a photograph of Chase and Colton and placed it on the table. Although she was too ashamed to look me in the face, she couldn't remove her eyes from the likenesses of the brothers, ages two and three. As Lori stared at the adorable boys, I described the butchery and pandemonium on the morning of the bombing. I relayed the decision of the coroner, who wanted to dismember Chase's and Colton's little bodies for scientific research.

I told Lori, in vivid detail, what my life had been like, living a nightmare that I once thought would never diminish. I told her I fought to *endure* life, with no thought that I'd ever again *live* it. I explained the difference. I told her that Edye and I had spent Edye's birthday picking out a casket for Chase and Colton's funeral. I told her about the birth of little Glenn.

By then, Lori was silent and attentive. Like most people, she knew few specifics about the survivors' agony, and how that blast tore away our minds, hearts, and souls in the same way it demolished steel, glass, and concrete.

Similarly, Lori had no idea that I had reached out to McVeigh and Nichols, and that the latter had warmly accepted my gestures.

I confided that I had truly forgiven Nichols, who had become my friend. Her face, which had at first been mostly expressionless, became a portrait of astonishment.

As she continued to gaze at the picture of my grandchildren, she suddenly shook and bawled, uncontrollably.

I found myself reaching across the table to hold her hand. I had been doing most of the talking, but then I wanted Lori to talk to me. I mentioned her own children, knowing that she, like most mothers, would be eager to discuss them.

Silently, I did the mathematics as to what age Chase and Colton would have been on that day, had they lived. I decided not to go there.

I learned that Lori's oldest child had become a social outcast at his public school. Children berated him because of his infamous parents. Lori herself was persona non grata at school events.

At her place of employment, she was known only as "Lori the Nail Technician." She didn't want people to know her identity. I'm sure that using her last name would have damaged business and exposed her to ridicule.

Once a month, she drove her children to Florence, Colorado, to visit their father in prison. Then they would all return home, where they lived with Lori's mother. Lori didn't earn enough money to afford a place of her own. Barring a miracle, she probably never would, I thought to myself.

As I lingered with Lori, I knew our discourse was touching her deeply—and me, as well. At that point in my life, I knew regret and I knew pain whenever I saw either. There are personal mistakes and errors in judgment that all of us regret and then repair. Yet there are others that seemingly cannot be repaired, no matter how much we regret them.

Lori appeared to be suffering that kind of remorse. No matter the depth of her pain and sorrow, she could not "unmeet" Timothy McVeigh. She could not withdraw her participation in a driver's license forgery. She could not undo the hateful mockery implied in decorating blasting caps like Christmas presents.

Few things make people as miserable as the yearning to retract their wrongdoings while knowing full well they can't. Lori Fortier was a contrite and broken woman. She had left a promising future behind her. It would remain there forever.

My heart broke for Lori and her children. Her obvious remorse made it easy for me to forgive. As I left, she followed me to the car and pleaded for me to write to her husband.

"What do you want me to say to him?" I asked.

"I don't know, but you'll know," she replied.

Later, inside my motel, I found myself writing to a man I had never met but had, at one time, loathed.

My letter confessed as much.

To Fortier, I identified myself as that redheaded grandmother who'd berated him at his sentencing hearing. My letter said I no longer had faith in our federal government and that I felt we were being deceived by government officials and by the bombers about what really happened.

I ended the letter with "Tonight, Michael, I prayed for your family." He had killed mine and I prayed for his—a bizarre turn of events.

In a few days, I received a written response from Michael Fortier. I thought some of it was sincere and some tongue-in-cheek:

Dear Mrs. Wilburn,

Thank you so much for your prayers and blessings on my family. . . . I had to fight the urge to weep. I am so glad that you got to meet Lori and came to see her for who she really is.

I am troubled by your statement that you no longer have faith in the federal government. I find it troubling that the federal government would deceive you in this matter. I also find it hard to believe. I don't know what you have uncovered but I have faith that the feds have uncovered everything, and I do not believe they would cover anything up.

Mrs. Wilburn, I am so sincerely happy that your dinner with Lori was a positive experience. I hope that meeting her has shown you that a person's worst mistakes do not always define that person as a whole.

My prayer for you is that you and your family continue to heal and that you all find the answers you want.

Sincerely,

Michael Fortier

God really does work in mysterious ways. In part, I had gone to Arizona seeking truth, and the truth I found was God's.

Chapter Fourteen

I braced myself whenever the phone rang in those days, and I tightened with anxiety about what he might say this time.

My priority was to keep my calls with Terry a secret, as no one knew I had authorized them from the solitary-confinement cellblock that held Terry Nichols.

I amazed myself by regularly communicating with Nichols as if he were just another casual caller, like my daughter or a neighbor.

By 1998, Nichols and I had shared scores of telephone conversations, contrasting his life in solitary confinement and mine in free society. Sometimes, he quietly fed on my every word.

I became Nichols's window to the world from which he'd been forever banished. In addition to the phone calls, Nichols and I continued to exchange personal letters.

Nichols was aware that soon after the bombing, I had discreetly befriended his mother and sister.

The more I got to know Nichols, the more I wanted to see him face-to-face. I must admit that my initial desire to meet him was driven by my nonstop desire to learn more about the bombing and who else might be involved.

The unanswerable question was simply, How would I ever get to him? Not even the mass media penetrated Nichols's maximum-security jail cell without his consent. He saw no outsiders except for his lawyer.

And, if I actually met with Nichols, how would I keep our meeting a secret? Most of the nation wanted him dead. Oklahomans would especially take a dim view of my visiting someone who'd taken so many lives, as well as the will to live from some of their family members.

I approached Nichols with the idea of a visit. He was excited and agreed to call Brian Hermanson, his defense lawyer, to obtain permission.

"Why do you want to meet Terry?" Hermanson asked me.

I told him that I had forgiven Nichols and that we had been corresponding by letter and conversing by phone for months. The line went quiet.

"I'm a Christian, too," Hermanson told me. "But I have never encountered this kind of forgiveness. This is extraordinary."

Hermanson agreed to make the arrangements and scheduled my first visit with Nichols. He told me I was forbidden to discuss Nichols's pending trial or his alleged crimes. We agreed that neither of us would disclose the visitation to anyone.

To be honest, I was not sure why the unprecedented visit was so important to me. Somehow I just felt that it was the right thing to do. This *was* Terry Nichols, one of the men who had slaughtered my grandchildren. Adding insult to injury, Nichols's bomb had stripped away the spirits of my late husband and deeply wounded my daughter. If Glenn were still living, he would have been outraged at me for merely speaking to Nichols, much less reaching out to him and his family.

I believe that quite often when God is speaking to us and through us, we are not consciously aware. We just feel strongly compelled to act. At least that is how it is with me. It is only later that I realize from where the inspiration came. In any case, I knew I wanted to talk face-to-face with this infamous man.

Hermanson and I met at a designated area inside the courthouse where I identified myself by my maiden name. I had a driver's license that corresponded. The clerk was not pleased when I wrote the name of the inmate I intended to see. He, like most Oklahomans, deeply resented anyone reaching out to Nichols, especially through a personal visit.

I prayed the clerk would not recognize me. Thankfully he did not, despite the fact that my image had saturated the television airwaves for months after the bombing—and continued intermittently to that day.

I knew I would have to be very careful to ensure that no one ever found out I pulled this off.

I recalled television news scenes depicting hostile threats shouted at Nichols and McVeigh. Most threats came as each man wore handcuffs and waist chains while being escorted by a platoon of lawmen to holding cells. Angry civilians seized with mob psychology yelled threats to kill, knowing that police were present and cameras were rolling.

Those hate-filled people seemed to have no fear of consequences; they were ready to take the law into their own hands if simply given the chance.

Hermanson, now inside the lobby, whispered that a guard would soon escort us to the fifth story of the jailhouse. I learned that all prisoners, except Nichols, had been moved from that floor.

The migration of the inmates had resulted in packed cells that worsened jail overcrowding. The prisoners' resulting discomfort aggravated their hatred for Nichols.

A floor that had once housed scores of criminals now housed only one: Nichols. He was totally alone, without radio or television or reading material. His future behind him, Nichols now had nothing to do and no one with whom to do it. His mind was surely locked on the unstoppable reprocessing of his despicable past.

Additionally, Nichols was loathed by inmates due to their intolerance of child abusers. Convicts will abide murderers, rapists, bank robbers, and the like, but they will not tolerate baby killers.

As if stolen by an invisible hand, my confidence suddenly vanished, leaving me with fear bordering on terror. My will to see Nichols had been overpowering while inside the safety of my living room. Now, all that desire somehow deserted me. At any moment I would begin my ride with Hermanson and a guard inside the elevator to the jail's virtually abandoned top floor. I would then be left alone with Nichols on the isolation side of security glass. Surely the silence would be deafening.

Nichols had been described as a frighteningly calm, inscrutable sociopath whose veins seemingly surged with ice water rather than the warmth of human blood. He had meticulously helped build a killing machine whose blast was felt six miles away. During the construction, he was reportedly void of emotion, as if assembling a toy jigsaw puzzle.

As the elevator slowly crept upward, I continued to feel my will to confront Nichols evaporate into the stale air.

They have moved the prisoners, but what if one managed to hide and stay behind? I asked myself. *The inmates supposedly hate Nichols. They're likely to hate me for seeing him. What am I doing here?*

My mind was playing games with me.

As the elevator reached the fourth floor, I fought to suppress my panic before my imminent encounter with Nichols. The more I tried to minimize anxious thoughts, the more they multiplied.

With the car still easing upward, my mind flashed forward to my impending conversation. I realized my intention was not entirely rooted in my testimony. Initially, I had pondered our time together as a fact-finding mission. I'd planned to ask Nichols, face-to-face, who helped him build the bomb that destroyed much of downtown Oklahoma City and lives within it. Yet, in order to pursue that question, I had promised Nichols's lawyer not to pose it! How crazy is that?

Have I acted too hastily? Who's going to protect me if Nichols comes through the glass at me? It's only glass. Couldn't he break it? As I imagined terrifying scenarios, my determination grew weaker.

By the time the elevator reached the top floor I was overcome by the desire to run. Had Brian not been with me, I would not have been about to step onto that floor. And I did something no other civilian had done since the bombing.

I sat and talked with Terry Nichols.

✒

"The culture of a thousand years is shattered with the clanging of the cell door behind you," said the late Johnny Cash, a singer often voluntarily locked inside prison walls to perform for inmates. Asked why he did, Cash replied he wanted men held against their wills to be visited by a man who willed to see them.

"Then they'll know someone really cares about them," Cash said. I wished I'd met the man. Even more, I wished he was beside me in that elevator.

Squeaking as it closed behind me, the elevator door resounded with a soft echo in the emptiness of the prison's fifth floor.

I saw no sign of life.

I suddenly understood Cash's interpretation of the clanging of a steel door and the resulting surrender of civilization.

Inside these walls, my identity before massive television viewers had no significance. Totally alone, I felt powerless and terrified.

I even recalled a frightening scene from *The Silence of the Lambs*, the movie where vulnerable FBI agent Clarice Starling walks down a prison hallway, then waits alone outside the cell of Dr. Hannibal Lecter, a mass murderer from whom she wants answers. I wanted answers to questions I had promised not to ask.

What have I done?! I inwardly asked the silence. Then, *Why isn't Nichols or someone on the other side of the glass?*

Had he changed his mind about seeing me? Did guards decide not to place him within my line of sight?

Before I could answer myself, Nichols appeared.

I heard the opening of a door I could not see. A guard who seemed as large as a California redwood stepped into my window's frame. Another, seemingly his towering clone, followed him. They stood behind Nichols looking over his shoulders, one on either side. They glared at me throughout the entire visit, making me extremely uncomfortable.

Between the uniformed men stood a slight man whose pasty complexion reminded me of fresh mayonnaise. Measuring up to a mere five foot nine, Nichols seemed much smaller standing between the giants.

He sported a vibrant-red jumpsuit, attire I would later learn was standard issue to prisoners inside the Oklahoma City county jail.

Not until Nichols was seated, and his handcuffs removed, did he raise his eyes to mine. Wearing thick glasses, Nichols looked more like a small-town librarian than a mass murderer. This guy was Barney Fife, minus the humor.

For a moment, he and I simply stared at each other. I looked into his face. He seemed to look through mine.

I began speaking for no other reason than to break the unbearable quietness. Nichols didn't reply. Actually, he couldn't hear me. One of the guards tapped the glass, motioning to the phone on my side of the glass. He pantomimed that I should pick up the receiver. As I did, Nichols lifted a receiver on his side of the transparent barrier between us.

What was I about to say? I asked myself. No matter, I couldn't remember, and this silence had to be broken.

Say something! my mind shouted.

"Terry," I said. "You look like Santa Claus in that red suit."

Nichols just laughed as his face turned crimson. I had embarrassed him.

Did I really just say that? What in the world did that mean? Was that the best I could do? I wanted to gain this man's trust, and the best I could offer was a gibe about his prison clothes? Why? Did I think he could have selected another outfit?

First impressions are the most lasting. Would Nichols forever think I was a smart aleck?

We finally began our conversation in earnest. In soft tones, he thanked me profusely for the kindness I had extended to his family. He said his mother and sister really liked me.

Then came another uncomfortable silence.

I asked about his comfort inside an entire cellblock reserved for him.

Immediately my words struck me as yet another dumb thing to say. What could he possibly reply? That the place is not as nice as a Holiday Inn? I was ill at ease, and by now he had to know it. But he didn't seem to mind. After all those months in solitary confinement, I'm sure he was happy to see anyone who was not an attorney or a guard.

As the conversation slowly came easier, I found that Nichols was not the monster I had envisioned. He seemed frightened. He told me he had trouble sleeping at night because he could hear other prisoners on other floors screaming and crying.

I wondered if Nichols ever screamed or cried all night; if he ever raised his voice hoping that someone would come, despite knowing no one ever would.

Looking at Nichols here in this cubicle, I had momentarily forgotten that the sprawling room behind him was designed to confine not a single prisoner, but throngs. It was the stark, cavernous home to which he'd soon be returned. The silent space was surely a vacuum as hauntingly void as its only inmate's life.

Speaking with an increased sense of freedom, Nichols said the worst part of confinement was not the place, but the people. "I do like *finally* being away from the general population," he affirmed.

Nichols was scared. And I knew it. And he obviously knew that given the chance, the other inmates would kill him.

Somehow his words just didn't ring true. Anyone enduring solitary confinement inside a cellblock for one hundred men would get lonely, especially if he knew, as Nichols did, that he would never go free.

Enough of this "nice-nice" talk, I thought to myself. I'd been writing letters to Nichols for two years. I'd befriended his family members. Wasn't I "close" enough to ask him anything, especially *the* question?

Nichols never took the witness stand in his first trial. He had never publicly confirmed or denied his construction of the fatal bomb. Circumstantial evidence and the testimony of others had established that fact in lieu of a confession.

Still, the slight, mild-mannered man before me just didn't seem capable. He seemed more like Mr. Rogers in crimson pajamas.

No one was here except those guards, and they couldn't hear me on my telephone. Who could stop me from asking Nichols who helped him build the bomb that killed all those people, including my grandbabies?

I had to know.

I had promised I would not address the slayings, but to whom did I promise? To the defense lawyer representing a convicted murderer? So what if I broke my word to him? A jury of twelve had decided that Nichols was guilty. Otherwise, neither he nor I would be here.

"Terry...," I began.

He peered at me, awaiting my next words.

But they didn't come—only a long pause.

I gave my word in order to get into this place. Now I decided to keep it, hoping I would have a later opportunity.

I was already planning my next visit when the guard said my allotted fifteen minutes had expired. I had been given one-quarter of an hour, and had spent most of it uncomfortable and spouting silly banter. Instantly, I determined to do better next time.

The most awkward part of my visit came during my exit. *What do I say? "Have a nice day"?* Right. He'll have a very nice day alone inside a silent cellblock. *"See you later"? How do I know?* I had to move mountains to get into the place the first time. Who really knew if I'd be allowed to return?

"It's time to go," the guard said again, politely but firmly.

Still bewildered, I put my hand on the glass that separated me from Nichols. I remembered seeing that pose in motion pictures. Right now, I understood—it's about the only thing a person in my position can do.

Taken aback, Nichols stared at my open palm and leaned back in his chair. Ever so slowly, he eased forward, and put his hand on mine, with nothing between our touch but cold glass. I turned and walked away, and when I looked back, Nichols was gone.

The only evidence of this improbable meeting were a couple of handprints on that cold glass.

Chapter Fifteen

⊷⊶

Getting that first face-to-face audience with Terry Nichols solidified our friendship like nothing else. The fact that I was willing to visit him in jail touched him deeply. It was as if I were the only friend he had.

No matter. I was reaching out to someone who needed to be touched. And he was reaching back.

That was yet another validation of my decision to forgive him. At times, while alone in a cell, Nichols seemed to have nothing but the spirit of Christ and memories of me. I wanted to be sure that the latter reinforced the former.

I promised myself I would honor all requests he asked of me, whether posed through letters, telephone calls, or in-person dialogues. The more I nurtured our friendship, the more Nichols trusted me. The more he trusted me, the more likely he'd be to eventually tell me everything about the bombing.

Nichols knew, of course, that I had befriended members of his family. Now, he wanted me to share Jesus Christ with the others, and to emphasize the peace of mind and satisfaction of soul I had found in His presence. I believe Nichols and my initial jail visitation became a real-life manifestation of everything I'd ever communicated to him. I think he had to see, with his own eyes, how my lifelong God of salvation had also become my God of restoration and forgiveness—even toward one of the Oklahoma City bombers.

My personal transformations had inspired Nichols. He wanted his family to observe my tranquillity firsthand.

I remember when, during one of Joyce Wilt's visits to my house, I explained what I had learned thus far about the bombing. When it came time to leave, she hugged my neck. As she was walking away, she stopped in her tracks, turned around, and put her finger in my face, saying, "Young lady, if you find out that my Terry was involved in that bombing, I want to know."

Up to that point, Nichols was denying that he had any role in the genocide.

After all was said and done, though—despite Nichols's convictions after two trials—his brokenhearted mother stubbornly believed that her son had been set up by McVeigh, or by the federal government. She earnestly insisted her boy was innocent because he wasn't "smart enough" to plan a calculated mass murder.

At one point Joyce brought her daughter, Susie McDonnell, to visit me at my home. Both were touched by the warm hospitality with which I welcomed them.

Joyce didn't know what to think of Nichols's newfound Christian faith. Such a thing seemed foreign to her, even though her daughter, Susie, was a Christian. I shared my testimony about accepting Christ as my Savior as a child. As I shared my experience, Susie enthusiastically chimed in, helping her mother to catch a meaningful glimpse of what she, at that point, did not understand.

"You're the real deal," she said. She thanked me for reaching out to her boy Terry.

We both knew that there was something special about our relationship. The fact that God's grace had enabled me to forgive Joyce's son and others involved in the bombing seemed miraculous to her. She wanted to hear more. I told her about God's love, and I tried to show her that love.

Joyce seemed humbly grateful that I had cooked dinner for her and Susie. She declined my offer of lodging for the night because she had already reserved a room at a hotel.

Although I had initially felt concerned about what my neighbors might think, I came to realize that I no longer cared. I knew that reaching out to the Nichols family was the right thing to do.

That said, I did take precautions to keep our visit a secret. I didn't want it to turn into a media circus. And I didn't want to give any of the good people in Oklahoma City another occasion to feel angry. We had all been hurt enough. Besides, Nichols and his family had become my friends. I wanted to protect them.

Nichols asked me to reach out to his wife, Marife. He said she didn't know the Lord. He knew I was a Christian and hoped I might be able to touch Marife's life, and that of their young children, Nicole and Christian.

Nichols told each of his family members that he or she would be getting a call from me.

He gave me the unlisted phone number for Marife. She trusted no one. But Nichols convinced her that she could trust me.

The former Marife Torres had married Nichols when she was sixteen or seventeen, depending on which account you read. He was thirty-five.

They met after he responded to an advertisement offering a mail-order bride in the Philippines. He traveled to Cebu City, home to about 80 percent of the country's domestic shipping companies and a significant center of commerce and trade, to meet Marife and her parents. The teenager, along with her mother and father, lived in a tiny apartment above a lumberyard.

There, Nichols actively wooed Marife to become his wife. He knew little about her, except that she wanted to move to the United States to pursue citizenship there.

I didn't know that the practice of mail-order marriage had continued beyond the 1800s, when men who settled the American frontier responded to newspaper notices from women on the East Coast.

Nichols and Marife were married on November 20, 1990, inside a Chinese restaurant in Cebu City—despite the disapproval of her father, a policeman. He scorned his daughter's union to a man twice her age.

Nichols returned to the United States to begin the process of securing her citizenship. Later, she deplaned for the first time in her new country, bearing a gift for her new husband.

She was six months pregnant by another man.

Nichols accepted his wife's condition. They named the baby Jason Torres Nichols.

Nichols drove his new, imported family to his hometown of Decker, Michigan. There, life continued for two people who had barely met, and for a third who wasn't conceived when they did.

Following a series of failed moneymaking endeavors, the three-member Nichols family broke up and Marife returned to the Philippines. Nichols moved to Marion, Kansas, where he labored as a farmworker, then on to Herington, Kansas, located seventy miles north of Wichita. Marife returned to him there.

Terry Nichols, Marife, and Jason, then two years old, had moved to Decker, Michigan, to live with James Nichols, Terry's brother. There, Marife taught Jason those special things that only loving mothers can teach.

She learned to recognize his different cries, including those that meant he was hungry, and those that meant he was sleepy. In time, she helped Jason with his first uneasy steps and more. Marife wore parenthood beautifully and naturally, like a crown of joy.

Then she, her husband, and her baby found themselves in the company of a friend of James and Terry. His name was Timothy McVeigh.

On November 22, 1993, the household was awakened not by

Jason's cries, but by Marife's. She burst into the first nearby room, which happened to be McVeigh's. Hysterical, she shouted repeatedly that little Jason wasn't breathing.

"How do you know?" McVeigh yelled.

"I just left him!" she said.

McVeigh leaped from his bed and scurried to Jason's room. There, he saw the toddler with a plastic bag over his head. The sack had lined the inside of a cereal box that someone left in the boy's room near his baby bed. It was later theorized that the youngster climbed over the railing on his bed during the night. Not knowing how to remove the plastic bag, Jason left it there until he died, McVeigh surmised.

According to sheriff's reports, McVeigh claimed to administer CPR while ordering Marife to tell Nichols to dial 911.

Marife's hysteria was utterly uncontrollable, McVeigh told authorities.

McVeigh and Nichols argued about the fastest way to get Jason to a hospital. Meanwhile, he was still not breathing. Nichols finally drove Marife and Jason to the nearest emergency room. A physician tried to revive the tiny, motionless body before pronouncing the child dead.

Jason was buried with a new Barney doll inside his little coffin, although Nichols had repeatedly denied his stepson's pleas to have that doll while he was alive.

Area neighbors brought food to the distressed household. One woman appointed herself as Marife's "helper." The small community's display of sympathy and charity was truly marvelous. But Marife would not be calmed.

She suspected her little boy had been murdered. How could a two-year-old child not know how to pull a bag off his head? McVeigh had been known to crack racial slurs about Jason. He had let it be known that he didn't want the youngster around him.

Marife called her father in the Philippines to say she wanted her son's body exhumed and given an autopsy. Over time, McVeigh convinced her to forget any notion of foul play.

But she didn't—not entirely.

While attending Nichols's trial in Denver, I heard Marife questioned about the death of her little boy, and if she actually thought his death was an accident. Her answer indicated that she still held her original suspicion, that her helpless baby was murdered.

Then she dropped a bombshell.

Convinced the child's killer was McVeigh, she had tried to extract his confession by lowering his emotional guard. To accomplish this, she claimed, she had sex with him.

Marife went further to say that her physical encounters did nothing to soften McVeigh's contention that her baby pulled a plastic bag over his head that he couldn't remove.

How would McVeigh know that? Was he in the room at the time? If so, why didn't he help the baby?

McVeigh contended that Jason made his way through the darkness to find a cereal box that happened to be in the bedroom. Then—in total darkness—the toddler pulled out the inner plastic wrapping. And, without making a sound, the youngster fit the plastic over his head and pulled it downward, where it remained until he died.

McVeigh's hypothesis hardly seems likely, to say the least.

Do I personally think the outrageous ordeal was an accident? No. Do I think McVeigh was capable of murdering a toddler? I'll answer that question with a question.

Did he murder nineteen children during the Murrah bombing?

Did McVeigh have an incentive to kill Marife's little boy?

Perhaps. Maybe his demented mind wanted to "rehearse" the murder of a child to see if he could subsequently live with himself. But most pointedly, McVeigh hated all races that weren't Caucasian.

Jason was not white. McVeigh had openly called him "that foreign little bastard," according to published reports.

There was never a conviction. Never a trial, never even an arrest. Never an investigation.

To this day, Marife's answer to lingering questions is that she has no definite answers. And it's likely that she never will. She can only live with those internal theories. They don't satisfy her.

They don't cry or seek a mother's comfort, and you can't watch them take their first steps.

✄

In 1999, at Nichols's request, I invited Marife to my Oklahoma City home. She brought her two children, Nicole and Christian.

I took Marife, her two children, and Glenn (my new grandson), to Chuck E. Cheese, a popular children's entertainment and restaurant chain with stores in Oklahoma City. I remained fearful about going into public with Marife and her children. She had testified at Nichols's trial, so her photograph had been flashed on many national newscasts.

I knew she felt skittish about our meeting. But if anyone needed a friend, she did. For all of our sakes, I wanted our visit to remain low-profile.

I selected a Chuck E. Cheese location far away from my house. I figured most adults inside the restaurant would be focused on their youngsters rather than on other adults. The atmosphere tended to be fairly clamorous. All the distractions would lessen the chance of Marife's presence drawing anyone's attention.

We ate pizza and watched the kids play. I knew in my heart that this relationship was a God-thing... something I couldn't explain.

After dinner, we returned to my house.

The evening of frolic continued and children's laughter filled my home—sweet music that I had missed.

Chase and Colton were long since gone. And now, playing in

their room, were the children of one of the men responsible for their deaths. That might seem crazy to some, but it seemed right to me, given my forgiveness of their father.

Without her saying a word, I knew Marife was hurting. I also knew that she felt touched by the kindness I was extending to her family. She was unaccustomed to warm receptions, and therein lay her brokenness. When might she ever be lovingly received again?

Glenn was three years old, almost the exact age of Marife's baby when the toddler died of suffocation. Like me, she knew the immeasurable agony surrounding the loss of a precious child. She knew the anger and frustration that murder inspires. She believed the murderer was McVeigh. She had gotten no satisfaction from law enforcement personnel charged with investigating a murder.

In an effort to protect the children, Marife had changed their last name from Nichols to Torres, her maiden name. Her daughter, Nicole, had been three years old at the time of the bombing—old enough to remember her father. When she was in my home in 1999, she was seven and living in Oklahoma City. But she had no idea that her daddy was associated with the Oklahoma City Bombing.

Christian, Marife's youngest, was three at the time of their visit. Marife told the Nichols family that Christian was Terry's child. He claimed at the time of the bombing that he didn't know she was pregnant. The Nichols family does not believe the boy is Terry's.

If that's true, I believe that Marife put his name on her son's birth certificate because she was desperate. She needed the financial support of the Nichols family to survive. Why else would you brand your child with the Nichols name? Marife told the children that their daddy had gone away and that she didn't know when he would be back.

Nichols was allowed to call and talk to his children for fifteen minutes twice a month.

Nichols's children and young Glenn spent the rest of the evening playing in Chase and Colton's room with their toys. Marife and I sat chatting quietly in the den so the children couldn't hear us.

"I don't understand how you could allow your grandson to play with Terry Nichols's children," she asserted in her Filipino accent.

I could tell when she spoke Nichols's name that she was angry at him. She was worried about how she would tell her children about their father and his connection to the Oklahoma City Bombing. I suggested she go to a counselor for advice. I even told her I would go with her if she'd like. She seemed amazed by my offer.

"Terry told me you are a Christian," Marife said. "He said he's a Christian, too." She understood Nichols's need for a Savior. She nonetheless thought he was just using God. She had no explanation for *my* Christianity.

She listened intently as I told her that I had forgiven Nichols. Her eyes widened in disbelief.

"Why would you do that?" she asked—which opened the door for me to share my faith.

And I answered, "Because that's what the Bible says I should do. He's worried about you and the children. He wants you to know the same Lord that he's found. He wants his children to grow up in a Christian home."

Marife sat quietly. I could tell that the wheels in her head were turning as she pondered what I was saying.

"How could you forgive him?" she asked.

"I don't really know, Marife," I replied. "After a certain point in trying to deal with my grief, it just seemed like the right thing to do. I really don't understand it myself. All I can tell you is my forgiving Terry lifted a tremendous weight from my shoulders and I slept much better."

As Nicole and Christian played, they asked me to identify whose toys belonged to whom. Marife's children had developed a fascination for Chase and Colton. They'd seen their pictures on the walls, bookshelves, and furnishings of my home. They knew the boys had died in the bombing. They'd heard me affectionately talk about my two grandbabies as angels who left this world too soon.

From out of nowhere, I felt led to do something that most would find strange. I then asked Nicole and Christian each to select a favorite toy, one of Chase's and one of Colton's. After shyness and a nod from their mother, each child settled on a toy.

I gave away two of Chase's and Colton's toys to Marife's children.

I thought the weary mother was going to cry. And so would I. Neither child noticed, as each was jumping and cheering.

I embraced everyone at the door. Each of our hearts seemed to overflow with warmth. Marife had seen enough hardship in her life to drive anyone to despair. But if seeing is believing, Marife had also seen God's transformative power infuse me with forgiveness for her and her former husband. For a few hours, the woman who had come to a strange and foreign land to seek her dreams might finally have felt peaceful and at home.

Thank God the address of the home just happened to be mine.

Chapter Sixteen

My efforts to access McVeigh continued to be thwarted at every turn by law enforcement personnel at the federal level. McVeigh remained as inaccessible to me as if he were still at large. His isolation was his legal right. I couldn't penetrate it, no matter what I tried, in or out of court.

Yet, the more I was told McVeigh wouldn't talk to me, the more I determined to seek him.

My desire to interview McVeigh regarding a number of related matters bordered on obsession. But, all things considered, I would have settled to ask McVeigh just one pointed question.

I had amassed biographical and circumstantial data about McVeigh that, once again, raised more questions than it answered. I feared that someday McVeigh would likely be put to death for his heinous crime. His demise would forever lock the door on truth I still yearned to know.

At his trial, eyewitnesses were called who placed McVeigh with numerous other individuals in the days before the bombing at the Dreamland Motel in Junction City, Kansas. I decided to go there, hoping to discover who those people were.

I pulled into the Dreamland parking lot, which was littered with old dented and rusted cars, vehicles belonging to economically challenged guests. I entered the registration office, where I met a delightful German woman who identified herself as the owner. I asked if she'd ever heard of Timothy McVeigh.

She said she had. She then told me what I already knew, that McVeigh had stayed at this very motel shortly before he killed all those people in Oklahoma City. Then, as if she were on my side, she said McVeigh had lodged in room 25.

I told her who I was and why I had driven from Oklahoma City. Within minutes, I checked in and slowly drove to a parking space outside that very room.

I stepped from my car and looked squarely at the number 25 door that needed painting. I opened the door and fumbled for a switch that activated a solitary, low-wattage lamp. Wanting more light, I started to open the curtains but hesitated, although I'm not sure why.

Perhaps I did not want to be seen. I knew what I was doing would seem bizarre to most people, but my probe had been laced with bizarre behavior.

The establishment resembled no place I'd ever stayed. The floor was covered with a musty shag carpet. I sat down on the bed and felt it sink, as if the mattress had worn out long ago. I ran my hand across a dingy floral-print bedspread that was nappy and worn thin.

"Oh dear God," I said to no one. My mind raced as I thought about what I was doing. "Timothy McVeigh was here. He sat on this bed, he slept in this bed. And now here I am."

I could hardly believe it myself. My presence seemed like a bad dream.

I tiptoed into the bathroom, where many of the tiles on the floor were missing and an old shower curtain that had hardened with age was hanging stiff and rigid.

I felt like the Janet Leigh character in *Psycho*. I ever so gently pulled the curtain back and saw two silverfish crawling around the drain. I never found the courage to shower.

Later that night, several cars pulled to a stop before some of the approximately thirty doors on the facade of the rectangular motel, which was reminiscent of a 1960s weather-beaten strip shopping center. Room 25's front wall quivered slightly whenever a guest slammed his door at one of the rooms on either side.

I slowly paced inside my room, which was scarcely larger than modern walk-in closets. Or jail cells. The latter description is most appropriate. I truly felt captive, albeit of my own volition.

I took no food into the room. I couldn't abide the thought of eating there. And besides, I had no appetite. By now, I was a nervous wreck.

I sat back on the bed where the scratchiest wool blanket I had ever felt lay beneath the bedspread. I hated its touch on my hand, and I did not want it against my skin.

I looked around at the dingy walls, at drab sheetrock seemingly browned by years of exposure to nicotine.

Just knowing that McVeigh was a former guest intensified my experience in this sleazy setting.

I had been retracing McVeigh's footsteps for almost three years. This ordeal was becoming just another milestone in my frustrating journey. As I was taking in this experience, I found it overtaking me. I could not get him out of my mind. I obtained McVeigh's phone records from his defense team and had them spread out all over the bed. I knew whom he called and when. But I did not know who was with him in this room. For all I knew, they could have still been out there somewhere. Or maybe in the motel. Or even next door. I was frightened. My mind was running rampant. But I was compelled to do whatever it took to get answers. Answers I hoped I would find at the Dreamland.

Now it was time for my self-imposed sentence.

I was going to sleep in McVeigh's bed, the last hotel mattress he ever lay on before hauling a bomb to the now demolished Murrah

Building. My behavior was a clear affirmation of the fact that desperate people do desperate things. In retrospect I can't imagine why I went and stayed in that room. But at the time it was a compulsion that I could not resist.

I could not believe that I was really crawling into McVeigh's bed. I would have entered McVeigh's skin to learn the truth about him. I turned off the lights and situated my head on a flattened pillow resembling cushioned plywood. Later, I moved to the other side of the bed. At one place or another, I'd surely place my head in the very spot where McVeigh's head churned with the final details of the crime. My brain struggled for McVeigh's thoughts the night before the bombing. Intermittently I wondered why I had even entered this vaultlike room, a soiled shrine to Satan's emissaries. In coming here, had I climbed to the pinnacle of my investigation or leaped over the edge into insanity?

I now felt so alone.

I wondered if I would always be a loose cannon whose behavior would always be this reckless. I feared it would, at least for as long as I could not resist this insatiable desire to know. But to know what? Honestly, I wasn't sure.

Sunlight was my cue to rise. I hadn't slept all night. I considered a shower to wash away that bed and whatever microscopic creatures resided inside its stained mattress. But I didn't shower, as I didn't want my bare feet to touch the surface of that disgusting bathroom floor.

I loaded my single bag and checked out forever from the Dreamland Motel. I had learned nothing from my stay in room 25 but had learned plenty from employees and former guests. They all confirmed that McVeigh was not alone at the Dreamland. There were men seen coming and going from his room. Unfortunately, those men remain unknown, and no one in law enforcement seems to care.

I was barely beyond the city limits of Junction City when frustration smothered me. I pulled to the side of the road and listened to myself bawl uncontrollably.

The elusive road to truth, or whatever I was looking for, would patiently wait before me. It always had.

Chapter Seventeen

❧❧

My ambitious plans to continue interviewing bombing-related personalities had originated inside my mind and within my home: my comfort zone. Confronting alleged perpetrators or accomplices was far outside it. The face-to-face dialogues with some apparently crazed individual would have frightened most people. But I didn't care.

Therefore, only five months after meeting Lori Fortier and writing to her husband, in September 1999, I visited the Aryan Nations compound near Hayden Lake, Idaho. What was I thinking? Or, more to the point, was I thinking at all? These people were dangerous and I knew it.

The Aryan training process would prove to sicken me.

Through reliable sources, I'd heard that McVeigh had undergone active antigovernment indoctrination at the compound where his hatred toward the United States and human equality had become well honed. The Aryan Nations' teachings might well have pushed McVeigh over the edge. I was determined to find out.

I flew to Spokane, Washington, and rented a car. At that time, I knew Ruby Ridge and Waco had sparked the hatred in McVeigh's heart for the government.

As I drove to the compound, my memory flashed to April 21, 1995, the first time I saw McVeigh's face on television. He had stared straight ahead like a good soldier, his eyes piercing and cold.

What happened to that young man that prompted him to do something so evil? I asked myself, for what surely was the thousandth time. *Was his hatred for the federal government fueled by the Aryan Nations?*

I intended to find out.

Filled with apprehension—and unarmed—I eased my car along the secluded and foreboding driveway toward a fortified gate, the first line of protection for alleged Aryan insurgents. At first sight, my eyes scanned a cluster of heavily tattooed young men with shaved heads. Then, as now, a shaved head served to signal identity as a "skinhead"—one of a group of usually white males who share an extremist ideology and claim to love our nation while hating certain of its minorities.

Inside the compound I saw the sinister group enjoying natural shade from towering trees and a building with a sign that read "Jesus Christ Christian Church."

Then I noticed another sign proclaiming "WHITES ONLY" in giant letters!

"I haven't even stepped on the grounds, and this is what I see?" I exclaimed to no one.

I reminded myself to stay calm as fear gripped my heart. I knew instantly that I could soon be in real trouble.

After all, they'd glaringly espoused their racism before I had said a word to them, or they to me.

Cautiously, I began easing my car door open. Then I slammed it shut as a ferocious, barking German shepherd leaped to the driver's-side window.

The giant, snarling dog's outburst prompted my scream. Only a thin pane of glass separated me from the savage animal whose saliva was streaking my car window.

Someone curtailed the dog as I struggled to regain my composure. My panic was obvious to the skinheads, all of whom were staring at me, chuckling.

What have I done? I asked myself. *Where have I come? Stay focused.*

I was thoroughly vulnerable. In that out-of-the-way place, I could have been killed and buried inside my car and no one would have found me. The Aryan Nations had the manpower and the acreage to make me disappear.

Think about it. I was a stranger who had traveled fifteen hundred miles from Oklahoma City to a controversial encampment, filled with misfits posing as militiamen, all heavily armed. I knew I could be in mortal danger if they thought I was a government plant. *Who else would come to this godforsaken place?* I wondered.

And yet, I was never threatened. To my knowledge, none of the many guns I saw—both pistols and rifles—were ever pointed in my direction. No one behaved improperly toward me.

Through the small slot in my lowered window, I asked one of the skinheads if I might see Pastor Richard Butler, head of the vile organization.

Privately, I questioned his title as "Pastor." Did he claim to be ordained? If so, I wondered what kind of seminary would ordain him.

To my surprise, a couple of the men wearing pistols like gunslingers agreed to lead me to Butler's home, which was located within walking distance of the church.

I was escorted to the front porch.

There I saw a withered, leathery old man who looked rather harmless. Butler's better days were, at this point, mostly blurry memories. A single red rose lay on his wife's chair. His life's companion had died a few months before my arrival. Butler was still mourning. I could tell by his somber stare. I had seen it countless times in my mirror.

I didn't immediately tell Butler I'd heard McVeigh had once lived at the compound, or that I was seeking information about his training or other experiences.

Instead, I took advantage of Butler's bereavement for his wife and

told him I'd lost two grandchildren in the Murrah Building bombing. His loss was from natural causes. Mine was from unnatural
and premeditated violence. Mentioning my loss implied as much to
Butler, I was sure.

When I told Pastor Butler about Chase and Colton, his eyes
teared up. He told me how sorry he was. He had seen them on TV
and had been very saddened by the deaths of "those two Aryan little boys."

He referred to them as "Aryan boys" because Chase and Colton
both had blond hair and blue eyes.

Though his response shocked me greatly, I didn't let it show. I
just said, "Well thank you, thank you very much; I appreciate that."
I was intent on learning all I could.

I hinted that my loss entitled me to know just who was behind
the murders of my grandbabies.

Knowing Butler's disdain for parts of the United States government, I applied a feeble attempt at reverse psychology. I spoke
harshly about the government, thinking Butler would regard me as
being like-minded. Then perhaps he'd share secrets about McVeigh
and his connection, if any, to the militia.

"The government lied to me about what really happened on the
fateful day," I said.

He simply replied that I couldn't trust "the feds."

He then began to open up, but not as I had wanted. From somewhere, he raised a King James Bible and began reading to me, while
giving the verses his own ideological slant.

Butler's interpretation of God's Word specified that only Cauca-
sians will enter the kingdom of heaven.

White people, not Jews, were God's chosen people, he said. I listened to his twisted theology for what seemed to be a monthlong
hour. I didn't argue. I didn't question. I didn't even respond.

I finally broached a subject far removed from the Bible.

"Did Timothy McVeigh ever come here?" I asked directly. Before replying, Butler stared at me long and hard, as if second-guessing a motive behind my question.

"It's certainly a possibility," Butler said—and nothing more.

Those four words would stand as Butler's only response to the primary, haunting question that had initiated my lengthy sojourn from Oklahoma to Idaho and back. I never again asked Butler about McVeigh's presence at the camp.

Then Butler asked me to attend church on Sunday.

"I'd love to," was my forced reply, spoken before realizing that Sunday was tomorrow.

Before departing the grounds for the night, I was shocked to learn something else about the Aryan Nations compound. Although Butler had not discussed McVeigh, he did reference Buford O'Neal Furrow Jr., the assassin who'd opened a seventy-round burst of automatic-rifle fire on the Jewish Community Center in Los Angeles in 1999. Five people were wounded. Shortly thereafter, Furrow murdered a mail carrier.

O'Neal had trained at this very compound while working as a security guard.

I instantly had second thoughts about returning Sunday morning. Although I felt I would be safe entering the compound, I was not all that sure about leaving.

～

I awoke from fitful sleep inside a Hayden Lake motel. I had come from the Southwest to the Northwest to learn about the background and mentality of McVeigh. Now, twenty-four hours later, I had learned nothing about the infamous killer, not if he'd ever visited the Aryan Nations compound, or even if he'd ever heard of it!

Why should I go back to that horrible, hate-filled place?

I didn't want to return, but I didn't want to leave.

I had not finished my mission.

After showering and applying my makeup, I donned my Sunday best and forced myself back to the Aryan post. I hoped I'd dressed appropriately, but my concern vanished the instant I pulled up to the gate. There were a few women and children; otherwise, the grounds were teeming with males of every age.

Yet all had something in common, something I had never seen except in movies.

Each male wore a Nazi uniform!

I wanted to gawk at the suits but didn't, as the men were watching me closely. I didn't want them to think I was staring, the very thing I yearned to do.

I felt sorry for the women and the children. I asked myself, *Why would anyone want to marry a wannabe Nazi?*

I eased toward the compound's church, where I jumped slightly upon entering the foyer. I didn't know where to step. The floor was covered with the flag of Israel.

Everyone else used it as a doormat, wiping their boots and shoes on it.

I said nothing, and not because I was at a loss for words. I was simply afraid to speak.

I eased into the auditorium, where I was again aghast. Immediately beside the pulpit stood a life-size bust of Adolf Hitler. Pictures of Jesus were hanging nearby.

I stared at my Savior and silently prayed, *Dear Lord, deliver me from this terrible place.*

On that Sunday morning in churches all across America, voices were raised singing "Amazing Grace." In that respect, this den of evil was no different, with these Nazis belting out the sacred words as if grace flowed only to whites who wanted to destroy all other ethnic groups.

What do any of these ambassadors of hate know about grace, whether God's or their own? I asked myself. Their hypocrisy was astounding.

God help me, I continued as my stomach became queasy and I prayed not to vomit.

The sacrilege went on as the congregational singing included "How Great Thou Art." Surely I had entered a place of worship instigated by Satan himself. What else could I think?

When the hymn was finished, someone asked the gathering to bow their heads in prayer. Once again, the action was identical to what happens in churches all over North America. Yet the sacrament of prayer seemed so misplaced inside this chapel of venom.

I bowed my head, but I didn't close my eyes, for fear I would miss something. I'm glad I peeked around.

Other than mine, each arm in the place, including those of women and children, was rigidly extended in a Nazi salute toward the bust of Hitler! All the while, someone vigorously prayed aloud. I was now so rattled I couldn't process his every word. "Christ died to *save* men!" I wanted to shout. "Hitler lived to *murder* them! What are you people doing, associating the memory of our blessed Savior with that of a human demon?"

Had I shouted those words, would they have allowed me to live long enough to ever speak anything again?

I'll never know.

Finally, Butler rose from his chair and ambled toward the pulpit. I had seen godly men preach under the anointing of the Holy Spirit all of my life. But there was no Spirit in Butler. And his words, at first, didn't shape a sermon.

Instead, surprisingly, he introduced me to the congregation. So much for my attempts to keep a low profile.

My cause in coming here was pure, I reminded myself. *So why do I feel like I need to scrub myself in the shower?*

I desperately wanted to wash this place and its despicable atmosphere off my body forever.

After introducing me, Butler launched an antigovernment dia-
tribe that included his rationale for why there *had* to be an Oklahoma City Bombing. *Did he really say that?* I listened, but I didn't
hear. I was deafened by my silent but raging fury. Then, to the
entire congregation, Butler regaled the man he earlier wouldn't
even mention to me: Timothy McVeigh.

"One man's terrorist is another man's freedom fighter!" he thun-
dered. "Timothy McVeigh was a *great* man! A *martyr* for the cause!"

The audience leaped to its feet, offering up deafening applause.

What cause?! I could barely keep myself from screaming. *The
cause of slaughtering innocent people and helpless babies? Who among
you is the most heartless?*

Even if I had screamed, my explosive words would not have been
heard above the zealous cheering and applause, their earsplitting
expression of idolatry for McVeigh.

Yesterday, I had asked Butler if McVeigh had ever come here.
Indeed, they *loved* him! Even in his absence, he remained their towering hero!

In my personal opinion, I decided most of the men lacked what
McVeigh had—determination. They coveted his "bravery" to step
out and annihilate a tiny part of America's civilized establishment.
Many wanted to do the same. And many were as smart as or perhaps smarter than McVeigh. But they lacked the wicked nerve to
follow through.

Most of these men had never found a place to fit into society. To
them, the compound was a sanctuary.

By now, I was breathing harder, and yet was somehow feeling
short of breath. I felt like the toxic atmosphere was actually suffocating me. I prayed not to pass out.

How much of this nightmare-come-to-life could I withstand?
In my quest for the truth, I had forced myself to listen to lie after
lie. The weight of hateful propaganda, and the twisted thinking

that produced it, was taking a toll on me. I wondered if the souls of Chase and Colton would forgive me if I abandoned this part of my search and ran from the hate-filled church.

When the service ended, I walked slowly toward the door and exited quietly, all the while wanting to scream.

And for all of my personal purgatory, I'd learned nothing new about McVeigh except that he'd probably once visited the Aryan Nations compound, where his memory was saluted with raucous adoration.

How could they love him? More to the point—could hate-filled hearts truly love anyone or anything at all?

Once outside, I was joined by Butler beneath a lovely tree. The leaves were softly stirred by a gentle wind. I welcomed the breeze and wondered if Butler knew I was hoping it would dissipate the putrid stench of hate that had nearly suffocated me in his place of "worship."

As if wanting to make sure I understood the motivation behind his rant from the pulpit, Butler confessed that he was, in fact, a racist. To me his confession seemed comical—and completely unnecessary.

"But," he went on to explain, "a racist is one who loves his race."

How utterly twisted! I thought to myself.

Silently, I mused, *What would happen to me—what would become of me right now—if I told this misguided zealot what I truly think of him?*

Meanwhile, Butler went on to illustrate his "reasoning" with a series of insipid analogies.

He pointed to "Eva" and "Fritz," two German shepherds that served as canine sentries for the compound. He praised the animals for the purity of their breeding

Then he pointed to a black dog.

"Do you see that old nigger dog?" he asked.

Once again, the coarseness of his words—of his heart, of his entire being—struck me dumb.

"That old nigger dog has no more soul than a Jew, an Asian, a nigger, or a homosexual," Butler proclaimed.

He went on to say what I already knew: that he and his followers were dedicated to keeping their race pure, according to their sickening definition of purity.

He proudly likened himself to Adolf Hitler and his followers to the army of the Third Reich. Those may have been the most ghastly of all the words I had heard during my entire visit to the compound.

I suddenly realized that Butler and his men were self-proclaimed warriors with no place to fight. Their enemies existed only in their hate-addled minds. They would have to settle for cowardly ambushes not against combatants, but against harmless civilians. They weren't brave soldiers on declared front lines. They were cowards playing army, hunkered down in a play fort. They were pretending to be soldiers the way little boys once pretended to be cowboys and Indians.

The Aryan Nations? What disillusioned, pathetic people. I struggled to keep up a good front. Once again, I braced myself at the thought of what they might do to me if they knew what was really in my heart.

I was terrified.

Butler and his followers asked me to accompany them to a local restaurant for Sunday dinner. Inside the café, I felt the frigid stares of people closely evaluating the strange woman accompanied by eight or ten of their local skinheads. Well outside the compound, some of the men still proudly displayed swastikas.

When the food was served, the Aryans bowed their heads and asked God to bless it.

I wondered what God must have thought.

I didn't eat much. I didn't want to test my stomach. The entire ordeal had nauseated me.

Butler followed me as I walked from the eatery to my car. There, he kissed my cheek and whispered, "Don't worry, honey, you will see your boys again."

Once Butler and his entourage were disappearing in my rear-view mirror, I forcefully rubbed a tissue on my cheek the way I would scratch steel wool against pots and pans. I could feel my skin turning red and I didn't care. I almost hoped it would come off.

I was disappointed and angry. I had suffered too long and too much to learn so little from my encounter with the Aryans.

I was physically, mentally, and emotionally depleted. No skin-heads were around to see how I truly felt about the Aryan Nations and the virtually brain-dead men the group comprised.

McVeigh was their hero. They had helped to warp his thinking.

And yet, I mused—though it was hard to imagine—at some time in his life, McVeigh had been somebody's pure and playful little boy. In my visit to the Aryan Nations, I realized for certain that McVeigh's innocence was long ago and far away.

My recollection of the singing in Butler's church continued to haunt me. The Aryans had sung of God's grace just like many other congregations. And yet the loathsome spirit of those people in that place seemed like such a blasphemy to the Lord, there in their far-away forest concealing their hideaway hell.

Chapter Eighteen

━━⟡━━

I found that forgiveness was changing my life more than ever. The happiness that had eluded me for so long was now with me. I don't know how to explain it, but I think the events of our lives and how we handle them sculpt us.

Though I knew I was doing the right thing for me, I wanted to avoid hurting others and criticism from those who didn't understand. I remembered a quote from Aristotle: "Avoiding criticism is easy. Do nothing, say nothing, be nothing." As you can tell from my story told in this book, I'm hardly content to "do nothing, say nothing..."

I initially wanted to see Joyce Wilt, Susie McDonnell, Terry Nichols, Lori Fortier, and Michael Fortier to complete my investigation into the bombing and its mass murder. Their willingness to speak to me seemed like a miracle in itself. After all, some of those people helped plan the national catastrophe.

Yet, during my time with all of the above, I think they sensed my sincerity. I believed they knew my compassion and forgiveness was God-given. I had sensed a lift in their moods and their personal assessments, however briefly. Our interactions had triggered some to evaluate their spiritual lives.

In the post-bombing flurry that had been my life, I'd done nothing significant with or for the McVeigh family. I had last seen McVeigh inside a courtroom, where he asked what I wanted from him. I wanted an appointment, which he declined.

Occasionally, I thought about that greeting card, with Chase and Colton portrayed as cherubs, delivered to McVeigh by a reporter. I remembered McVeigh asking the journalist what he was supposed to do with the card.

I remained determined to find an alternate way to get to McVeigh. After extensive study, I wanted to know everything McVeigh could tell me about Murrah's massive slaughter, which was still being analyzed by the best and brightest minds probing domestic terrorism.

Working with wardens, lawyers, and law enforcement personnel *always* led to a dead end. I decided to pursue communication with McVeigh's father, Bill. The father and son had lived together in Lockport, New York, until McVeigh had left home for the Army.

I found a private investigator who was sympathetic to my cause and gave me Bill's home telephone number.

Upon Bill answering his telephone, I told him my name, and that I had lost two grandchildren in the Oklahoma City Bombing.

I didn't mention his son.

All my life, I've heard that first impressions are the most lasting. I've also heard that most first impressions are formed in a few seconds.

If that's true, then my instant assessment of Bill McVeigh as a depleted man proved to be accurate. His possible knowledge about the bombing prompted my curiosity. His seclusion activated my sympathy.

Merely identifying myself triggered Bill's wordy stumbling as he stuttered through an apology about my losses. Even through the long-distance line, I felt his sincerity.

I earnestly told him what I had told other parents, spouses, offspring, and siblings—that I felt he was a forgotten "victim" of the bombing—that I was sorry for his pain.

In part, I was trying to get inside and empathize with the family member's agonizing world in order to make sense of mine. I was getting audiences with people that no one else could—not even some of the top investigative journalists in the world. And the reason was that I was a victim. Who would have the heart to tell me no when I called?

Bill and other intuitive people could tell I had been deeply hurt. Our uncommon pain became our common denominator.

I told Bill I was coming to Lockport, and that I wanted to take him to lunch. He hesitated. I could tell that he felt as uncomfortable hearing my request as I felt making it. He agreed to meet me but explained that he didn't have much time to spend with me due to a previous commitment.

Except for McVeigh, everyone I had approached had accepted a meeting with a meddlesome woman staging her own inquisition.

Those statistics told me I was doing something right.

Bill and I met at a restaurant near Niagara Falls a few miles from his home. Our conversation started out stiff, but the strain gradually eased.

I found out that Bill was a Catholic, retired from GM and just a good-old blue-collar worker who did the best he could by his three kids. When he and his wife split up, he tried to take good care of them. He was very active at his church, where he played bingo on Friday nights.

Our chat was not unlike a couple's on a first date. When our meal came, we talked about food. He told me he liked to cook in Crock-Pots. He asked if I knew that buffalo wings originated in a little bar in Buffalo, New York. We chatted a long time simply getting to know each other. After all, we had something in common: we both were grieving the loss of loved ones.

McVeigh was not dead, of course. But he was certainly removed from his father's life forever.

Once tall and imposing, Bill's presence now seemed bent and

humbled. I would say he was humiliated. McVeigh's time behind bars, and Bill's time as an unfairly disgraced father, had been hard on the man. A blind person could see it; anyone could understand it.

Well into our lunch, I learned that Bill and his former wife had divorced when McVeigh was ten. Bill was of little help to his young son, a quiet child who felt abandoned.

McVeigh's relationship with his grandfather, Bill's dad, was the best relationship he ever had in his life. He loved his grandpa and spent a lot of time with him. McVeigh had a very strong work ethic, and his grandpa probably instilled that in him. The old man died shortly before the bombing.

If McVeigh's grandpa had not died, I wondered, *would there have been a bombing?*

As a teenager, McVeigh earned modest wages as an unskilled laborer. He had wanted to go to college, and, like many poor young people without prospects, he could have used some financial aid. But, as a white male, he didn't qualify for the government's Affirmative Action program, which favored females and minorities.

That may have been why McVeigh enlisted in the Army. Without a craft, trade, or profession, guys like McVeigh often joined the military for need of something to do. Wages for an enlisted man were ridiculously low, but were accompanied by "three hots and a cot," slang describing the Army's daily meals and bunk beds for soldiers.

Bill hoped that one day, McVeigh would be able to retire on a military pension. But, of course, that never happened. McVeigh became disillusioned when he couldn't get into the Special Forces. He didn't have the physical strength.

So he quit the Army and simply began to drift long before he became politically radicalized.

Meanwhile, Bill remained a reliable and consistent member of America's working class, the noble and human fabric of American commerce. Eventually living on a pension from General Motors and Social Security from the federal government, Bill's "golden years" were tarnished. His lifelong income, or the lack of it, didn't allow for serious travel.

As a senior citizen, Bill's recreation consisted of three activities: vegetable gardening, cooking, and bowling. When his days ended, he usually shifted into personal-privacy mode.

Not long after the bombing, Bill posted a handwritten sign on his garage door that read "No Media."

Not every reporter obeyed.

If a journalist had traveled a substantial distance to meet Bill, too bad. The bruised father had plans, sometimes to play golf, and couldn't be interrupted. His ironclad stance, however, had a softer side. He'd occasionally tell journalists when they could come back and how long they could stay.

If a reporter capitulated, he usually got his interview, but little more. Bill usually resorted to facts, the few that he knew about his son's darkest day. Many of his statements had been previously published.

Bill said he'd never discussed the bombing with his son. Perhaps the thinking was *If we don't talk about it, maybe it didn't happen.* The issue was avoided almost completely, except when Bill asked his son if he planned to apologize for what he'd done.

McVeigh said he would not. An apology would be a lie, as he had no remorse for anything surrounding that fateful day in Oklahoma City.

How did Bill handle his son's hardened attitude? The father's love was unconditional; it did not matter what his boy had done.

During my visit so far, I hadn't learned a great deal about the bombing, or about McVeigh. I had pressed hard and traveled far to get this meeting. I wished it were taking a different direction and yielding things more substantial.

But, amid Bill's recollections, I felt too sorry for him to be pushy. I had hoped he might have something pertinent that could explain why McVeigh had blown away a major section of a major American city.

There had to be a reason behind the madness. But it was becoming clear to me that Bill was uncomfortable discussing his son.

Then, when I least expected it, Bill's talk turned to McVeigh. He affectionately called him "Timmy," his only son. The boy's childhood had been solid, Bill said even before he was asked. I wondered how he defined "solid."

I had once heard Joyce Wilt blame Nichols's misguided behavior on his association with "the wrong crowd." Now I was hearing the same evaluation from Bill.

Whether right or wrong, those parents' convictions were understandable. Had Nichols or McVeigh been my son, I'm sure I, too, would have found a reason, sound or flimsy, to rationalize his behavior.

Bill took McVeigh's plight a step further.

He said his son would not have gotten in trouble had he been able to find a job after leaving the Army or if he had gone to college.

I discerned Bill's contrition about McVeigh's inability to pursue higher learning. Did Bill therefore feel responsible for McVeigh's involvement in the bombing? I hoped he didn't.

During lunch, I realized it would have been impossible for Bill to discuss the bombing with McVeigh. He didn't want to acknowledge his son's involvement.

His position was not denial, it was secrecy: believing that some things are best left unmentioned.

To me, that was Bill's defense against dealing with the reality of his son's participation in the most unthinkable display of terrorism of his lifetime.

Bill told me that Jennifer, his daughter and McVeigh's sister, had started using her mother's maiden name before moving out of state. She was trying to get away from everything.

When I asked Bill for Jennifer's telephone number, he gave it to me without hesitation, something he wouldn't have done for a reporter.

Bill's wearisome rationalizing on behalf of his children fell apart before we finished our meal. Throughout, he had tried to be strong. Now, tears overtook him.

And the facts couldn't be denied.

There had been a monstrous bombing. His son had been convicted. My grandchildren had been murdered. I was the face of accountability sitting within Bill's reach. Although I was Bill's "welcome" visitor, I was also his nemesis, someone who'd touched his heart while shredding his paternal optimism.

My own heart broke as Bill, in a surprise change of attitude, began to apologize profusely for what his child had done to my grandchildren. He wasn't stuttering. He simply could not speak fluently through choking tears.

The next time I visited with Bill McVeigh was weeks, maybe months, later. I had just learned that McVeigh's execution had been scheduled for June 11, 2001. Although I kept up with the latest news, I found out *before* the news broke. A reporter told me.

Immediately I thought of Bill.

Oh, man—he's got to be crushed! I surmised. There was a considerable amount of time before the date, so I thought, *My God, how horrible to have to spend all this time waiting for your son to be killed.* I could not imagine anything worse. I picked up the phone to call Bill:

"Hi, Bill, this is Kathy Wilburn. I'm so sorry, I just heard."

"What did you hear?" Bill queried.

"Well, I heard they've scheduled a date for Tim's execution."

"Oh...I didn't know that," Bill responded.

"Bill, I'm so sorry. I did not want to be the one to tell you this. I'm so sorry."

"Well, when is it scheduled?" he asked.

No one had told him, and he had not asked. The father who knew his son had been sentenced to die did not know when. How could that have happened?

I knew Bill was not going to attend his son's execution. I don't think McVeigh wanted him there. Thereafter, I sent Christmas cards for a few years, but that was the extent of my communication with Bill McVeigh.

By my design, the broken father never had to answer another question from me. That was the least I could do. A man who had done all he could for his solitary son deserved more than that.

Chapter Nineteen

❧❧❧

In 2001, I called Jennifer McVeigh, Timothy's sister, while she was living in North Carolina teaching school under an assumed name.

Previously she had lived in New York City, where she had been harassed and humiliated by unsympathetic New Yorkers. It was not a good time to be a McVeigh. And once her role in the bombing became public knowledge, she was reportedly forced out of town.

When I called Jennifer she was caught off guard. She stumbled for words when I told her who I was. I explained that I had been writing to her brother, but he hadn't answered any of my letters.

I said I had gotten her unlisted telephone number from her father, hoping that his confidence in me would be instilled in her. I also had an ulterior motive. I wanted her to tell me what she knew about the bombing. As we chatted I learned that she was coming to Oklahoma City in a few weeks. I questioned the visit.

Why would a McVeigh want to come to Oklahoma? I thought. She said that she had become friends with members of McVeigh's defense team and that she had spent the past four summers vacationing in Oklahoma City. How peculiar. I concluded that this girl was desperate for friends. I found myself inviting her to dinner.

In many ways, I expected that Jennifer might be the most beneficial source of information among all I'd questioned. But first, as I had done with others I had spoken to, I wanted to make Jennifer feel welcome in my home.

I wanted her to see the room where Chase and Colton once played. I wanted her to meet my new grandchild.

I wanted to show her that I was a survivor and a great deal more.

Thinking back, I wonder what she must have thought when I told her I wanted to prepare her a meal. Had I been her, I might have suspected that I intended to poison her.

Before reaching out, I had researched Jennifer's life. I discovered she was bright and accomplished. And I knew she looked up to her older brother.

Unlike McVeigh, Jennifer had pursued her education at Niagara Community College, where she graduated with an Associate of Arts degree less than a month after the bombing, which perplexed me.

McVeigh had been arrested a few days earlier. By then, she was being questioned by the FBI. I couldn't imagine having the presence of mind to study for final examinations.

"Most schools would be very proud to claim her," said Arthur Taylor, her former college instructor, according to a *New York Times* profile by Joseph B. Treaster, published August 4, 1995, almost four months after the bombing.

There were considerable similarities between Jennifer and her brother. I intended to casually mention them. If I could simply put her at ease, perhaps she'd intercede on my behalf to her brother. Getting so close to Jennifer actually intensified my yearning to talk to McVeigh himself.

Jennifer, like McVeigh, reportedly felt the federal government had become an enemy of the American public at large. She allegedly shared McVeigh's bitterness about the FBI's assault on the Branch Davidians' compound near Waco, Texas. She wrote a letter to that effect that was published in an upstate New York newspaper.

In 1992, three years before the bombing, Jennifer had reportedly attempted to send McVeigh seven hundred rounds of military ammunition that could be used in machine guns or assault rifles. The FBI got wind of her effort and told her she'd likely face federal charges. To my knowledge, she never did.

When Jennifer first heard her brother's name mentioned in connection with the bombing, she immediately panicked.

On her back porch, inside a charcoal grill, Jennifer was burning letters written to her by McVeigh when the FBI came unannounced to her house to interrogate her.

"I'm not going to help you kill my brother," she reportedly told a federal agent during a search of her home. Ultimately, she did testify before an Oklahoma City grand jury. She had been granted immunity from prosecution in exchange for her testimony regarding her brother.

Even so, Jennifer's standing up to the federal government, and her publishing of antigovernment sentiments, led me to believe she was no pushover.

The night Jennifer arrived at my house, I was instantly overwhelmed with a mixture of emotions as the significance of her visit hit me.

I would be cooking for a woman who had, in all likelihood, known in advance that her brother was preparing a bomb—a high-powered explosive that would kill my grandchildren. She might have stopped the bombing had she alerted authorities to what she knew.

But, as I said, she did eventually collaborate with authorities to craft the terms of her immunity. She negotiated well, as she avoided all charges.

Even people who hated McVeigh said Jennifer sold him out.

I felt a need to know that could not be quenched. Perhaps Jennifer could help me get answers that I had found nowhere else. Even better, maybe she could connect me with McVeigh, my ultimate objective.

Anticipating her arrival at my home became a high-anxiety countdown. There I was, a widow living alone in a big house, waiting for a woman heavily connected to the Murrah bombing.

Only Edye knew Jennifer was coming.

Despite my expectation of Jennifer's visit, the doorbell startled me. I nervously rose from the chair at my desk and eased to the front door. I opened it to find a harmless-looking girl.

How could she have been involved in something so diabolical? I asked myself.

Jennifer and I exchanged small talk inherent to strangers meeting for the first time. I was on my best behavior—and totally boring.

My guest and I sat at a dining room table for eight people. A crystal chandelier hung above us.

I've forgotten the menu, but it included Cajun coleslaw. After dessert had been eaten, she asked for more coleslaw. I retrieved it from the refrigerator, and Jennifer ended the dinner with a second helping of the same dish with which she had begun it.

Trying not to put my guest on the defensive, I mustered the courage to ask her about her brother's political views. Jennifer told me she didn't know anything about her brother's extreme political opinions. She said the two had never discussed them.

I felt internally enraged by her dishonesty.

What about her published ideas that were similar to his? What about her sending McVeigh ammunition? What about their mutual disdain of the Branch Davidian fiasco?

Unbeknownst to Jennifer, I had read her handwritten confession. I knew a great deal about what she knew. Why was she lying?

To me, her lying implied that I could not withstand the truth.

In those days, I felt as though I could withstand anything. After all, I had lived through a massive bombing and the deaths of my grandbabies! I could certainly handle the spewing of deceptive words, no matter how angry they made me.

"I felt she knew about McVeigh's plan for the bombing. Why isn't she on trial along with her brother?" I once asked Richard Reyna, lead investigator for McVeigh's defense team.

That's when Reyna first told me about Jennifer's immunity deal. His pronouncement had infuriated Glenn, my late husband.

"If that little b——h knew something and didn't try to stop it, she's as guilty as her brother," Glenn had fumed.

"I know, but that's not how the justice system works," Reyna replied.

"Some justice," I exclaimed bitterly. "Our boys are lying dead in the cemetery and she's free."

I had read the letters Jennifer received from her murderous brother.

"Something big is going to happen in the month of the bull [April]," one of the letters had intimated.

I had also seen Jennifer's May 2, 1995, sworn statement to the FBI. There, she admitted that McVeigh had asked her to exchange three one-hundred-dollar bills for "clean" money. According to the FBI, the money had been acquired from a series of bank robberies.

As if that weren't enough, McVeigh had constantly appealed to his sister to adopt his way of thinking. He urged her to read *The Turner Diaries*, a 1978 novel with a sinister, anti-American plot that was used by McVeigh as "instructions" to blow up the Murrah Building.

The novel portrayed a saboteur who rented a truck filled with cases of explosives, just as McVeigh had done on April 19, 1995. The explosives included ammonium nitrate fertilizer. McVeigh had used that in real life. It was implemented to blow up a federal building shortly after 9 a.m. and to kill hundreds of people, which is exactly what McVeigh did, almost to the hour.

The Turner Diaries also contained other sensational similarities that preceded the Oklahoma City Bombing.

Jennifer had no idea I knew she'd been urged to read this story with a plot propelled by a fictional white supremacist guerrilla army. In real life, her brother saw himself as a soldier in just such a militia.

I knew that the aura of the woman sitting across my table rang of insincerity. So why was she lying?

I was surprised that she would act innocent. After all, some of her political and social convictions had actually been printed in her letters to a newspaper.

After Jennifer and I had eaten, I asked if she would like to meet Edye and see my new grandson. (*He's someone your brother* didn't *kill*, I angrily thought to myself.) She consented.

Baby in arms, Edye received us at her door. Jennifer fussed over little Glenn and extolled his cuteness.

I asked Edye to show Jennifer Glenn's room. I knew Jennifer would have to walk down a hall whose walls were adorned with photographs of Chase and Colton.

Earlier, I'd taken her on a similar tour of my house. Inside one home or the other, I had hoped Jennifer would melt at the sight of the toddlers killed by her brother.

But at Edye's house, Jennifer showed no sadness, just as she hadn't at mine. Her lack of what I considered appropriate emotion deeply offended me.

Unbeknownst to me, one more strenuous ordeal had yet to unfold.

Daylight saving time meant an extra hour of sunlight as I departed Edye's house en route back to mine. Many of my neighbors and others within my subdivision were strolling the streets, puttering on lawns, and going through the motions of suburban living.

Some waved at me, and I waved back. I saw one or two stare at the passenger in my car's front seat. I kept driving, not wanting to talk to anyone.

I did not want them to know I had Jennifer McVeigh in my car.

I wondered how they'd react if they knew. Somewhat holding my breath, I maneuvered my car to a distance within a few feet of my driveway. I was almost home.

Suddenly, a good friend stepped into the street. She'd recognized my car and wanted to visit.

I rolled down the driver's-side window and she stuck her head inside my vehicle, just as she had always done on such occasions. Then she looked at me, waiting for me to introduce my passenger.

I didn't, not at first. Instead, I began to prattle. Her eyes, only a foot or so from mine, looked squarely into mine. She was pausing for me to fulfill common courtesy. By now, Jennifer was awkwardly looking directly at my friend.

"This is my friend Jennifer," I said to my neighbor, intentionally withholding a last name.

The two nodded, and my neighbor extended a polite greeting. I think she asked Jennifer where she lived, or what brought her to Oklahoma City. I didn't wait for an answer.

"Well, see you later!" I abruptly announced to my bewildered neighbor.

I revved the engine, a hint I hoped my friend would accept. She pulled her head from inside my car. Before she could say another word, I put my foot on the gas pedal, and Jennifer and I were out of her earshot.

In my rearview mirror, I could see that my neighbor had been baffled by my rudeness.

Jennifer and I reentered my house, where she extended her farewell. I continued to talk, hoping she would not notice my stalling that would have kept her there until darkness fell on the neighborhood.

But then she was gone.

I had spent approximately two hours with a woman whose brother had changed my life forever.

The nervous energy I had expended while preparing to receive her had been an exercise in futility. From her, I had discovered nothing new about the high-profile crime of the decade in America, and of the century in Oklahoma.

I confess I didn't instantly extend my forgiveness to Jennifer. And, unlike so many others, she had shown no contrition that would indicate her desire for my forgiveness.

That was then; this is now. Were I to meet Jennifer McVeigh today, I would hug her neck.

And I would tell her I've forgiven her every transgression.

At this point in my life, I relish each and every day. I refuse to disrupt my God-given peace by holding grudges. Holding a grudge is like being a psychological hostage, and I enjoy my mental and emotional freedom too much for that.

Chapter Twenty

⚜

Timothy McVeigh died by lethal injection on June 11, 2001, at the U.S. Federal Penitentiary in Terre Haute, Indiana. He became the first person to die at the hands of the federal government in thirty-eight years.

Prosecutors had won a conviction against McVeigh for the murder of eight federal employees. The number was small when measured against the 168 lives that McVeigh had actually taken.

Yet eight was enough to justify the killing of the killer.

Besides, the United States Department of Justice couldn't prosecute McVeigh for the additional murders. Those deaths were relegated to the jurisdiction of the State of Oklahoma.

Oklahoma did not actively pursue the death penalty for a man who was going to die anyway. The taking of McVeigh's life was therefore reduced to a matter of practicality.

Did I rejoice? No. Did I regret the execution? No.

McVeigh believed himself to be a patriot and fancied himself to be a modern-day Patrick Henry, who said, "Give me liberty or give me death." When he was arrested, he was wearing a T-shirt bearing a quote from Thomas Jefferson: "The tree of liberty must be refreshed from time to time with the blood of patriots and tyrants."

McVeigh knew the penalty when he broke God's and man's laws against murder. And, although he had at first refused to see a priest while on death row, he did ask for one to come in and give him last rites before his execution.

With McVeigh's death, I had forever lost the opportunity to ask him what I didn't know—the why behind his actions—and who his accomplices were. Most of all, I would never get to hear McVeigh disclose facts that the federal government might be concealing.

I was not alone in this sentiment.

A sizable faction of Americans felt that McVeigh had secrets that died with him, according to published and broadcast reports, as well as my personal mail and telephone calls.

Meanwhile, many if not the majority of Americans were blood-thirsty regarding McVeigh's death. Someone actually petitioned the federal court to stream his killing on the Internet. A federal judge denied the request.

Though McVeigh had waived his appeals and seemed to want to be executed, his lawyers sought a stay of execution based on the FBI's admission that thousands of documents had been withheld from them during the trial. Fifteen days later, Judge Richard Matsch denied the petition. The execution would proceed as scheduled.

I struggled with whether or not to attend. I didn't want to see a man die, but someone needed to represent Chase and Colton.

I therefore joined two hundred people who beheld a giant screen as we watched McVeigh die on a closed-circuit, live telecast from America's heartland. The ordeal was true reality television.

McVeigh lay motionless beneath a sheet that partially covered his torso. He said nothing and stared vacantly at the ceiling.

The room where I stood had fallen quiet. Muffled coughing and the shifting of restless feet were the long and short of the audio.

McVeigh slowly turned his head and noticed a television camera pointing directly at him. He no doubt realized that he was being watched a final time by people he didn't know inside a place he'd never been. He looked scared.

Apparently, knowing exactly what he was doing, McVeigh looked directly at the camera and gave the victims of his crime a demonic stare. The piercing look shot daggers through the camera lens, through the cable conduits, and into the communal room in Oklahoma City.

People all around me gasped and a few women shrieked, as if McVeigh would break his restraints and lunge a thousand miles into our faces. His power of hatred and rage had transcended the distance, penetrating the glass between him and his final observers.

McVeigh had evoked fear into innocent people a final time.

His arms were situated on extensions of his gurney-like lair. I watched an intravenous needle slide into one arm, then a second needle into the other.

Except for that terrifying stare, McVeigh neither said nor did anyhing to acknowledge himself.

He was asked if he had any last words.

My optimism shot skyward.

Maybe he'll at last say why he murdered all those people, not one of whom was his adversary, I silently hoped.

I flashed back to his earlier appraisal of his victims. He'd called them "collateral damage."

Surely now, with eternity hanging in the balance, he would utter a sorrowful explanation about his slaughter of men, women, and children undergoing their mundane lives, which he instantly and collectively extinguished, like so many unwanted dogs at a municipal pound, or so I thought.

But McVeigh said nothing.

People beside his table, and those in Oklahoma City, were handed a final slap of secrecy from the consistently silent killer.

"Let the execution begin," someone said from inside the death room.

The process began at 7 a.m., when three poisons began weaving throughout McVeigh's circulatory system. I saw the fatal fluid trickle into his stiffened frame. The first rendered him unconscious. The second halted his breathing. The third stopped his heart.

His skin was ashen, his eyes were open. Even in death, McVeigh seemingly stared at people whose lives he had ruined by taking the lives of those they had loved.

The process was finished at 7:14 a.m. McVeigh's months of planning the bombing, his years of "fighting" for his hateful ideals, had culminated in less than a quarter of an hour.

Was that all there was to it?

What transpired before McVeigh was wheeled into the execution room? I asked myself. *Surely McVeigh had told someone something about his motives.*

He said nothing about anything, I was told.

Like someone lounging on Sunday after church, McVeigh had watched television, then fallen into restful sleep after indulging his final meal, two pints of ice cream.

His last meal was as cold as his doomed soul.

Chapter Twenty-One

❧

My initial meeting with Lana Padilla, Nichols's former wife, took place in Las Vegas on April 20, 1999, at the Sunset Station Hotel where she worked in hospitality.

While walking through the lobby, I noticed a cluster of people crammed around a small television. The shooting at Columbine High School in Colorado was the horrifying subject of live coverage.

As I formed my first thought, I shuddered at the timing. It was Adolf Hilter's birthday, something I had learned from my visit to Elohim City.

The Columbine massacre was also one day after the four-year anniversary of the Murrah bombing.

I had gone to Las Vegas primarily to visit with Lana about the bombing, as I was still pressing to get to the bottom of what remained America's bloodiest act of terrorism to date. Sometimes I wondered if I would be chasing answers for the rest of my life. My haunting questions lived on. My grandbabies did not. If I was expected to live with that sad fact, then people would just have to live with my persistent questioning.

Lana understood.

I may have formed preconceptions of Lana as a misfit like her former husband. Lana and her son, Josh, still endured their "guilt by association" discrimination.

In fact, Lana had been a successful Las Vegas real-estate agent.

But her business plummeted after media accounts identified her as the ex-wife of Terry Nichols. Hence her change of jobs, and her affiliation with the hotel.

My expectations about Lana were wrong. She wasn't the least bit odd or strange. Instead, she met me with an upbeat, outgoing, cheerful personality that put me instantly at ease. Talking to her was like talking to an old friend.

I also took a liking to Lana because of her transparency. She made it her aim to project, not censor, the entire truth. Her delivery was whole.

During our time in Las Vegas, and eventually at my Oklahoma City home, my memories of Lana painted a picture of life after marriage to a notorious public figure. Lana was guilty by association in the public eye. Regrettably, the same could be said about Josh.

Never mind that Lana and Nichols had been divorced six years before the bombing, and that Josh had last seen his father several months before the explosion.

Lana and especially Josh were sometimes targets of violent threats from total strangers. Many had called them filthy names in diatribes laced with obscenities. Josh had often been bullied by public school classmates and adults, people who attacked in groups that left him crying and bleeding in the streets. The mistreatment began when he was twelve.

By the time Josh was a teenager, he fought back publicly against his assailants and privately against his demons. Drugs and alcohol allowed him temporary escape. Often, police found him drunk and high while aimlessly wandering the streets of Las Vegas late at night. Feeling sorry for the troubled youth, cops took him home, usually forgoing processing to prevent a paper trail of his alleged infractions.

Physically speaking, Josh matured early and grew to become an imposing figure. At age thirteen, he stood five foot eleven inches tall and weighed 240 pounds.

Despite his stature, after his first day in the eighth grade, a loud-mouthed classmate confronted Josh as soon as he stepped from the school bus to walk home.

Josh had seen and heard it all before, and he braced for the heckler's predictable onslaught after calling him out as the son of Terry Nichols.

The aggressor shouted that his own father had been a fireman in Oklahoma City, where the Murrah bombing had shattered the fire station's windows.

The aggressor was obviously looking for any excuse to attack Josh and remarked that he could kill him.

But when the blowhard came to appreciate Josh's towering physique, he hurriedly walked away. Josh let him. He'd had enough fighting in his short lifetime.

"Josh was beat up lots of times by people who didn't really know him; they just knew who he was," Lana recalled. "They would leave him bleeding on the sidewalk. They'd threaten to beat him again if he didn't move out of town."

Eventually, Josh became unofficially stripped of his first and last names. To many, he was known simply as "the bomber's son." They did not know his real name and did not care to learn.

In their investigation after the bombing, the FBI initially considered Josh as "John Doe II," a bulky man thought to have accompanied McVeigh in the Ryder truck that carried the deadly bomb to Oklahoma City.

I couldn't imagine a twelve-year-old boy under interrogation by the FBI when his father was identified on television news programs as one of the Oklahoma City bombers. How much stress could one child endure?

While Lana's recollections were as sensational as tabloid journalism, I never doubted their accuracy. People who fictionalize usually talk with hesitations in order to contemplate what they're going to say next. Not Lana. She spoke calmly and continuously. She did not repeat or contradict herself.

That was another reason why I liked her.

Additionally, I believed Lana because I barely had to question her. She knew I wanted to learn the truth, and she volunteered information freely.

When I left Las Vegas, I told Lana to give me a call if she was ever in Oklahoma City. I never really expected that she would.

Two years later, on June 30, 2001, a call from Lana took me by surprise. She and Josh were coming to Oklahoma and she wanted to let me know. They intended to stay in Oklahoma a few days, Lana said. Josh wanted to visit his father in the Oklahoma County jail. By this time, the two had not seen each other in four years.

I invited Lana and Josh to dinner at my house. They came, then stayed for four days.

Even before their arrival, I had a giant problem.

I had forgotten about my commitment to do a comprehensive radio interview at the hour when Lana and Josh would arrive. How would I do that as the two of them sat in the room? I didn't want them to hear what I might say. I certainly didn't want them to participate, as I didn't want to thrust them or their whereabouts into the spotlight.

But I had to do the interview. I had given my word. Besides, if I didn't, how would the moderator explain my absence to listeners?

My determination to keep Lana and Josh's visit a secret was shattered. Like it or not, I needed help with occupying my mystery guests while I was in the next room speaking on the air to countless households.

Circumstances were forcing me to reach out and trust someone. I called Christy Rush, my neighbor, who had helped me search for Chase's and Colton's bodies after the blast six years earlier.

My neighbors were the very people I did not want to know about my controversial and out-of-town guests. When I explained my dilemma, Christy became silent. I can only guess that she paused in disbelief.

I don't remember exactly what I said to her, but I can assume how she probably translated my words:

"Hi, Christy, it's Kathy. Would you mind dropping by my house to play hostess to two highly controversial people? You know them, at least by reputation; Lana and Josh, the former wife and the son of Terry Nichols—one of the men who blew up much of the downtown of our city and killed my grandchildren."

In retrospect, my spontaneous request to my unsuspecting friend was comical. I wish I could have seen her body language on the other end of the phone line.

Despite what Christy did or did not feel, she secretly came to my house and even agreed to help feed Lana and Josh.

Food had to be prepared. I had to gather my thoughts for a broadcast. The flurry was mounting as Lana and Josh were running late. They had yet to appear. Ten minutes before airtime, they rang my doorbell.

Much of my anxiety proved to be in vain, particularly the part about my wanting to protect Lana and Josh from whatever I might say.

I did the interview, and they went to another room where they simply turned on the radio. Hearing me would not be difficult.

The two were listening when I said I believed Nichols was involved in the bombing of the Alfred P. Murrah Federal Building in Oklahoma City, something Nichols had been denying to his family.

I knew he was guilty, but I did not know to what extent. I was not convinced that Nichols was aware there would be people inside the building when it was bombed. This aspect of Nichols's alleged involvement hadn't even been addressed, much less answered, at Nichols's federal trial.

When the telephone interview was over, I had to walk into the next room and face Lana Padilla and Josh Nichols.

Neither said a word about my remarks. Therefore, neither did I.

≈

I cooked for my guests because I was uneasy about being seen with them in public, including in a public restaurant. I feared for their safety as well as mine.

Lana had earlier told me how she and Josh had been abused with shouted threats and profane name-calling from Oklahomans during their last visit to the state. I did not want them to experience that again—or worse—during their trip, which was partially motivated by my invitation.

I wanted their visit to be low-profile. I also wanted to spend time with Lana and Josh out of the public eye.

I knew opening my home to the mother and son would be seen as unusual to some, but I also knew they were among the forgotten victims of the bombing and I wanted to reach out to them. I opted to show God's love rather than to talk about it.

While I didn't agree with some Oklahomans' hateful thinking, I understood it. Still, I knew they'd never understand my logic in visiting Nichols in his downtown cell, or sending him letters, or talking to him on the telephone. How would they feel about my harboring his ex-wife and his son?

How could I expect anyone to understand what I was doing? Especially when I really didn't understand it myself? It just seemed like the right thing to do.

By this time, more than half a decade after the bombing, many people had grown weary of my campaign to reveal the truth. Many people just wanted me to finally let it rest. They'd told me so.

Although I had peace about my personal losses, my restlessness regarding government lies and the probability of accomplices remained in high gear. I determined to never rest. I felt I owed it to Chase, Colton, and Glenn to get all of my questions answered.

Inside my home, Lana was as wonderfully forthright as she'd been in Las Vegas. Her words included a disclosure, at least to me. Federal agents had barged into her real-estate office only two days after the bombing!

Astonished, she had reeled with shock. But agents gave her no time to process. Instead, they'd instantly wanted to hear about Lana's most recent activities with Nichols.

Many folks, myself included, might have asked for a lawyer. Others would have done nothing, as they would have been paralyzed by panic.

Lana didn't flinch.

Forgoing an attorney, she told agents what she later repeated in my home, that only five months before the tragedy, as Nichols was leaving for the Philippines, he had entrusted her with a package that he ordered her not to open for sixty days. Shortly after dropping Nichols off at the airport, she defied him and opened the mysterious bundle.

It contained notes from Nichols to McVeigh. One urged McVeigh to "go for it" and ended with the words "This letter would be for the purpose of my death."

"I bawled," Lana told me. "I was convinced he was going to commit suicide."

"Terry's note also ordered me to clear out a storage locker in Vegas," she said. "When I did, I found a stash of wigs, masks, panty hose, and other stuff used to change someone's appearance."

Lana's findings were tools of disguise, and strongly suggested that Nichols and McVeigh were a part of an Aryan group that robbed banks wearing disguises and used the proceeds to finance terrorist activities. Jennifer McVeigh admitted as much in her handwritten confession to the FBI. That's when she told them she had been laundering one-hundred-dollar bills for her brother— money that he told her came from a bank robbery.

Lana disclosed that she had found something else in a secret locker: sixty thousand dollars' worth of gold and silver bullion.

I was still trying to process Lana's information when she issued more.

"I hadn't heard from Terry since he had shown up at my house three months before the bombing," Lana recalled. "He was furious because I had opened the package. So what does he do? The next day, he clears the rest of the stuff out of storage and disappears. Again!"

Solely on the face of Lana's reports, I was sure I would get answers for some of my questions. Lana was on a roll and I wanted her to keep talking.

"I answered all of the FBI's questions, and I let those agents question Josh, too," she said. "It went on and on and I never once asked for a lawyer. Why should I? Josh and I had nothing to hide."

Finally, she said, agents rested their general questioning and asked Lana point-blank who was really behind the bombing.

"I told them it seemed to me that Tim was the leader and Terry was the follower," she said she told them.

"Then everything changed," Lana said she told agents. "They acted like they were concerned for Josh's and my safety."

Lana revealed that she and Josh, who was then in middle school, were hidden by agents at various Las Vegas hotels.

The mother and son, while under federal protection, were mostly alone. The silence of the nights seemed too much of a contrast for them after the rapid-fire questioning from the FBI.

When darkness showcased the glistening radiance of Las Vegas by night, Lana and Josh stood side by side, staring blankly through curtains at the bustling nightlife below. In protective custody they felt more like prisoners than guests.

"Josh and I hadn't done a thing," she said. "But there we were, listening to each other cry while the rest of the city was having a wonderful time."

Things got worse for the innocent mother and child. I continued to listen without interruption, all the while filing mental notes. Eventually, not many questions remained to be asked. Lana seemed to disclose everything she knew and everything she experienced during her hand-in-hand walk with Josh through those trying days.

Federal agents continued to move mother and son through a maze of alternate locations. I never fully understood from whom they were being protected. McVeigh and Nichols were in jail. Besides, at that time, Lana's knowledge about the bombing included few hard facts. Mostly, her opinions were based on that stash of money, the materials for disguise, a handwritten note, and mass media updates.

After two weeks in hotels, Lana and Josh were allowed to go home, where the FBI had tapped their telephones, Lana later learned. Whenever questions arose from their monitoring or taped phone conversations, FBI agents would come unannounced to their house. At that point, the agents focused on Josh, Lana recalled.

As a lad, Josh had spent a couple of weeks with his dad in Kansas blowing up bottles and things at the Nichols family's Herington farm, she said.

At age twelve, Josh had no idea his dad was experimenting with how to build a bomb. The boy watched Nichols use gasoline and ammonium nitrate to disintegrate tree stumps. It was all fun and games for a boy who didn't get enough face time with his dad.

The youngster was hardly privy to any plan for an explosion at an Oklahoma City federal building. His mother said he had little to say to agents. At first, Josh was certain the agents were mistaken—that they simply couldn't be talking about his dad. The boy loved his dad and wished he had come around more often.

Why didn't he? Josh wondered.

As Josh had told his mother, he and his dad had blown up tree stumps and other neat things that seemed to be just harmless fun.

❦

By the second day of my visit with Lana and Josh, Lana began to reminisce about her marriage to Nichols. I saw a bittersweet glisten in her eyes as she recalled the life and times of a young couple falling in love.

The passing of time had seemingly idealized good times into great ones for Lana.

She met Nichols in 1980 when she oversaw his purchase of 120 acres of land around Decker, Michigan. He seemed to be a country boy, and she was herself a daughter of the heartland. She had already seen romance's dark side after two failed marriages.

While Nichols had many appealing traits, Lana was drawn, foremost, to the fact that he did not drink at all. In lieu of hanging out in taverns, Nichols liked to paddle canoes and even had an athletic side in his enjoyment of volleyball. Mostly, he liked to walk hand in hand with Lana through the woods of the upper Midwest.

The tranquil forest was the background for blossoming romance. Lana was falling in love, and she indicated that she relished the ride.

In January 1981, Lana and Nichols went away and returned to Michigan as man and wife. Josh was born ten months later.

Home life was like a scene out of *Little House on the Prairie*, according to Lana's descriptions. Nichols was soft-spoken and gentle, helping with household chores without being asked. Lana had never previously met a man who ground wheat to make bread.

I supposed it could be argued that, eventually, the marriage suffered from success—Lana's.

She triumphed as a real-estate agent and insurance broker. Nichols played the role of stay-at-home dad, taking care of Josh and of Lana's two children by a previous marriage.

Lana felt a bit troubled by Nichols's seeming lack of ambition. She was forever asking him what work might capture his passion, probing him to discover exactly what he wanted to do with his life. To her way of thinking, Nichols needed to be earning an income.

By May 1988, the couple was separated.

Lana persuaded him to join the Army, partly to defend his country and partly because he needed something to do and somewhere to go. She wanted him to have a career.

During his basic training at Fort Riley, Kansas, Nichols met McVeigh, she said. Lana told me she felt guilty for insisting Nichols join the Army. Had she not done so, Nichols would never have met McVeigh, and he wouldn't be spending his life behind bars.

Josh was in need of his father, and the need was enough to justify Nichols's hardship discharge, Lana explained.

As too much of a good thing can ruin everything, Nichols's penchant for patriotism became extreme. He joined the Michigan Militia, Lana remembered.

She divorced Nichols in 1989 and made plans to move her real-estate business to Las Vegas. Lana started Esquire Realty and entered her fourth marriage in 1993, two years before her third husband would become an infamous personality.

By the end of 1995, only months after the bombing, Josh was dealing unsuccessfully with his classmates' harassment. He fell into depression that prompted psychological therapy. He almost never mentioned the Oklahoma City Bombing.

"I miss my dad," Josh told me, regarding Nichols's imprisonment. "It's going to be hard for me to get through this life without him. He used to take me hiking and hunting. We laughed a lot. We did things together."

⸙

Edye called me on the third day of Lana and Josh's visit. She nonchalantly asked what I was doing.

"I'm sitting here talking to Lana Padilla," I replied.

Silence.

"Oh," Edye finally said, as if Lana were a frequent guest in my home.

Lana overheard my conversation and excitedly interrupted.

"Oh, Kathy," she implored, "please invite Edye to join us for dinner. My treat."

I said nothing of my apprehension about going out in public with them. Actually, I was surprised that Lana wanted to go out, given all that she and I had discussed regarding the hostility formerly handed to her by strangers. But that was four years earlier. Perhaps Oklahoma had forgotten them.

I asked Edye, still on the phone, if she'd join us for dinner. Hesitating, her voice said "yes" while her tone said "no." She came anyhow.

To no one's surprise, Edye and little Glenn were the objects of Lana's and Josh's affection. Their adoring remarks segued into talk about eating, and we discussed restaurants.

"Has my cooking been that bad?" I teased, hoping my guests and I could avoid public notice for another night.

Edye took her own car because she planned to leave the restaurant early. Little Glenn wanted to ride with his grandmother, leaving Edye to drive alone.

"Hey, Josh, come and ride with me!" Edye yelled.

The young man was stunned and so was I.

Moving in disbelief, Josh slowly got out of my car and into my daughter's. Given all of the persecution he had endured, the son of a bomber could not believe he'd ride next to a mother of the bomber's victims.

As Lana and I rode in my car behind Edye's, I shared an ironic thought.

"Wouldn't the media have a field day if they were to see those two together?" I asked, giggling.

Josh later told me he couldn't believe that Edye, of all people, liked him. I understood his implication.

His father was at least partially responsible for the deaths of Edye's sons, and yet she was extending friendship. His mind appeared to be short-circuiting—but in a good way.

His enchantment with the situation also rang of loneliness, the result of being disliked by so many people for what must have seemed to be an eternity to the teenager.

My sense of Josh's mind and emotions was heightened due to the fact that we had bonded very deeply and quickly. Our connection was not based on my cooking for him or my opening my home to him.

Josh and I had opened our hearts and shared our souls with each other. He was as easy to approach as his mother.

At fourteen, he had dropped out of school, not only because of physical attacks on him, but also because of "Bomber," the nickname assigned to him by other students.

I knew how sensitive teenagers were regarding their sense of identity. Stripping away Josh's name and replacing it with a slur had pushed indignity too far over the line, especially in the wake of everything else he'd undergone.

After all, I wondered to myself, *how many innocent boys are grilled by the FBI? How many have seen their names plastered all over the newspaper in connection with mass murders partially planned by their fathers? How many have faced major-league journalists, such as Diane Sawyer or a reporter from the* New York Times?

Josh had suffered through all of the above.

He and I spoke nightly into the wee hours as he braced to testify against his father at Nichols's state trial, which began not long after McVeigh's execution. He did not want to be responsible for saying anything that might help send his father to his death. He just did not think he would be able to stretch his emotions that far without breaking them. And I feared for the same thing. (Ultimately, Josh's testimony was not required by prosecutors—reportedly due to his young age.)

Throughout our nightly conversations, I tried to draw on my experiences with Danny, my own son, whom I had adopted when he was thirteen.

Danny's life started out rough, too. The first time I met him I was the director of a boys' ranch. I answered the door and there stood a total stranger with a thirteen-year-old boy. She looked me in the eye and told me that if I would give him a good education, I could have him. She turned and left. She had just given me her son as one might give away a stray puppy. I was dumbfounded. I cannot imagine how Danny felt.

He was one of eight children. In the years after I would allow Danny to return to his birth mother's home to visit his brothers and sisters. He would come home smelly and dirty. I asked him why he didn't bathe. He told me, "Mom, I couldn't. The bathtub there is crawling with cockroaches."

One Christmas I sent money with him to buy his siblings presents, and his mother stole it from his wallet as he lay sleeping.

He told me horrific stories from his childhood. He said that once his mother picked up a hitchhiker and Danny walked in on the man lying on top of his younger sister, sexually molesting her.

When Danny ran to his mother for help, she simply walked into the bedroom and told the man to get off the child. She amazingly let the man spend the night in her home without calling law enforcement. So I knew about innocent boys being catapulted into horrifying situations.

While my experience with my son helped me to understand Josh's turmoil, my solutions to his problems remained elusive.

I finally realized that simply listening was probably the best thing I could do for him. In retrospect, I think my overall ability to empathize with people was greatly enhanced by those late-night huddles as much as or more than anything else.

Wee hours and darkness seem to inspire heart-to-heart personal exchanges. People tend to abandon pretense when they're awake and the rest of the world is asleep.

Yet, on the third night of his visit, Josh's words caught me squarely off guard.

"Could you take me to the memorial for the people that died in the bombing?" he asked.

He was referring to the monument consisting of 168 "chairs"—one for each victim.

I felt that Josh's expressed desire to see it indicated how much he had grown to trust me. The young man who had at first feared the wrath of people in Oklahoma City wanted to visit their memorial garden, their most sacred terrain. And with me—a grieving victim whose grandchildren were represented by two of the chairs!

Many Oklahoma City residents were finding it hard to move on with their lives. I was unsure what people would think if we were recognized. That's why I had used my maiden name the first time I snuck to the glass wall framing Nichols's jail cell.

Josh had heard too much hateful talk about his father while outside my home. He would never hear it inside, not from my lips.

Nevertheless, Lana, Josh, and I went to the memorial.

I felt awestruck as I walked up to the giant gate. It was blowing my mind that I had Nichols's son with me.

What would Glenn be thinking? What would anybody I knew be thinking? Of course, I knew the answer. They would think I had lost my mind.

I looked around to see if anyone recognized me. I felt confident that they would not recognize Josh. He had changed so much. He was inches taller and pounds lighter since his last exposure by the media circus. He didn't look anything like the kid he was at that time.

But Lana was with me as well. And I was also hoping nobody would recognize *me*. I did not want anybody talking to me. If they did, social graces would require that I introduce my friends.

When we got to the memorial, I walked over and escorted Josh and Lana to Chase's and Colton's chairs. They paused. Josh stood in reverence with his head bowed. This seemed to be a very powerful moment for him.

On the eve of Josh and Lana's fourth and final day with me, I was strongly inclined to talk about what, up to that point, I had only tried to show: my forgiveness of Nichols based on grace from the One who had forgiven my sins.

"Josh, I'm sure you've heard all about your dad's newfound Christian faith," I said. "Do you have thoughts about that?"

"That's what gets him by," he instantly replied.

Then he shared something I already knew, that his dad had formerly refused to acknowledge God.

"Instead, my dad referred to Mother Nature as the person behind good things," Josh said.

"But now he uses the word 'God,'" Josh continued, as if the change had pleasantly surprised him.

"You know, Josh, there might be more to this than you think," I said. "Your dad is a different man now than he used to be. He invited Christ into his heart and asked Him to forgive him of all his sins. When you do that and mean it, God changes you."

Josh looked at me quizzically and shrugged his shoulders. He said, "Whatever gets him by."

I knew Josh was angry with his father. He had every right to be. Nichols had not only blown up the Murrah Building and the people inside it, he had destroyed the life of his son.

I told Josh that Edye and I had forgiven his father. I suggested he should, too. He responded as most teenagers respond to words of guidance—with silence. But I knew he heard me. I knew my suggestion had hit home. For a moment, he seemed very deep in thought.

I decided not to belabor chapters and verses from the Bible. I wanted to share my testimony, not preach it.

Josh and his mother were about to depart my world, where they had been my houseguests for four days.

The more I had tried to give to this mother and son, the more they'd unknowingly given to me. I had been strong during their entire visit. I wanted to remain that way as it came to a close. I knew Josh was struggling with his dad's newfound faith. I also knew he was fighting with the idea of forgiving his father.

Suddenly at a loss for words, I again considered giving voice to biblical Scriptures.

But instead, I shared an old Native American adage.

"Josh, there is a black dog and a white dog inside each one of us. One wants us to do good and the other evil. Inside you, there's a battle taking place for your soul. The dog that wins is the one you feed the most." Josh listened intently.

With that, I told Josh he might understandably make wrong choices during his life. All of us do. Understandable or not, some of those choices could ruin his life. I asked him not to take the easy way just because he could.

Is that *all I can say?* I asked myself.

I wished they didn't have to go. I had enjoyed having them. Their visit to my home had been a healing experience for all of us. Josh gave me a hug in the kitchen, then I walked my guests to their car.

I listened to Josh's footsteps as he slowly made his way to his mother's car.

Staring directly at me as he climbed in, he slowly and softly closed the car's heavy door behind him.

Instantly, the door sprang open.

Josh darted across my driveway and gave me another hug, then returned to the vehicle. Then, yet again, he reopened the door and ran back to me.

"You're the nicest lady I've ever met," he said, his voice cracking with emotion. Like most teenage boys, he didn't want me to see him cry.

As I considered his words, Lana got out of her car to join Josh and me in the driveway. We embraced in a group hug. By this time, we were all crying.

"Kathy," she said, "the last time we were in Oklahoma City, we were booed and heckled. Thank you for giving Josh some good memories."

She kissed my cheek, and with that, the uplifted mother and son left.

Standing alone, I watched their taillights fade out of sight and thought about what a remarkable visit this had been.

Nichols had been instrumental in the of deaths of my grandsons. Yet I had received and nurtured his son. And it felt wonderful.

After that, no one would ever convince me that God doesn't work in strange, miraculous, and merciful ways.

Cradling that thought in my mind, I walked alone into my silent house.

❧

After Josh's visit to my home, he seemed to turn his life around. He went to drug and alcohol rehab, and he even served as a mentor to others.

In April 2005, Nichols admitted to his role in the bombing. Up until this time, he had denied that he had any involvement. He had convinced his family that he had been set up by McVeigh and the government. This new revelation sent Josh reeling.

His life took a nosedive and he began to get in trouble again. Apparently, he turned passionately against society and its laws.

In 2006, Nevada district judge Joseph Bonaventure acknowledged an eighteen-page letter he'd received a month earlier from Nichols. The bomber pleaded for leniency for Josh Nichols, who was awaiting sentencing for conviction on two counts of assault with a deadly weapon, resisting an officer, battery of an officer, and possession of a stolen vehicle.

Josh, then twenty-three, was sentenced to nineteen to forty-eight months in prison. Under Nevada law, he could have been given twenty-two years.

In handing down the lesser time, the judge cited Josh's sad and stormy past.

"I have to look at what this kid has been through since he was eleven or twelve years old," Bonaventure said, as reported in the May 18, 2006, edition of the *Las Vegas Review-Journal*.

The judge then said the Nichols family history was no excuse for Josh's crimes. For me, the news came five years after my four days with Josh. My heart broke for him. I wondered about Lana, and how she had fared during the trial and sentencing.

On May 1, 2009, Josh, then twenty-six, pleaded guilty to one count of grand larceny in connection with the theft of a motorcycle in 2008.

I understood Josh's scrapes with the law, but I did not want to believe it. I turned back to the page in my memory that held the image of that tall, impressionable young man who graced my home in 2001. I relived those emotionally charged, boyish embraces as Josh struggled to tear himself from me while leaving my home.

In 2012, while talking to Lana, I learned she was thrilled because Josh had just gotten out of prison in the fall of that year and was finally ready to embark on a new life.

Once again, she was optimistic about his future.

Chapter Twenty-Two

❧

On September 11, 2001, as commercial jets were crashing into New York City's World Trade Center, broadcast live on TV, the first frenzied phone call I received was from Christy Rush.

The second was from Terry Nichols.

I suspect mine was the first voice he heard after the Twin Towers fell in on themselves and thousands of people fled in fear. Manhattan was gripped by mass hysteria.

Even before my phone rang, I had surmised that this was a deliberate airborne attack—as had millions of other viewers across our nation.

Will missiles be next? I wondered. *Will terrorists strike other American cities? Will this be the end of the United States as I've known it?*

I shared my wild thoughts with Nichols, then told him, "I wish McVeigh was still alive. He could see what a real terrorist could do."

I don't know why I made such a ridiculous statement. Perhaps I wished that McVeigh could feel the kind of terror I was going through. I felt the world had gone mad.

I told Nichols I hated being alone inside my home—so empty, so silent. My always protective husband, Glenn Wilburn, had been dead for four years. I longed to hold and be held by him. Glenn's presence was but a tender recollection. I could not curl my arms around a memory.

Nichols listened quietly, and I did not realize the role reversal that was subtly under way. For years, I had listened to his laments. Now, he was hearing mine.

When Nichols finally spoke, I sensed his caution. I knew his fear when I heard it. And I understood why.

The man whose act of terrorism had taken lives now feared terrorism would take his. If the fanatical attacks on the East Coast should spread to the heartland, Nichols might be targeted for retribution, even though his act could not be directly associated with this one. While imprisoned, he couldn't cheat death by running for his life.

Should there be an explosion, Nichols was trapped. Rescuers would find his corpse still locked in an impenetrable solitary-confinement cell.

Even if he survived the blast, there would be no hope of escaping the resulting fire. He would likely be burned alive in his small cell, which would radiate heat like the walls of an oven.

Free people like me could fantasize surviving an attack by running into a basement or beneath a highway bridge. Not so for those incarcerated inside maximum-security prisons.

I knew those imaginary doomsday scenes were searing Nichols's fearful mind just as they were ravaging mine. After all, each of us had seen the effects of a terrorist bombing up close and personal.

The media were reporting that another aircraft had been destined for the United States Capitol building. The flight was foiled when determined passengers physically overcame the hijackers, but not in time to prevent the plane's crashing into a field near Shanksville, Pennsylvania, killing all forty-four people on board.

The fact that another plane had also been on a mission of death instilled new fear in the hearts of terrified Americans. Another hijacked aircraft—number four—had targeted the Pentagon. Several attacks mounted simultaneously, in what seemed to be a highly coordinated effort, seemed to suggest a possibility of other planes attacking other locations across the United States; perhaps even Oklahoma City where Nichols was being held in the county jail.

His fifteen minutes of allotted calling time were ticking away inescapably. Our conversation would soon be cut off. Then, when my voice vanished, Nichols would wonder if he'd ever hear another human voice from "outside."

After several hours had passed, I began to feel safer for us all. The federal government initiated a no-fly zone nationwide. If a hostile aircraft were to enter U.S. airspace, it would have quickly been shot down.

Thank God that never happened.

Soon after that horrible day, Nichols resumed his phone calls and letterwriting to me, his friend who was also safe in the heartland where amber waves of grain still blew free and unharmed by the perpetrators of 9/11.

The national temperament was one of gratitude, as people were gloriously thankful to simply be alive. Nichols and I were among them.

✎

On September 13, when U.S. air traffic officially resumed, a producer from NBC's *Today Show* asked me to do a return interview with the program's host, Matt Lauer, regarding similarities between the Twin Towers attack and the Murrah Bombing.

An apprehensive spirit settled over me. New York City seemed like a war zone. I wasn't sure I should enter it.

The more I thought about it, though, the more I realized that was just what I had to do. God had given me a gift more precious than gold—my peace of mind—and I had to share my testimony with New Yorkers who were being tossed about in a sea of sadness and confusion.

Survivors of the vicious attack on the World Trade Center needed to know that God was with them. His invisibility need not diminish His power to comfort. Some New Yorkers' shredded lives seemed to be open wounds that they believed no balm could soothe. They saw no avenue of comfort.

It was my calling to try to provide it. I knew about that of which I spoke. I had been there, and I needed to tell them so.

Once again, I thought back to John Walsh and the brutal murder of his son. Walsh was totally candid when he told other Murrah survivors and me that we would grieve and grieve deeply.

"But," he also promised, "you *will* survive."

At the time, his proclamation gave me hope, something that had vanished with the news of my grandsons' deaths. I thought I was doomed to a life filled with pain.

Just because he got through his misery doesn't mean I'll get through mine, I once thought. *Not all people are made the same; not all recover identically.*

But God and time had proven Walsh to be right.

My passion to go comfort New York's battered souls was mounting. There, I could share my story. I could share with credibility, as my grief had been exactly where theirs was now. If nothing else, I could physically hold them, and let the strength of my love ease into their hearts where love for anything was temporarily missing. This would not be a trip, it would be a mission. I was certain I was supposed to take it.

I called my friends Larry and Frances Jones, who had coincidentally been in Manhattan on September 11 and had been unable to leave the city due to those government-imposed flying constraints. Larry and Frances were the founders of Feed The Children, a benevolent charity.

"Is it safe for me to come up there?" I asked Larry.

"Get here right away!" he said. "I need you!"

I knew that meant he had determined I would be safe. Meanwhile, since Larry had just happened to be inside the tragedy, he did what he always did amid catastrophes: he initiated disaster relief in a big way.

Before I ever got to New York, Larry committed me to visit exhausted firemen at a kitchen and bunkhouse he had quickly procured exclusively for firefighters. He had also committed me to speak the following Sunday morning to survivors of the World Trade Center massacre. Most of the people in my audience would be family members of firemen and survivors of private citizens whose bodies were missing in three stories of debris that filled Ground Zero.

I called Edye and asked her and young Glenn to come to my house. I wanted to tell them both how much I loved them. I wanted to feel their embrace and let them feel mine.

I was rocking Glenn when he astonished me with his awareness. After all, he was only three years old, the exact age of Chase when he was killed.

"Nonny," Glenn said, "some mean men flew an airplane into a building and it made a big crash and there was lots of fire."

I think the child sensed my despair, as he slowly put his tiny hands on my wet cheeks.

"Don't worry, Nonny," he continued. "When I get big and get some big muscles, I will build the building back."

I thought about the irony. An innocent child's first impulse was to build back what satanic mens' obsession had sought to destroy. There was a lesson somewhere in that contrast. I would have three hours to process it during my flight to New York City. I could think of nothing that would stop me now.

And if it was my time to die, I would rely on a priority lesson I had derived from Murrah: "If you're not prepared to die, you're not prepared to live." I was prepared for both. My anxiety about flying was dissolved by my enthusiasm for my mission. I did not know then that my personal peace would actually enable me to sleep most of the way.

Upon entering the Oklahoma City Will Rogers World Airport, authorities expectedly interrogated me as to why I was flying to New York at such a perilous time. Their questions prompted more questions, and I felt somewhat like a grand jury witness.

My person and my baggage were thoroughly searched and X-rayed repeatedly. I was then taken to a back room where every-thing in my luggage was examined one piece at a time. Airline agents had plenty of time for the meticulous probe, as virtually no passengers were inside the once teeming airport.

In fact, I boarded my flight with only a handful of people. The flight attendants and pilots outnumbered the uneasy passengers.

During our descent into New York, the pilot took passengers almost directly over the still-smoking Twin Towers. Days after the event, the black smoke continued to billow forth.

The scene reminded me of cars passing a bad traffic accident. The passengers wanted to look away, but none could remove his or her eyes from the view. I was glad no one sat beside me. My thoughts were pushed back six years by the smoldering building and I had no desire to talk just then.

Lost in my thoughts, I began to sing "Amazing Grace," thinking that the noise of jet engines would prevent anyone from hearing.

Quietly, in a seat in front of mine, a woman of foreign descent turned to look at me, her eyes tenderly staring into mine. She had heard my hymn.

Ever so gently, her eyes filled with tears and maintained their lock on my face. Not knowing what to say or do, I continued to sing:

When we've been there ten thousand years,
bright shining as the sun,
we've no less days to sing God's praise
than when we'd first begun.

Perhaps she and I had a language barrier. Perhaps she just didn't want to speak. When I finished that holy melody, she slowly turned away. We had connected on a spiritual level without saying a word.

I can see her face to this day. Her eyes spoke fluently. Yet I'll never know what she said, not until I see her in a life without carnage, a place where everyone shares the universal language of goodwill and eternal love.

Upon deplaning, I saw a chauffeur holding a sign bearing my name. The *Today* show producer had sent a town car—a welcoming gesture that had been common throughout my visits to national talk shows.

But this car's driver was different from the scores of others I had encountered during the six years since Murrah. He was extremely nervous and visibly shaken by the Twin Towers attack. I was actually uneasy about entrusting my safety to his motoring skills. But I let him place my bags in the trunk, and I uneasily entered his car when he opened the back door.

He tried to communicate with me, but the process was impaired by his Russian accent. About all I could discern was his remorse about the extreme terrorism in New York City, site of his new homeland.

He maneuvered the vehicle through Manhattan's crowded streets, where a lot of unexplained and frenzied activity still prevailed. I saw fifteen to twenty United States marshals standing in the middle of bumper-to-bumper traffic. Sirens were blaring, seemingly from all directions, and Manhattan's main thoroughfares were jammed with emergency vehicles, including ambulances and fire trucks.

I realized I had not heard a radio or seen a television since leaving Oklahoma City three or four hours ago. My stomach seemed to be in my throat as I thought the unthinkable.

Had another attack occurred during that time? Might my daughter and my grandchildren be terrified back home? My imagination was running wild, just as it had been on April 19, 1995.

But this time was different. I was not panicked. I felt more curious than fearful. I realized that my sense of calm affirmed God's work in healing my mind and soul.

Alone in the backseat of a town car, I quietly thanked Him.

As the driver eased into the passenger unloading zone outside my hotel, policemen instantly surrounded the vehicle. They explained nothing but loudly ordered the driver to move his car.

He said he'd be parked less than a minute and simply wanted to unload his passenger.

The cops would not hear of it, and the Russian actually entered a shouting match with the determined policemen.

One cop ended the conflict when he screamed that the car would be impounded if the driver dared to let me out.

"What on earth?" I remarked aloud, to no one who could have heard me. "I have traveled this far, and now I can't get out of the car?"

So we departed. There I was, riding alone in the rear of a vehicle that was dangerously weaving through clogged traffic, with no idea where I was going or what my driver was saying.

Then, as if I'd been taken hostage, he pulled the town car into a vacant space beside the curb and bolted out of the car. He stormed around the back of the carriage toward my side of the vehicle.

At last, I thought to myself. *I can get some answers as to what's going on here.*

That was not to be.

The driver physically jerked me out of the town car. Standing on the curb, I dodged my bags as the driver threw them my way. All the while, he said nothing. He got back into the car as rapidly as he'd gotten out, and the tires squealed as he pulled away.

By myself with suitcases at my feet, I stared at passersby as they walked briskly around me.

I still had no idea what was under way, and no one stopped when I asked. To make matters worse, rain began to fall. I wished to be dry and in the safety of the car with the mysterious man who drove it.

For a moment, I thought about leaving my bags on the sidewalk and falling in with the moving pedestrians. I had no reason to flee down the street, but they obviously seemed to feel they did— and that many people could not be wrong. Perhaps frozen by my increasing fear, I didn't move after all.

Then I began my walk back to the hotel where Larry and Frances had procured my reservation. There, I would meet familiar friends and retreat to a silent room. So I continued, dragging my luggage through the rain, amid the chaos. Once I entered the hotel lobby, Larry and I noted the gradual removal of emergency vehicles that had been clustered around the hotel's parking zone, that place I had been forbidden to enter.

Larry asked several policemen to explain the pandemonium I had just endured. Not one would answer his questions, or mine.

Had there been another bomb threat? Were thousands of people again in harm's way?

It had seemed like a replay of the white-hot fear that had gripped the city only days before my arrival; citizens seemed mobilized by the terror that it might all be happening again. As I and others pressed for an explanation, I shook my head in disbelief that I couldn't get answers. More important, I couldn't believe that two gigantic passenger jets had been flown into the heart of America's financial and cultural hub, and had toppled two icons of concrete, steel, and glass, each of them having risen more than a thousand feet above New York's financial district streets—all on what began as a peaceful morning on a bright fall day.

During the next seven days, I appeared nationally on the *Today* show and *The Joan Rivers Show* as well as on several television news programs broadcast only in New York and New Jersey. I talked of the heart-wrenching empathy I felt for World Trade Center survivors and their families, and I described how interacting with other Murrah survivors had gradually helped me reclaim my peace of mind.

I said nothing about the forgiveness I had extended to the Murrah bombing's perpetrators and their families. I said nothing about having traveled to see them, or inviting them into my home.

It was much too early to talk about forgiveness.

I knew that the broken survivors of the Twin Towers massacre needed hope that they could survive the devastating loss of their loved ones. Having been in their place six years earlier, I understood perfectly.

On talk shows, I primarily discussed my identification with people who struggled—feeling helpless and hopeless—following the deaths of their dearly beloved. Intensity of feeling was especially pronounced among those whose loved ones were still missing.

Although most of those survivors struggled to live, they were doing no more than merely surviving. They had no appetite for food, no ability to sleep, and all their misery was dramatized by memorial services that were under way mornings, afternoons, and evenings. And even if they did not attend the funerals, they nonetheless saw them on round-the-clock news coverage. There seemed to be no escaping a constant awareness of the magnitude of death and destruction.

No matter how many ministers preached sermons of comfort, most survivors of friends and family seemed unable to feel comforted. Instead, they struggled to continue breathing and putting one foot in front of the other as each individual stumbled in a daze, one person in seven million inside a city gripped by a toxic sense of grief and loss.

Larry took me to Ground Zero, where he and I were allowed to pass beyond the "No Trespassing" barrier. There, I stepped to the brink of a pit filled with twisted steel girders—the only parts of the wreckage that were not burning.

I felt as if I were teetering on the edge of hell. The scene was surely reminiscent of Hiroshima, where an atomic bomb ended World War II by incinerating the city.

The makeshift plywood wall surrounding the devastation was covered with photographs bearing inscriptions that begged, "Have you seen my dad?"; "Can you help find my mother?"; "Have you seen this person?"

And then there were photographs of entire families with captions stating that one person was missing and pleading for information on the missing person's whereabouts. So many people were searching, searching so their family circles would not remain broken.

I thought I would suffocate in the sorrow.

I recalled Mother Teresa's comment when she was in Calcutta with dying babies.

"What will you do with so many babies?" a reporter asked her.

"Give them to me," she replied. "I will take care of them one at a time."

I was no Mother Teresa, of course. But I relished the opportunity to hug and to hold desperate survivors. There is something to be said for sorrowful, sincere embraces, as people of like minds feel their hearts beating against one another's.

I gave those distraught and precious people my love, my words, and my prayers as I shared my faith. I regretted that I could not offer them instant comfort, as they would have preferred. There is no quick remedy when you lose a loved one.

I confess I often felt totally inadequate in trying to ease anyone's sorrow. So I turned to God for His wisdom, but it didn't come. And I wondered if the human ravages of this demonic event were even too repulsive for Him. This thought was a bit crazy, I know. But many thoughts are when you don't know what to think—or even how.

I then went with Larry to FTC's improvised kitchen and sleeping quarters that he had set up for firemen. Larry had personally arranged procurement of the premises—a temporary home to hundreds of arriving and departing firefighters. They ate, showered, and slept in their home away from home, a secret respite where they could recharge a bit before returning to their seemingly endless task at Ground Zero. People begged them to find their loved ones. Three hundred forty-three firefighters were among the lost.

I had heard about Larry's tireless work at rescue sites, but I had never seen firsthand just how he is a man in perpetual motion—he almost literally never stops to rest.

I later learned he had made an unofficial deal with a New York City policeman to get FTC trucks directly beside Ground Zero. Larry arrived with four long-haul trucks filled with food and water. He asked firemen what else they needed, and their requirements included boots with steel toes and heavy-duty gloves.

Within a day, Larry, who had contacts with manufacturers, produced gloves and shoes in bulk. Being aware of the added efffectiveness of diamond saw blades when cutting steel, Larry again got on the telephone, and the saw blades appeared within hours.

Larry Jones proved himself to be an unparalleled master of extremely practical emergency response where there otherwise would not have been any—at least not that rapidly.

His rescue and relief efforts were not sanctioned by any government agency or organization's board of directors. There was no time for "taking issues under advisement" while firemen were literally falling on their faces from heat and exhaustion.

I didn't criticize Larry's unofficial, secret pact with a cop. I applauded it, as FTC trucks subsequently arrived at the disaster only four hours after the second tower toppled. Other rescue organizations were conspicuously tardy when compared to Feed The Children.

~

There's power in numbers.

The magnitude of human agony was concentrated in a standing-room-only gathering at the Glory Zone Church, a suffering congregation situated in Long Island, New York—past and present home to thousands of NYC firemen and their families. Inside the rubble of the World Trade Center, many local firemen were missing or dead. Many grieving family members were wishing they were dead as well.

I was asked to speak to those emotionally shattered survivors on the second Sunday after September 11, 2001. My arrival had been postponed by the air travel moratorium levied immediately after the Twin Towers toppled. Parishioners at Glory Zone understood. Their own lives had not merely been disrupted, they had been utterly devastated—and to a degree that many of them thought was beyond repair.

The church members showered me with a rainbow of expressions of warm hospitality. They were a widely diverse, multicultural group, and yet they all shared one question in common: How would they ever recover from the wounds in their hearts caused by such overwhelming loss?

As I stood before their helpless faces, I could offer no quick-fix answer. There wasn't one. But I could share the process that worked for me—someone whose emotional healing was, after six years, still a work in progress.

And yet all my senses again told me not to share the deliverance I'd found through forgiveness of my enemies, specifically Nichols.

That message would be too much too soon for these fractured people.

The fires of rage toward Osama bin Laden and al-Qaeda—the self-proclaimed perpetrators of the WTC terrorism—were burning inside mourners' hearts as intensely as combustible jet fuel igniting fires that caused the Twin Towers to collapse.

Forgiveness comes in its own time, an interval needed for God to miraculously soften the heart of the giver and the defenses of the receiver. For someone to claim forgiveness toward mass murderers without first allowing time for God's healing would be, at best, self-deception and lip service. Many of the torn souls before me at that time frankly felt outrage toward God. They did not want to ask Him for help to forgive the guilty. They sought God for nothing except an explanation of how He could allow such an outrageous horror to take place.

"God, just where were You on the cloudless morning of 9/11?" many had brazenly asked aloud.

Through mass media and face-to-face dialogues with survivors, I had heard other impolite queries to the Almighty, including, "God, just where was Your protective Holy Spirit?"; "God, why would a Christian nation lose to a satanic stronghold?"; "God, You said You were going to be with us at all times. What good is Your presence if You don't protect us?"

Were I to return to that church today, nearly thirteen years after the bloodiest act of terrorism ever inflicted on the United States, I would talk about the blessed and dramatic peace given to me by a God who's all about forgiveness. After all, He, too, lost a Son—under different circumstances, of course. God's loss was premeditated by Him, for all humankind, before His beloved Son, Jesus, died on the cross.

Today, I would tell the congregation that my mustering of forgiveness surprised me more than anyone and did not come without

God's intervention. But it came as my own mercy extended to men who did despicable things. And it resulted in tranquillity for them and joy for me.

Today, I would explain that my forgiveness may not have extended any of the forgivens' lives, but it most definitely saved my own. Otherwise, I would have succumbed to the emotional cancer of hating people whose dastardly deeds I could not undo, and the consequences of which I could not erase. The hatred and frustration combined to form a poisonous cocktail sure to cause a fatality: my own.

At Glory Zone Church, I silently prayed that the Holy Spirit would enable me to know just what to say—as well as what not to say—to these desperate people who had spent almost two weeks with their lives on hold.

Now, those same exhausted people were going to hear me, someone they had never before personally seen or heard, a transplant from the heartland where terrorists had not flown jets into highrise buildings to eventually leave nearly three thousand dead and more than six thousand wounded. While the act of terrorism that took down the Murrah Building was heinous, this one, in terms of raw numbers, was many, many times worse.

What does this woman have in common with us? This seemed to be the unspoken question on most faces in that congregation. *How can she help us? No one else has been able to.*

Having prepared nothing formal, even I was eager to hear what I would say. My first words to the grieving involved my truthful declaration that I had no answers.

"But I know who does," I said, advocating my God to everyone. "Six and one-half years ago, I didn't know it would be possible to recover from such a mortal wound," I said.

I could see the New York audience was listening. More important, I could *feel* that they were.

I gave details about the Murrah bombing, and how I, like them, knew the misery of walking amid a mountain of shaky rubble while searching for loved ones. But, unlike those in the Twin Towers, my fallen people were not robust and gallant men. They were not independent, driven women with careers.

"They were grandbabies, ages two and three," I said.

A faint gasp floated across the hushed gathering.

I was now thinking out loud, imparting a saga with a story line I could recite by heart. And that's how I spoke—heart to heart—to the suddenly rapt attention of the assembly.

I touched on returning to my house on April 19, 1995, when I saw toys and breakfast food just as they were when Chase and Colton were earlier taken to the Murrah nursery, never to return. I confessed my intense inclinations toward suicide only days after the toddlers' funeral. I sensed common thoughts of self-destruction among a few startled faces. I shared my gnawing, nonstop frustration with the unfairness of it all.

"Glenn, my late husband, would see parents of surviving children on television and would hear them say they had prayed to God to spare their child and He had," I told the audience. "Glenn would be furious because God hadn't spared *our* grandchildren. Why hadn't He?"

I could see that some people were pondering the stark inequities of a real tragedy.

To those whose faces seemed etched with skepticism about God's existence, my words began to involuntarily proclaim the reality of an omnipotent being, even when He seemed distant or inactive. I likened His presence to the wind, something I had never seen but had often felt.

I recited numerous Bible verses taught to me in childhood. And I mentioned how they had felt empty and meaningless to me when at first I was trying to deal with my sense of loss.

As the gathering remained attentive, I began to recall my post-bombing inability to enter grocery stores. There, I would see mothers and grandmothers pushing youngsters inside shopping carts. I had once done that same thing. I thought I never would again.

The little things often carried the biggest sting, I explained to the aching people.

While speaking, I was confronting the presence of overpowering grief, and I felt kinship with the wounded parishioners who wept without restraint. The mood was thick, like summertime humidity before an Oklahoma thunderstorm. I caught myself monitoring my breathing. It was punctuated by soft sobs.

I did not know even one of the listeners. I felt for all of them. Personal loss had become our common denominator, our unbreakable bond.

As I wound down, those precious and loving people, despite their own travails, applauded my closing words. "Today, as I look out on this sea of broken hearts, I know that my words cannot ease your pain. That is not important. What is important, and the reason that I am here with you, is that, as one who has suffered in the same way, I can tell you that your loving Father did not take your loved ones. He simply received them when they came. I want you to know that in the days and weeks ahead, He will renew your spirit and bring you peace." I felt their love, and, for a few moments, I basked in it.

My departure from Glory Zone was stop-and-go, as more people I had never seen before, and would never see again, took time to embrace me. They told me how my presence had blessed them, with no idea that I felt the same, in reverse. Sincerity shone through their glistening eyes, and I know they spoke the truth.

Unavoidably, I thought about another childhood Bible verse, one asserting that Christ's followers will know the truth, and the truth will set them free. Inside that church, where truth was spoken, many listeners were set free of torment, if only for a few minutes.

The fact that they had caught a glimpse of the light of relief suggested that, in time, the light would become brighter. Now I am sure no one left that church having overcome pain. But they did leave with slightly raised hopes that someday the pain would be less intense, and come less often.

As I flew out of New York a few miles from Manhattan, I could still see a tiny thread of smoke trickling from embers still burning at the WTC. The cloud was markedly reduced from the billows I had witnessed on the day I arrived.

The fires ignited by the terrorists' hatred were, in fact, dimming in reverse proportion to the rise of the survivors' hopes. Their lives would go forward one delicate step at a time—like walking on the ruins of a burned-out building that would someday rise again.

Chapter Twenty-Three

❦

Like most Americans, I was enthralled by the resilient New Yorkers' obsession to rebuild their once thriving city. Even while grieving, they attacked the towering mountain of rubble that had been the World Trade Center and eventually resolved to build a monument that became an architecturally stunning and wonderful commemoration to the fallen.

I underwent a giant step forward in the reconstruction of my own emotional wreckage that resulted from the terrorist act that had destroyed the Murrah Building, my grandchildren, and the lives of many others in Oklahoma City six years earlier.

Glenn had been dead for five years, and I discovered that loneliness is cumulative—the sense of it becomes stronger year after year. By 2002, I was lonely to the bone.

Dale Phillips, a member of the Oklahoma City Bombing Investigation Committee, was in business with Tom Sanders, a Little Rock, Arkansas, financial planner whom I had never met. Phillips insisted that I accept a telephone introduction to Tom.

I was not looking for anyone to play matchmaker for me. I didn't like blind dates. But a telephone chat couldn't hurt, I reasoned. Besides, Dale and I had worked closely on post-Murrah issues, and I felt I owed him the courtesy of granting his request. Reluctantly, I took a call from Tom.

Even from the sound of his baritone voice, I decided he was a classy guy. He said he was coming to Oklahoma City for a board meeting the following week. He asked if I would have dinner with him. I accepted.

As the date approached, I decided I did not want to chance a relationship with someone living 345 miles away from me. On the day of my first scheduled date with Tom, Edye asked me to babysit my grandson Glenn, and I consented.

Over the phone I told Tom why I could not meet him, and he graciously offered to let me take Glenn to dinner with us. I refused and had no reason to think I would ever hear from Tom again. After all, I had canceled a few minutes after he had driven from Little Rock all the way to Oklahoma City, although, as I said, his primary incentive was to attend a board meeting.

Nonetheless, my last-minute cancellation was rude, and I knew it.

The next day, Tom sent me a sweet e-mail. He complimented me for putting my grandson first and thanked me for taking time to visit with him.

Between the lines, the e-mail communicated that he knew I had brushed him off. And still he complimented me?

How great is *this guy?* I thought.

I felt like a total witch.

I apologized, and I told Tom I would see him if he ever returned to Oklahoma City. (I knew he would be back. He had business here.)

Tom returned to Oklahoma City the next weekend—and it was not for a business meeting. I deduced a lot from that. I told Tom upon his arrival at my house that he could pull into the driveway. I would admit him through the garage.

Why did I do that instead of receiving him through the front door? He probably thought his visit was unimportant to me. To this day, I often admit guests through the garage. I don't know why.

Understand: at this point I still had never seen Tom in person, and he hadn't seen me. He stood in my driveway when I raised the garage door, and it was like the raising of a curtain for a theatrical production.

I liked what I saw. He looked the way he sounded—dignified. Is it possible to look brilliant? If so, he had that appearance, too.

We went to dinner, and on our first date I asked him if we could share one meal. He teases me to this day about it. He says that I was a cheap date and that sealed the deal for him. Besides not being hungry, I did not want to take advantage of him.

In a short time, our relationship took a romantic turn.

But then I broke up with him.

"I'm sorry, but you live so far away from Oklahoma City where my daughter and grandson live," I told Tom. "I don't want to be in a long-distance relationship."

Then I cried about my stupid decision for a week. Love, after all, does not always respect geography.

Tom, a bachelor of twenty years, didn't give up. He convinced me that we would make it work. He owned a condominium in Oklahoma City that he had bought earlier for his mother. She no longer lived there due to her declining health. He said he would keep it for me to stay in and that I could go back to Oklahoma from Arkansas to visit my grandchildren any time I wanted.

I resumed seeing Tom Sanders and married him one year later. He was a blessing I was not expecting. He accepted me for who I was and, just as important, for what I was.

Tom and I had been totally candid during our courtship. He knew, for example, about my obsessive mission to discover what *really* happened before and during the Oklahoma City Bombing. He was aware that I had befriended and forgiven Nichols, the convicted murderer who, I was sure, would one day tell me everything about Oklahoma's killing field.

I even told Tom I had once been seriously suicidal.

He knew I intermittently sat up late to watch a home movie of

Chase and Colton as they played with Edye. He knew that sometimes, when I least expected it, I cried myself to sleep.

How many women with baggage like that are accepted into a
storybook marriage? How many men would grant the acceptance?

Tom Sanders was my godsend.

✄

My transparency with Tom also included his knowing about Nichols and me exchanging letters and our secret telephone conversations. He knew that besides my hoping that Nichols would confess
everything about Murrah, I was also offering true friendship to the
lifetime inmate.

Nichols was languishing in solitary confinement with no chance
of pardon or parole. I felt sorry for him. I never knew when Nichols
might phone me while incarcerated in Oklahoma, I told Tom. But I
always took his calls, I added.

On March 1, 2004, jury selection began for Nichols's second trial,
this one in Oklahoma. Jurors would hear evidence regarding 161
counts of murder.

I entered the district courtroom of Judge Steven W. Taylor
in McAlester, Pittsburg County, Oklahoma. A change of venue
had been granted at the request of Nichols's lawyer, who said his
client could not get a fair trial in Oklahoma City due to pretrial
publicity.

The venue change did not bother me, but it seemed like a dumb
idea. Nichols's pretrial publicity had saturated the national and
international media. An impartial jury could not have been found
in McAlester or anywhere else in the continental United States, I
believed. So why look for one in Oklahoma?

Nichols conspicuously waved at me from the defense table at the
pretrial hearings in Oklahoma City.

"Hi, Kathy," Nichols had mouthed silently.

I was taken by surprise. There was nothing subtle about his

greeting, particularly when he continued to pantomime sentence after sentence, only some of which I understood.

Then came the sentence that almost knocked me off the spectator's bench.

Nichols said he wanted me to visit him.

I think I paused, and I prayed no one heard his request.

He wants to visit with me? I pondered.

"How am I going to do that?" I asked him, while pantomiming myself.

"Through them," he mouthed, pointing to his defense team.

I slowly turned my head to see if anyone had noticed our silent dialogue. Virtually every eye in the courtroom had turned my way.

Total strangers were eyeing me with hostile curiosity. Nichols was staring at me to see if I would resume our dialogue.

I was embarrassed.

The discomfort ended when the judge entered the courtroom and banged the gavel to begin the hearing.

The instant that day's testimony ended, I all but ran to my car, hoping to avoid confrontations with reporters. My attempt at escape was futile. I was quickly surrounded and bombarded with questions about my conversation with Nichols.

"No comment," I said. "I have nothing to say regarding Terry Nichols." The journalists continued to pry and directly asked about my relationship with the defendant.

"No comment!" I said repeatedly.

A reporter from the *Daily Oklahoman*, the state's largest newspaper published in Oklahoma City where I lived, was especially aggressive. His query even seemed to carry a veiled threat.

Uninvited, he walked beside me toward my car. My pace did not diminish.

"Look, Kathy," he said, "you better tell me what's going on with you and Terry Nichols. It's not going to look good when the families

232   KATHY SANDERS

[of other victims] pick up their morning papers and see that you and Terry are friendly."

"I've been investigating the bombing for years," I replied curtly. I told the reporter that I was willing to walk through fire to get to the truth, and who would know more truth than Nichols?

"Has he told you anything?" the reporter asked.

"I don't want to talk about it," I responded.

"Well, can you tell me how you correspond? Have you been to see Nichols?" he asked.

"We write," I said.

Instantly, I had reservations about what I had just said.

Will my words wind up in tomorrow morning's newspapers? I wondered. *What will people think of me?*

I soon felt sorry for Nichols again, this time for something comparatively insignificant. He continued to wear the same shirt he had worn to his federal trial and to his pretrial hearings for his state trial. I felt sorry for him and hated to see him wear the same garment to yet another trial.

So I bought him two new shirts. I gave them to Nichols's lawyer, who promised he would not divulge the giver.

There I was, regularly attending the pretrial proceedings for Nichols's second murder trial. Earlier, I had been writing him. I sent him a cassette player and now I was dressing him.

What in the world would people think? I asked myself. Little did I know that question would resurface for years to come.

On May 26, 2004, Nichols's Oklahoma trial ended after his conviction on 161 charges of first-degree murder. He'd been found guilty on each. The jury deadlocked on the death penalty.

The controversial defendant was remanded to federal custody and sent to Federal Supermax Prison in Florence, Colorado.

More than ever, I urged Nichols to go public about what really happened the day of the Oklahoma City Bombing and to tell what he knew about the others who were involved. I reminded him that his story could be a deterrent to young people who might otherwise pursue a criminal life like his.

As a favor to my cause and to me, Tom had asked Jay Bradford, a former Arkansas state senator and close friend of former President Bill Clinton, to see if he could cut through the red tape of the prison system so I could arrange an interview with Nichols. I had been trying for months to get in to see him, but I had a problem.

In order for anyone to interview a prisoner at ADX, he or she had to have known the inmate before he committed the relevant crimes. I had not known Nichols then. It didn't matter to prison officials that I had visited with him numerous times while he was in state custody.

I also contacted Michael Radutzky, senior producer for *60 Minutes*, America's premier program of investigative journalism, and explained my dilemma. *60 Minutes* wanted the story and agreed to help.

Ed Bradley, arguably America's foremost television journalist who appeared regularly on *60 Minutes*, was assigned the story.

My struggle to pair Nichols with the broadcast powerhouse became a running battle between the federal prison system and the CBS television network.

Tom was with me every step of the way as we waded through the quagmire of penal system bureaucracy that eventually suppressed the truth about Nichols and the bombing.

Later, in a letter from Nichols dated June 15, 2005, I learned that a part of the prison system's lack of cooperation lay in Nichols himself:

Dear Kathy,

...I believe the BOP [Bureau of Prisons], as instructed by the DOJ [Department of Justice], is not going to allow any type of media interview by anyone until at least they get the information from me

*which they [DOJ] want—which I have refused to divulge to them.
So, until I do, I don't see any interview happening.*

*In fact the FBI even dragged me up to Denver on June 9th against
my will and put me in front of a Grand Jury to try to extract the
information from me. They tried to use the Grand Jurors to intimi-
date me by bringing me before them and thus tried to use this pressure tactic to get me to talk.*

*But I did not because as I told the [DOJ] prosecutor and jurors
that this was NOT the proper forum to do so because of the inherent problem that exists with the FBI and DOJ. Plus I questioned the
validity of using a Grand Jury in Colorado rather than one in Oklahoma where the bombing occurred. It didn't seem right to me.*

*I did not take the 5th. And I told them I wouldn't, but rather I sim-
ply told them that it's not the proper forum and that I would simply
wait for an independent Congressional hearing and investigation.
The prosecutors didn't like this.*

That short, verbal bombshell was casually dropped in Nichols's
letter between offering his best wishes for the healing of my grandson's appendicitis and his expression of happiness over recently
chatting with his mother.

The results of Tom's and my tireless work seemed to instantly
evaporate. To say I was disappointed that Nichols did not cooperate
with the grand jury is a giant understatement; rather, it was perhaps my biggest disappointment so far, in all my years spent searching for the truth.

But I did not give up. How would I get into the prison to do the
interview? Prison officials had consistently denied each of my previous requests to see Nichols.

Working with CBS provided an adventure for me.

Working journalists were often allowed to interview an ADX
Florence prisoner. So I approached prison officials again, this time

as a *journalist*. I met the prison's guidelines as a special correspondent for *60 Minutes*.

60 Minutes has a rule that prohibits anyone other than their regular correspondents from doing interviews. Because Terry Nichols refused to talk with anyone but me, they made a special exception. And the CBS legal department agreed to take on the prison system. I thought, *Surely, this is it!*

My request for permission to enter ADX Florence prison to interview Nichols was met with the following reply:

Dear Ms. Sanders,

This is in response to your correspondence in which you request permission to meet with inmate Terry Nichols.

The Bureau of Prisons makes every effort to accommodate media personnel as long as the request does not negatively affect the security and operation of our institutions. It is my determination based on my sound correctional judgment, that to grant your request at this time could pose a risk to the internal security of this institution and to the safety of staff, inmates and members of the public. Therefore, your request has been denied and you will not be permitted to meet with inmate Nichols at this time.

Robert A. Hood
Warden

"...risk to the internal security of this institution and to the safety of staff, inmates and members of the public"?

This particular maximum-security prison housed the worst of the worst, including Ramzi Yousef, mastermind of the first World Trade Center bombing; Ted Kaczynski, the "Unabomber"; and former inmate Timothy McVeigh as well.

And yet I, a housewife from Little Rock, Arkansas, someone who had visited Nichols before, someone with no criminal record, might suddenly pose a security threat to the staff and inmates? Just how might I do that? Beat them with measuring spoons?

How would I endanger "members of the public"? The public wasn't inside the prison. The public was locked outside!

I did not have the wisdom of Socrates, but I did not need it to suspect that the federal government's fingerprints were all over my rejection letter. Why would the prison care who Nichols talked to?

After all, *60 Minutes* had already aired an interview with McVeigh when he was incarcerated at this very prison.

But I, a surrogate Betty Crocker, couldn't interview the tiny and timid Nichols?

What a joke—an *unfunny* joke!

I had been communicating with Nichols for ten years. Why was I not seen as a problem during all that time? Clearly, the prison's decision to deny my interview had come from higher up.

Somewhere, some agency with power wanted to keep Nichols quiet. Perhaps Nichols's interview would explain why the Oklahoma City bomb squad was downtown the morning of the bombing before the bomb went off. Did they have prior warning? ATF agents were brought in from around the country before the bombing. ATF officials admitted to me that they were working on a sting operation the night before the bombing. But they would never admit that the Murrah Building was their sting's objective.

Why had the hunt for John Doe II been called off when twenty-two eyewitnesses saw McVeigh downtown, accompanied by another man, the morning of the bombing? Not one witness said they saw McVeigh alone.

Earlier, in the courtroom, I had listened as FBI agents admitted they never ran fingerprints recovered from McVeigh's car. They said it was not cost-effective. Really? The federal government spent $82.5 million investigating and prosecuting McVeigh and Nichols.

The cost of processing fingerprints would have been markedly minor by comparison.

What were they hiding? Could identifying additional John Does and their fingerprints reveal the identity of government agents who were involved in the failed sting operation?

The *60 Minutes* lawyers repeatedly contested the prison's virtual gag order against the news organization, and now me. They sent letters to Warden Hood, and they initiated other procedures that I was not privy to.

Meanwhile, I continued to pray that God would let the interview happen. Nichols wanted to come clean by finally revealing the truth. Surely God wanted the same thing, I reasoned.

So, together with *60 Minutes* producers and lawyers, I resumed submitting interview requests to Warden Hood. Each was denied.

Chapter Twenty-Four

A strong "grapevine" prevails inside prisons. The word was out that inmate Terry Nichols wanted to rip the lid off the Murrah bombing and who, including himself, was involved and why.

Inside the walls, Nichols had gotten feedback implying his life was in danger. His self-imposed pressure to do the *60 Minutes* interview was mounting. More than ever, he wanted to do it soon.

In October 2006, Nichols called me unexpectedly while Tom, Jay Bradford, and I were riding in Tom's car. I knew it was Nichols by the caller ID. This time, Nichols insisted he wanted to do the interview *now*, with or without prison approval.

"Tom, it's Terry," I said to my husband, who was sitting behind the wheel.

Of course, Jay knew about my peculiar friendship with Nichols. But now the former senator was sitting three feet away as I talked to the high-profile prisoner. I was uneasy. While Tom and Jay could not hear Nichols on the other end of the telephone line, I sensed that they were hanging on my every word.

Both were respectfully quiet, but I could feel their tension. I had never previously talked to Nichols in front of anybody, including Tom. It felt painfully awkward.

When I announced who was calling, Tom had abruptly veered our car to the shoulder of the road and turned off the ignition to reduce road noise so I could hear. Nichols was surrounded by thick walls of steel and concrete nestled in the foothills of the Rocky

Mountains. Depending on the weather, and reception, cell phone transmission was sometimes spotty.

After we had exchanged a few pleasantries, Nichols blurted the words Tom and I had been waiting all year to hear:

"Kathy, we can't afford to waste any more time. Who knows what might happen to me. Let's make this interview happen! If they won't let you inside the prison to see me, let's do it by phone," Nichols said to me. "I'll tell you everything!"

Nichols had given the green light to his full disclosure about the Murrah bombing's planning and implementation, all to be broadcast from Maine to California. He had just sanctioned everything I had pursued for years, traveling thousands of miles to interview a dozen people and more. I was sure Tom's and my recent work would now enable Americans to learn what really happened on that fateful day. People would hear why the bombing planners did what they did, and exactly who helped them. Nichols was going to reveal the motives behind the madness. Via news networks, the world was about to know what really happened and who was involved!

My heart was racing. I wanted to rejoice, but knew I had to remain calm.

Nichols seemed excited to a degree I had never seen or heard from him. I was convinced he truly intended to give a full disclosure, trusting his newfound faith to see him through whatever was in store for him.

His vow to tell the whole truth to the world was already setting me free from the agony of unanswered questions, those lingering mysteries that had plagued me since 1995.

I wanted to shout praise to God aloud for what Nichols was promising.

Instead, I remained low-key and methodical, mindful of the need to keep him calm.

Nichols knew that I had met Ed Bradley. He also knew I had been engaged in an ongoing dialogue with *60 Minutes* producers. Perhaps that was the reason he finally decided to come forward, or maybe the Spirit moved him, or perhaps the Spirit was working in all of us.

I told him I would tell the *60 Minutes* people about his long-awaited decision. He was happy with that.

And so—an unexpected and matter-of-fact telephone call by the side of an Arkansas road was going to change the world, I thought to myself. Nichols's story might finally implicate some other people. They might finally be arrested and tried.

Before the telephone conversation ended, Nichols and I chatted about insignificant matters. Then, as he was easing into his farewell, I braced myself to say what I wanted to say.

"I love you, Terry," I said.

"I love you, too, Kathy," Nichols answered.

Unavoidably, I felt embarrassed. The car seemed to become pressurized in a way I could feel. The one-time Arkansas senator remained completely silent, except for what might have been a gulp. As soon as Nichols was off the telephone, I began to explain our conversation.

I told Tom and Jay that Nichols wanted to get the interview done—now.

Since he and I couldn't get clearance to do it live, we would do it by phone, using Nichols's monthly allotment of two fifteen-minute phone calls. We would record the phone calls back-to-back.

Nichols had set the date for November 9, 2006.

On that day, the world would hear the rest of the story about the Murrah bombing. Nichols had said so.

꒰

The day after my excited call from Nichols, I resumed my coordination efforts with CBS and the *60 Minutes* production team.

Months earlier, Nichols had made it clear he did not trust his story to anyone but me.

He was afraid that a direct interrogation by Bradley "might make him look bad."

For lack of a better word, I was amused.

Nichols was serving life without parole after multiple convictions for murder. His name and face had been plastered across print and broadcast media around the world. But he did not want to be made to *look bad*? At this point, was it possible for anyone to make him look worse?

60 Minutes wanted the story so badly that they agreed to let me do the interview. I would interview Nichols, and then Ed Bradley would interview me, as I said earlier. That procedure was unprecedented in *60 Minutes* history. To me, the plan showed how passionately producers wanted this interview with Nichols. They thought it would be the story of the decade. So did I. Think of it: a surviving *victim* of a horrific crime interviewing one of the perpetrators! High ratings surely *had* to lurk in that scenario.

After a point, someone inside the prison apparently began to manipulate my mail to Nichols. My letters were regularly and mysteriously "lost."

Once Nichols and I were certain someone routinely tampered with our mail, we devised a scheme.

We would begin each letter with the following statement: "I received your letter dated 'such and such' on 'such and such' date." I wrote this to Nichols, and he to me. We could thereafter determine which letters were missing.

I wrote to Nichols and said I would resend my last three letters. I sent a copy of each by regular and by certified mail.

The certified letters would provide a "record" of the prison's having received the letters, including those not forwarded to Nichols.

Tampering with U.S. mail is a felony, even among prison officials. After I began following the regular mail/certified mail procedures, my letters to Nichols were suddenly delivered to Nichols in a timely manner.

Nichols was very guarded as to what he said in his letters because he knew they were read by prison officials. He was scared he'd be killed if they knew what he intended to reveal to *60 Minutes* and to me. Our phone calls were also monitored, we felt.

Brian Hermanson, Nichols's attorney, wanted this incredible interview to happen. He did everything in his power to help.

Prison policy allowed Nichols to call Hermanson frequently. Before each call, the attorney notified me. I then told Hermanson what to relay and what to ask his client. Nichols responded to Hermanson, who in turn communicated the prisoner's messages to me.

The three of us were persistent in nonstop scheming about how to make this blockbuster interview a reality. Through it all, Nichols and I were bonding to an unprecedented degree. The man who had always been so secretive about the details of his criminal escapades was now systematically collaborating to make them public. Nichols and I had a common cause: we both wanted to expose the truth.

In our hearts, we were confident that, with CBS's help, this interview would take place. Nichols even went so far as to ask me to prepare a list of questions I intended to pose on national television once the permissions and logistics had finally been arranged. Our plan called for me to give the list to Hermanson, who would, in turn, give it to his client.

I began crafting the following interview questions:

- Are you going to tell the truth?
- You and I would have never met if my grandchildren had not died in the Oklahoma City Bombing. How would you like me to remember you?
- Why have you waited so long to come forward with the truth?

- Eldon Elliott, owner of Elliott's Body Shop, and two of his employees testified that Timothy McVeigh was accompanied by a man when he came to rent the Ryder truck (used to haul the fatal bomb). Do you know the identity of that man?
- Why do you think everyone involved in the crime was not prosecuted?
- Do you believe people inside government agencies participated in or knew about the bomb before it was detonated?
- Is there a Middle Eastern connection to the Oklahoma City Bombing?

These are only seven of the forty-eight questions I prepared for Nichols. In all, I left no stone unturned about Nichols's and McVeigh's roles in the bombing. I also cited names of people who were implicated in various other investigations yet were never charged.

As Nichols's legal counsel, through privilege, Hermanson read my questions. He shared them with no one but Nichols.

He simply told me I was going to be "amazed" by Nichols's answers.

I had come to know the lawyer as someone who did not exaggerate.

Nichols finally became impatient with the prison's overt efforts to prohibit the interview. So he devised a plan to subvert the penal system.

Like all inmates, Nichols had to schedule his phone calls in advance. He was approved for two fifteen-minute telephone conversations with me on November 9, 2006. While prison personnel had committed to the day, none would commit to the requested hour.

I called *60 Minutes* and spoke to a producer. I relayed all the previous information. I had tried for eleven years to get this interview, and *60 Minutes* had tried for a year.

Now it all seemed to be coming together in one fell swoop.

The news show's producers officially summoned me to New York regarding a pending interview with Nichols. They knew Ed Bradley was ill, and that we had been working this opportunity for a year. They did not want to postpone it any longer. Who knew if we would ever get it coordinated again?

The plan was for me to use the *60 Minutes* studio. There, by telephone, Nichols would talk to me under prison officials' noses! Then, at a later date, Ed Bradley would interview me about my interview with Nichols.

I boiled with my excitement. Rushes of adrenaline felt like fire in my veins. I had spent untold sleepless nights mourning the losses of Chase and Colton. And now I couldn't sleep due to runaway feelings of anticipation.

The little silver lining on my cloud of human loss was finally going to glisten. Just as I'd always been told, there really is a God, and He really does move.

But not until *He's* ready.

Brimming with excitement, Tom and I arrived in New York City on November 9, 2006. During previous visits to America's largest metropolis, I had felt a bit overwhelmed by confusion at the airport and the logistical nightmares of trying to negotiate my way in the city. This time, I was oblivious to all of it. Instead, I just pushed through the congestion while yearning to get to CBS and to hear Nichols's answers.

After hailing a cab, Tom and I sped from the airport in Newark, New Jersey, to the network's studios on West Fifty-seventh Street in Manhattan. The cabdriver picked up on our sense of urgency and really put the hammer down, so to speak. But I wasn't scared. Sheer excitement about reaching my destination numbed my fear.

Upon arriving, Tom and I signed in and plopped down in a waiting room. For the first time since leaving Little Rock that morning,

I was not in motion. But my head did not feel that way. My world was spinning fast and I could not get off. And I did not want to.

While awaiting *60 Minutes* senior producer Mike Radutzky, Tom and I saw reporter Lesley Stahl as she walked toward the ladies' room. Big deal, eh? Actually, it was to me. I was admiring Ms. Stahl—and anyone else who was remotely a part of the news organization that was going to help me answer the haunting questions behind the Oklahoma City Bombing.

Employees were gathered at the front desk laughing. It seemed that Mike Wallace, a legend in his own time, had been sitting behind the CBS telephone switchboard taking calls, as if he were the receptionist. Someone said the actual receptionist could not be found, so Wallace walked from his office to her seat and fielded random incoming calls himself!

Imagine the callers' surprise when they dialed a listed number answered by Wallace's unmistakable voice.

Soon, Tom and I were approached by Radutzky, who led us to his messy office. Radutzky had to literally push piles of paper off his couch to make room for Tom and me to sit. The room looked like an indoor landfill. I loved it.

My eagerness to see Ed Bradley again was percolating. I had not seen him since an earlier show done with Murrah survivors, including me. How many times had I watched him bust corrupt politicians and underhanded officials on national TV? He was a champion of the First Amendment.

Bradley was a handsome man who looked incredibly trustworthy. And I was excited to work directly with that celebrated journalist! I longed to thank him for taking an interest in my probe of the bombing and the principal players behind it.

Yet he had no idea that I had been host to them in my home, or that I had visited them in theirs.

I felt this telecast was a miracle in the making, a God-thing. I yearned to thank God aloud, but I did not want to scare Radutzky.

He obviously had a lot on his mind, and I was about to hear why.

Ed Bradley was very ill, the producer said.

I could feel my sprits sinking, and Radutzky must have discerned it.

Quickly, he seemed to rush to restore my morale, and said the Nichols story would be shot today, as it had been too long in the planning, and no one wanted to start over. If Bradley could not do the story, then Katie Couric would, Radutzky said.

I wondered if she would remember our first interview on a windy rooftop the day after the bombing, or our second interview on the five-year anniversary of the explosion.

Any lull in my mood was lifted when Radutzky and I began evaluating my questions for Nichols. The senior producer initiated a crash course on how I should steer the interview, how I should not allow Nichols to go off track or to linger on any one subject.

No one in the studios knew when Nichols would call, just that he would call today.

Nichols had been unable to specify the time of our interview, as he had to wait for the prison officials to bring the telephone to his cell. As the day ebbed along, the stress among the technicians, cast, and crew rose slowly but palpably. They went about their various tasks like the professionals they were, including the adjustment of the lighting around a "sit-in"—a man sitting in my assigned chair.

I received facial highlights from a studio makeup artist, and someone else dabbled with my hair. I simultaneously felt special and out of place. All of this behind-the-scenes activity seemed a bit dramatic to me. I would have enjoyed it to the maximum had I not been stressing about a call from Nichols, awaiting a conversation that would be recorded in one take.

The arrangement did not allow for mistakes. I had not felt this type of pressure since my time at the white supremacy compound in Idaho.

What if Nichols doesn't call? I asked myself. I'd sparked all of this activity among all of these important people. And I was depending on a man who had nothing to gain but the clearing of his conscience? He once had no conscience. Would his spiritual conversion be enough to prompt him to keep his word, and to call me within the time frame he'd promised? Nichols had to be fragile, given his separation from the entire world. Now I was trusting him to speak out on the nation's most powerful television news program! Had I asked too much of him?

I was ashamed of my doubt underlying some of those thoughts. But the notions were spontaneous—and resistant to my efforts to suppress them.

Technicians altered my cellular telephone—the phone with the number Nichols had been given to call. I was then shown how to work a device that would enhance the audio quality of my interview.

Finally, there was nothing left to be done. Everyone in the studio had executed every necessary task. Nothing remained but time and creative ways to pass it.

A quiet settled over the studio as people uneasily stood at the ready, awaiting a ringing telephone that would again throw them into action performing their respective roles.

Personally, I felt like I was dressed up with no place to go. I had been told not to leave my designated studio spot, not even for a restroom break. And so I waited, and waited some more, feeling the nervous energy of a teenage girl waiting for the phone to ring.

The sound of a ringing telephone exploded into the room. It seemed louder than a fire alarm. The twenty or so CBS crew members bolted to their assigned places. With all in place, I was given the cue to answer my phone. I nervously fumbled a little, trying to press the right button.

The telephone caller was a close friend from Texas. She was calling to thank me for a painting of Mary and Jesus that I had done for her. When I told her why I could not talk, she was stunned. I told her I would call her back. For an instant, the room fell silent. Then someone chuckled and soon the whole studio broke into laughter. As it happened, Vickie's call provided a little tension relief for all of us.

Soon enough, though, Radutzky had had his fill of waiting. Sternly, he ordered an associate producer to call the prison to see if Nichols was actually going to go through with the interview. These CBS people were accustomed to rigid deadlines, and they were unaccustomed to unduly waiting on anyone. Now they were stalled by bureaucrats in a faraway prison who might be flexing their control over Nichols simply because they could. That theory was confirmed when the associate producer called the prison and asked if Nichols was going to call, and received an indefinitive answer.

I could see Radutzky's patience wearing thin. Nonetheless, he continued to wait with the rest of us—until he received notification of what must have been an emergency. He shared the news with no one, but darted from the production room.

"What will we do if Nichols calls now?" I said to no one. "Who's going to run this show?" I felt sure that *someone* was second in command—and surely he or she could do the job.

But Radutzky returned within minutes, asking Tom and me to follow him back to his office. He didn't seem to be in as big a hurry as he had been earlier while awaiting Nichols's call.

"Kathy, I have bad news," the senior producer said behind a closed door. "Ed Bradley has died."

I could see Radutzky's lips moving, but, for an instant, I did not hear his voice.

"We knew Ed was sick, but we didn't realize the severity of his illness," Radutzky continued. I think he continued talking, as I saw his lips continue to move. Perhaps he had lowered his voice, as I could no longer hear a thing.

In minutes, I would see the most esteemed people in the dispassionate world of television journalism as they really were. Despite their sometimes-jaded personalities, they had another side, a human side, as evidenced by flowing tears as they heard the news of Bradley's death.

By now it was late afternoon, and the grief-stricken broadcasters shut down the set without a call from Nichols.

I totally understood. I knew what it was like to lose family, and the 60 Minutes cast and crew clearly were family with different last names.

Tom and I expressed our prayers and condolences and left the now sad building. The day that had begun with so much promise and excitement now shifted into slow motion, replete with sadness for the loss of a great American and the loss of what might be the only opportunity for Terry Nichols to tell all. During our tranquil flight home, I thought about Bradley, specifically my experience of him when he interviewed me and some other disheartened bombing survivors. Then and there, I had seen his empathy for the emotionally wounded. I had looked forward to making another memorable recollection with Bradley. But now it was too late. He had passed from life to legend on the very day that was to happen.

Understandably, I heard from no one at 60 Minutes before Bradley's funeral or during the days afterward. I did not call anyone at CBS out of sheer consideration of their bereavement.

A few days later, I received an unexpected call at my home from Joyce Wilt, Nichols's mother.

Nichols had told Joyce to apologize to me for his not calling on the appointed day. He felt awful about it. He said that officials notified him, on the day he was to make the call, that my name had been removed from his calling list—*permanently*.

My conversations with Nichols were officially and forever terminated in 2006.

Nichols had found out about the permanent ban as he prepared to dial my phone to start the *60 Minutes* interview.

All that work by all of those CBS people, and eleven years of my life spent chasing the truth known only by Nichols, had instantly evaporated by the erasing of my name from an in-house calling list. I felt stunned, numbed, and totally defeated.

Now, how would I ever procure information that only Nichols possessed? I had proven that prison officials had censored his and my mail. I knew he could never reveal what he knew in a letter. And now I could not talk to him on the telephone!

Lost in a swirling fog of competing emotions, I suddenly felt very sentimental about my relationship with Nichols. Then, for seemingly the thousandth time since the Murrah blast, I suppressed my emotions and composed myself out of habit and determination.

I pondered what might be my next scheme to transform the very private Nichols into a public oracle of truth regarding what really happened on that fateful April morning of eleven years before.

꙳

Following Joyce's shattering announcement, we devised yet another plan. She expected Nichols to call her at her Michigan home on the following Sunday. She said if I was there, I could get my interview.

"I'll be there!" I almost shouted. "I'll be there!"

"If prison personnel want to play games with me, I'll play. I won't let them beat me," I said.

In short, in the wake of Joyce's call, I was instantly rejuvenated. I could have gone bear hunting armed with only a switch. Mine was an adrenaline *high* times ten, or so it seemed.

Joyce was willing to let me come to her home in Michigan to use her call for my purposes. The tireless people at *60 Minutes* promised to meet me at her house. I somehow felt they wanted to do this for all the right reasons, as well as a new one. They apparently were determined to commemorate Ed Bradley and the last story he never told.

This would be the second chapter from the same playbook. Only this time, Nichols would call his mother and I would answer the phone. Prison big shots would have no idea that I would be on the line. At that instant, perhaps while collaborating with Katie Couric, I would begin my questioning of Nichols as *60 Minutes* recorded the phone call.

My queries would be fast and direct. Nichols, no doubt angry about my removal from his calling list, would spew his truth with all the force and fury he could muster.

This interview could actually be better than the one planned inside the 60 Minutes *studio*, I realized.

One more chance. God surely does work in mysterious ways, but it's His show. I was ready for the next step.

Joyce had been wonderful to call me. I had lost my grandbabies to the grave, and she'd lost her son to lifetime confinement.

But there was a difference, I realized, once my euphoria began to subside.

Granted, our offspring were gone forever from our lives. And one day, I would talk to my grandchildren in heaven. But Joyce could still talk to her son by telephone now.

If I let her participate in my plot to record Nichols, the prison that took me off Nichols's calling list might remove Joyce's name as well.

How would she ever live with that? How would I live with that, knowing it was my fault?

As Sunday got closer, I became convinced that these bureaucrats, who, for reasons not yet known, denied a grieving America the truth, would certainly not hesitate to deprive a mother of talking to her son. I called Joyce, I called *60 Minutes*—I called off the entire plan.

I could not go through with the interview, and I can't to this day, not as long as Joyce is alive.

As a result of my decision, Americans have never heard Nichols speak for himself for the first time, and I have never heard his voice again. My years of passion to reveal the truth had taken me to the brink of success, only to see it undermined by my own hand. And heart.

From one mother to another, I just could not go through with it. I hope Americans understand. At times, to this day, I am not always sure I do.

During the passing of years, Joyce has suffered an intensifying battle with cancer. As of this writing, she's still alive but in failing health.

I am satisfied the Colorado warden did not take me off Nichols's calling list because I was a security risk. The very thought is laughable. He was merely following orders from someone else higher in government bureaucracy.

Of this, I'm entirely confident.

After all, nothing Nichols could have said to me and to *60 Minutes* would have impacted the prison. It would have impacted people who are still at large.

But who? And why?

I've heard the echo of these insatiable questions ever since the Murrah bombing, an event now receding into the history of the previous century. Yet, inside my heart and mind, if only as a whisper, I still hear the voices of the two little boys who once graced my life—the ones for whom I so doggedly pursued the answers—and I wonder, *What really happened?*

What *really* happened?

Chapter Twenty-Five

Someone recently asked if I'm still able to correspond with Terry Nichols since I was taken off his official call list at the ADX Florence Supermax prison. The ruling abruptly undermined the fabric of our friendship, sustained for years by telephone communication. What had taken years to build was instantly undone with a flippant stroke of someone's pen.

Earlier, during Nichols's days in the Oklahoma City jail, I spoke to him more frequently than anyone else. He had nothing to do. I routinely put whatever else I was doing on hold whenever he happened to call.

That pattern was repeated three or four times a week. These telephone conversations took place mostly during his confinement a few miles from my house. And, without telling anyone except his lawyer, I visited Nichols face-to-face on a few occasions.

Later, when my visits to Nichols were prohibited at Colorado's maximum-security prison, I received one of his two fifteen-minute calls that were allotted every month. These conversations were augmented through letters sent between us.

Nowadays, I send Nichols an annual Christmas card. When he rarely sends me a letter, I answer it.

Good or bad, nothing lasts forever, and my visits with Nichols, whether spoken or written, are now few and far between. Passing time brings people into our lives, and it eases them out.

I have often wondered what loneliness Nichols must feel, trapped inside a prison space he can never leave. I have been curious about the effect of the letters I wrote him long ago. Did they help at all? Did they really reach Nichols on the human level of an open mind and trusting heart? If not, they were written in vain.

Thankfully, my apprehensions were unfounded, as evidenced by a letter I received while preparing to write this book. It came in response to a letter I had sent Nichols, asking his permission to publish excerpts of his correspondence to me.

The emotional transparency of this letter clearly shows the trust born of our long and constant correspondence. Trust is the precursor to lasting friendship. The following excerpt shows how truly trusting Nichols had become of me through my missives. Inside the ensuing paragraphs, Nichols is totally candid about his family and his wishes. And that fulfills me. He was not always this forthright.

While living in the room where he will likely die, Nichols's interactions with outsiders are relatively few. But in me, he has a friendship that he deems reliable.

Is there any other kind? Is there any greater gift I could have given him?

March 12, 2012

Dear Kathy,

Greetings, my friend. Signing your permission form is the least I could do. I wish I could do more in some way for you and others. I hope your book does well. . . .

As for my family, if all goes well, Josh should be out of prison this October. The last incident he was involved in the judge had given Josh probation, but if [he] violated it he would serve 3 years minimum. Sadly, a week or two later he violated it by having a girl over at the house who was an ex-felon and his parole officer had stopped by and discovered it. So Josh has been in prison the past 2 years—*staying out of trouble. He's doing well and hopefully when he gets out he will make the right choices and make a better life for himself.*

Sadly, the home situation with Nicole and Christian has been quite chaotic and far worse than I was aware of. Shortly after Nicole turned 18 she moved out and is living with her boyfriend. She, hopefully, graduates this May. October of 2011 is the last time I talked with Nicole. I happened to call while she and her Mom were involved in a heated argument. My heart broke knowing I could do nothing to resolve the situation nor comfort her. I hope and pray Nicole is well and that she comes to realize that shacking up with her boyfriend is wrong and that she starts making Godly choices. Sadly, I've lost all communications with Nicole.

Christian is doing well the last I knew but that was back in September 2011 when I last talked with him. Since my conversation with Nicole in October I have not been able to get thru by phone. I don't know if Marife changed her phone # or if it was disconnected, or what. But I've had no contact now for months. I've written, but hear nothing back.

Sadly, my brother had to file bankruptcy with his trucking and excavation business due to the devastating economy in Michigan. Michigan was the hardest hit by this depression. Yes I know, the govt. calls it a recession but the facts clearly say it's a true depression. It's comparable in many ways, esp. financially, to the Great Depression of the 1930s. Even billionaire Warren Buffett says it's a depression. It's sad Les [another brother] is losing his business. He's worked so hard to build it and sacrificed so much.

My dad is doing all right but is losing his hearing and it is extremely difficult to talk with him. He also has some other health issues but it hasn't stopped him from farming. He will probably die in a tractor seat in the middle of a field. He's 86, no, 87.

Mother is 81 and surprisingly has made a full recovery from her latest bout with cancer. This makes the 3rd time she's had cancer, each a different type and location, and each time the doctor said she had only days or a few weeks to live. I was sure last Fall we would lose her but she overcame it and is doing well—health wise.

Yes, I did hear that Jannie Coverdale was looking for a part time job. I'm glad to hear she found one. I think it will be good for her. Jannie is a special person for sure. I'm glad you two stay in contact with one another.

As always, it's good to hear from you, my friend. I do understand you do have a busy life and it's not easy to find time to write. Writing takes more time than a phone call. If I could, I'd use the phone more myself rather than letters. In fact I've gotten burned out writing so much. So I do understand. Be well. And God's best to you and your loved ones. And I hope your book is a giant success.

Blessings,

Terry

As I write these words, my life is rich and busy with Tom in Little Rock, Arkansas. Between the two of us, we have six children and fifteen grandchildren (including Chase and Colton).

Edye lives in Washington, Oklahoma, with her children, Glenn (sixteen) and Emjay (eight). Edye went back to school and is now an equine dentist. We share mother/daughter secrets in person and on the telephone, and lace our communications with texts.

Danny is corporate director of Valley Health System in Bergen Country, New Jersey. He is currently completing his Director of Science degree at New Jersey City University in Jersey City, New Jersey. His daughter Caitlin is now twenty-one and is attending the University of Oklahoma.

I've studied art for the past eleven years and now have my own art studio. Scores of my paintings have been sold to collectors and aficionados.

In addition, I indulge my collection of heartfelt memories of Chase and Colton, who would have turned twenty-two and twenty-three in 2015, the twentieth anniversary of the Alfred P. Murrah Federal Building bombing.

And, now and forever, I continually have intimate times with Jesus, including silent offerings when I'm en route to somewhere, or inside the prayer closet each morning.

Those haunting, unanswered questions about the Murrah bombing present themselves less frequently. I have grown to live with the little I know, and the much that I don't know, about Murrah. The obsession for truth that once drove me to people across the nation is now little more than mild curiosity.

It's true—passing time changes everything—God's peace calms a troubled soul. I have experienced both.

After the bombing, I tolerated life before I painfully evolved to live it again. Now, I love life, and I would not want to be anyone but me.

I still feel there are others out there who were never prosecuted for the bombing and that government personnel could have stopped it. I believe that after Waco and Ruby Ridge, government agencies wanted to clean up their tarnished image and ride in like John Wayne on a big white horse and save the day. Their operation got out of hand, and that cost 168 people their lives. I am not sure I will live long enough to see it, but I pray that one day the truth will be revealed—all of it.

Over these years I've learned that time not only heals, it also sculpts. It's the constant push and pressure of everyday life that forms character ever so slowly—so slowly that we do not even notice it happening.

My life was overturned by the bombing, an event beyond my control. Now my life is divided into before and after. I live in the after, but I am a product of the before.

This lesson was among my final ones as I wound down my interactions with Nichols, my bombing-related investigations, and the recurrent tribulations I felt during those emotionally packed years after Murrah.

A few years ago I slipped away to visit my cousin in another state.

While en route by air, the captain authorized the reclining of passengers' seats. Traveling at 500 mph, 30,000 feet above the ground, I closed my eyes and absorbed the hypnotic purr of tandem jet engines. Seconds earlier, I had gazed down on billowing clouds that looked like cushions of cotton, blocking my sight of the earth and its stressful demands.

I drifted off into pleasant dreams, none of which were as soothing as reality in the moment.

K-a-b-o-o-m!

I was shaken from slumber by a loud explosion. My surprise made it seem all the louder and more violent. During that split second between sleep and awareness, my mind raced back to the Murrah explosion. As my eyes focused, I noticed a letter in my lap that I had been reading before dozing off. The return address belonged to Nichols at the Florence, Colorado, prison.

Over the airplane's audio system, the pilot announced that we had lost an engine.

The captain's voice returned, offering reassurance. His voice was even and measured as he repeated the words I knew he had been trained to say. A ripple of fear spread through the cabin. As some of us began to pray quietly, others began chatting nervously with their seatmates.

Meanwhile, the plane was in a subtle but definite descent. The comforting clouds were suddenly above me, and the ground was visible before me. With no basis for measurement, I guessed I was still a mile in the sky. I wondered how rapidly tons of metal could fall when missing half of the power that enabled them to be airborne.

As I prayed for all of us, I could hear subdued crying from some of the passengers.

By this time, the captain had ordered all flight attendants to take their seats. A passenger across the aisle appeared to be reading one of those airline pamphlets about how to prepare for a crash.

Following the captain's directive, one of the flight attendants hurriedly sat down beside me in the back of the plane and strapped herself into her seat. Within a few seconds her eyes focused on the envelope and the words "Terry Nichols," as well as the prison's address.

She said nothing. She didn't have to. Her face said it all.

"Is that letter from *the* Terry Nichols?" she finally asked.

"Well, yes it is," I replied. "I was just thinking how ironic it would be if this plane goes down and all that is left of my personal effects is this letter. I wonder what people would think."

Before she could answer, I followed up by telling her I had lost my grandchildren in the Oklahoma City Bombing and that Nichols and I had corresponded.

Conspicuously perplexed, and probably a little nervous and chatty because of the situation, she wanted to hear more about my relationship with Nichols.

I explained almost apologetically that I had not set out to forgive Nichols; that it had just happened. I told her that I had found it easier to forgive Nichols than to hate him.

"How could you do that?" Her surprise was obvious.

"Because I'm a Christian, and my Bible tells me to forgive others," I said.

By now, the flight attendant was caught up in my story. My explanation was clearly beyond the woman's understanding, I could tell.

Christ may have told Christians to forgive, but did He tell them how? Her countenance clearly communicated that unspoken question.

What was it that enabled me to forgive a murderer of my family members? Why would I want to do that? I'm pretty sure she thought I might be a bit crazy—or at least mentally deficient.

The flight attendant said she would never forgive anyone who willfully killed innocent people, much less her family members.

Obviously, she was not comfortable with what I had done. I told her that I understood how she felt. Most people feel as she did. But I also asked her to think about it and pray about it. I told her that I was confident that our pilot, with a little help from above, would bring us down safely. But one day will be the final one for each of us, and we have only an unknown, limited time to forgive. I hope she heard me.

As the aircraft limped toward the Denver airport, I saw a runway overrun with emergency vehicles, all aglow with swirling red lights. The plane's cabin, meanwhile, was now virtually devoid of human sounds.

I saw heavy machinery, and operators who had mounted them, at the ready. Still, no one inside the aircraft said anything. I watched the ground as it sped by below, but also "rose" upward toward us, indicating the plane was getting closer and closer to landing—and, hopefully, safety.

I heard the welcome scream of rubber meeting concrete, and finally the noise of humanity in the cabin, formerly silenced by suffocating fear. When we arrived at the terminal the passengers stood and applauded and cried. We were safe!

I am not a reflective person. I don't spend a lot of time trying to determine why I do things. When someone hurts, I comfort them. When someone grieves, I console them. When someone is mean, I pray for them. But as I worked on this book, I could not help asking myself why I comfort and console and pray for those in need. And the "elephant in the room": How could I have forgiven the murderer of my grandchildren?!

Part of the answer lies in my upbringing. Jesus said that we should come to Him as innocent children. Actually, I was a little girl when we met. From that simple beginning my love for and relationship with Jesus have sustained me through all that you are reading about and much more.

The rest of the answer comes from God's mysterious and majestic process of transforming hate and revenge into love and forgiveness.

There was not one magic moment when God said to me, "Go, Kathy, and forgive Terry Nichols." No, His process transforms us in ounces, not pounds or tons. My journey led from unbearable grief to bitterness and despair, then to a compulsive desire to know why, and finally to forgiveness and love. The journey has been long and frustrating. But now that I look back, I see that the wisdom and love of our Creator were always there to guide me.

Throughout this book, I've tried to present a testimony, not a sermon. I'm not a preacher. I've always preferred to live my Christian faith rather than talk about it. Here, I have struggled to share the entire story of my trauma, from the 1995 detonation to today's restoration. The most profound changes of my life were birthed by an explosion.

I can never be what I was before April 19, 1995. Even now, I grieve at times. The tears flow as I remember Chase's and Colton's laughter. Sometimes I can see their sweet faces as vividly as if I had touched them yesterday. There is a hole in my heart that will follow me to the grave.

Nevertheless, today I am at peace. I have quit mourning the babies and now bathe myself in their sweet memories. The nightmare is over.

Proverbs 22:6 certainly proved true: *"Train up a child in the way he should go: and when he is old, he will not depart from it."* I thank God for my Christian parents.

God's Word has sustained me. As I've written earlier in these chapters, my forgiveness came as a slow process. Eventually, I realized that Christ, when advocating forgiveness, had the forgiver in mind just as much as the forgiven. I fortified Nichols by extending forgiveness. He uplifted me by accepting it.

My prayers for others changed my life. I simply could not in good conscience approach a loving Savior with bitterness and resentment in my heart.

After all, the only conditional prayer Christ gave us was the Lord's Prayer, the most famous prayer in the world: *"Forgive us our debts, as we forgive our debtors. And lead us not into temptation, but deliver us from evil: For thine is the kingdom, and the power, and the glory, forever. Amen. For if ye forgive men their trespasses, your heavenly Father will also forgive you: But if ye forgive not men their trespasses, neither will your Father forgive your trespasses"* (Matthew 6:12–15).

There's no option there. Christ told His disciples in His day, and now He tells us in ours, that we are to pray for His forgiveness as we forgive those who do wrong against us.

I have learned that anger can change you. When people who love you see you say bitter and hateful things, it affects them. As I explained earlier in these pages, I saw that firsthand through my grandmother.

When Mother Teresa was asked how she and her sisters could spend their days and nights in the streets of India with the impoverished, forgotten masses, literally helping them die with companionship and prayer, she said, "The miracle is not what we do, it is that we are happy doing it."

While looking for the truth about the Oklahoma City Bombing, I found something much better. It has restored my joy and put a smile on my face. Had I gotten all my questions answered regarding the bombing and not learned how to forgive, all I would have now is more information—and still, two dead little boys.

My victorious life is wrapped in forgiveness.

Terry Nichols and I are now family without being relatives. We share an invisible bloodline, made possible through Christ.

At last...*Now You See Me* as I am...abounding in truth.

Epilogue

For me, painting is a wonderful way to express my thoughts—about my family, my friends, and sometimes those I don't know when they come into my life.

On May 20, 2013, just as I arrived home from my studio my neighbor called. "Kathy, turn on your television. There is a huge tornado in Oklahoma."

I'm from Oklahoma. I still have family and many friends there. I switched on the set, hoping it was not as bad as Mary described. It was worse. An F-5, the largest, most violent type of twister, was ravaging Moore, a southern suburb of Oklahoma City. Oklahomans are used to tornadoes, and so am I. But the power and fury of this storm shocked us all. Even the weather and news reporters seemed shaken by the devastation. Soon my husband, Tom, was at my side and we watched in disbelief as the cameras panned block after block of the total destruction of homes and businesses. The most disturbing pictures were of the Plaza Tower Elementary School, which was virtually leveled.

Our first thoughts were that there might be hundreds dead and thousands injured, no matter how well prepared the storm-savvy people of Moore might be. And that school—how could any of those children have survived in that pile of steel, bricks, and glass?

My thoughts flashed back to 1995. My mind's eye refocused on the pile of rubble that once was the Murrah Federal Building where my two grandsons died. True: this was a tornado, not a terrorist act. But the damages looked much the same.

The first reports indicated that twenty-four children were dead with many more injured. As the evening unfolded, the reports were modified. A day or so later, the final report confirmed that the lives of ten children and fourteen adults had been lost. It was certainly a miracle that there were so few casualties, a tribute to early reporting and effective storm plans by most residents of the area. But to those families who lost their loved ones, especially those who lost children, the loss was total.

As the emergency crews dug through the wreckage and helping hands descended on the stricken city, I knew I had to go to Moore as soon as possible.

Within days, I was on my way to Oklahoma City. Upon arrival, I tracked down my good friend Evelyn Seaton, who has devoted her life to helping those in need. I was not surprised to find Evelyn in the heart of the relief action, ministering to families at one of the many churches that had opened their doors to survivors.

When Chase and Colton died in 1995, an artist from Austin, Texas, offered to do a portrait for us. There has always been something about that painting that touches me deeply. I view that painting often. It brings me comfort. With that in mind, I decided to contact each of the families who lost children in the storm; I would offer to paint portraits for them. But first I wanted to share their grief and offer them hope. I prayed for guidance because I knew that sometimes well-meaning people can actually offend the survivors who are still in shock. With those prayers in our hearts, Evelyn and I decided to start by attending the funerals.

On May 29, I went to the service for Ja'Nae Hornsby, age nine, who once had lived with her grandmother, mother, and auntie. In her young life, Ja'Nae had lost her grandmother and her mother before she was eight years old. Her auntie lost her eyesight due to diabetes. At the time of her death, Ja'Nae was living with her father.

Following Ja'Nae's funeral, Evelyn and I met the mother of eight-year-old Kyle Davis. I told her my personal story about the loss of Chase and Colton, and she gave me a photograph of Kyle without hesitation. Ultimately, I shared my history with all the stricken parents—but not all were instantly receptive.

I visited the home where nine-year-old Nicolas McCabe had lived. It was one of only a handful of houses still standing in the neighborhood. His mother told me that he made headlines when he was born on the driveway of that home. Tearfully, she said that he left the world the same way—in the headlines.

The next morning, I visited with the mother of Emily Conatzer, who died in the storm at age nine. On the night she learned Emily was dead, the mother watched her husband break down, while she and her daughter struggled to cope.

I visited the parents of Antonia Canderaria, age nine, who died beside her best friend, Emily. When the bodies of the girls were found, they were still holding hands.

Antonia's grandmother was told of her grandchild's death by a medical examiner. Frantically, she drove to a makeshift morgue, all the while praying that it wasn't *really* Antonia. She realized if it wasn't her granddaughter, it would be someone else's child. The thought sickened her.

On June 2, day five of my mission, I felt myself psychologically weakening under the strain of so much sorrow. I am not a trained grief counselor. I prayed and trusted the Lord to give me the strength and wisdom needed to share with the remaining families. That same day, I went to the funeral of Karrina and Sydnee Vargyus, ages four years and seven months. The double funeral of the two sisters brought back memories of my grandsons'. No one should have to bury *one* child, much less two at the same time.

Karrina and Sydnee's grandmother and mother had placed them inside a bathtub, and then clutched them in folded arms when the May 20 tornado struck. The vacuum effect of the wind blowing at more than 200 mph literally tore the children from their arms. The grandmother was subsequently hospitalized with massive injures, hence the lapse of thirteen days before the funeral.

Evelyn and I went to the funeral home that had been chosen for their service but found the place empty and without electricity. There was no sign of life. Guests were arriving. I walked through the premises and eventually found someone who was working inside a room filled with caskets. He said the service had been relocated to a building down the street. There, the reading of the eulogy competed with the noisy hum and clang of an electrical generator. The distraught family deserved so much more.

Later that day, I went to visit a man whose wife and baby had been killed when they sought refuge from the storm's wrath by hiding in a walk-in cooler at a 7-Eleven convenience store. The man busied himself by clearing his yard. His mother spoke with us as he continued to work. Everyone handles grief differently. Not wanting to intrude, we left quickly with a photo of his wife and child.

Afterward, I could not even find the family of another nine-year-old victim. I was told that many families were too broken to endure the presence of journalists wanting a story. Although I was not part of a press crew, I did not argue with anyone who did not want to see me.

My last visit was with the mother and family of Christopher Legg—another child who died inside the Plaza Tower Elementary School.

As Christopher's mother received me, his father sat in a daze. The mother searched through papers, hoping to find family photographs. Her pictures had been scattered by the storm. Upon finding a solitary picture of her lost boy, I asked if I could take the photo and have it reproduced, promising to return it promptly.

When I returned, she stepped out onto the porch so we could talk privately. She told me her husband had been laid off from his job two weeks before the storm. She said that she was a teacher at a school three miles from Plaza Elementary. After the tornado, she could not leave *her* students until their parents came.

When she was finally able to leave her post, she ran the three miles across Moore to find her own children. She stepped over dead bodies along the way. Her husband, also en route to his son's school, came across a woman who'd been impaled by debris through her back and out her chest. The husband held the woman as she died in his arms.

He then renewed his quest and was covered with blood when, at last, he met his wife. She thought he was badly injured. He told her the blood wasn't his, and with no further explanation they began to search for their missing children.

She told me her husband was concerned that I would leak the photo of Christopher to the media. I asked her if I could go back inside to assure him that I would not.

As I walked inside the father spoke to me for the first time. "How many pictures you painted?" he asked. I answered, "I don't know, maybe a couple of thousand." I asked if he would like to see some of my work. He nodded. I pulled out my phone and began showing him paintings I had done. He said nothing. As I prepared to leave, he arose from the couch with his eyes fixed on mine for the first time. "When you going to bring me the painting of my boy?" he asked. "Probably in July," I answered. I had fielded only two questions from a man who otherwise did not speak during my entire visit. His finally breaking his silence had spoken volumes to me. He had been touched and so had I.

I learned lessons from my mission in Moore that will last throughout my lifetime. God has given each one of us a little chunk of eternity called time. Each one of us is the steward of what time we are given. These precious moments of opportunity are given to us for our benefit and God's glory.